DATE DUE

FEB 0 9 1990	APR 1 2 1995		
	FEB 2 6 1997		
FEB 2 4 1990	SEP 1 7 1997		
MAR 2 2 1990			
MAR 2 9 1990			
APR 1 9 1990			
MAY 1 5 1990			
JUN 0 7 1990			
JUL 0 2 1990			
AUG 1 4 1988			
AUG 2 7 1990			
AUG 1 9 1991			
JAN 1 9 1993			
MAR 1 9 1993			
FEB 0 9 1995			

DEMCO 38-297

PEARL S. BUCK

The Final Chapter

by

Beverly Rizzon

An ETC Publication

CIP

Library of Congress Cataloging-in-Publication Data

Rizzon, Beverly E., 1931–
    Pearl S. Buck : the final chapter.

    1. Buck, Pearl S. (Pearl Sydenstricker), 1892–1973––
Biography. 2. Novelists, American––20th century––
Biography. 3. Rizzon, Beverly E., 1931–   .
I. Title.
PS3503.U198Z79 1989   813'.52 [B]   88–7002
ISBN 0-88280-120-1

Published by ETC Publications
            Palm Springs
            California 92263-1608

Pearl S. Buck
by Karsh, Ottawa

DEDICATION

*To my husband, Bob, for understanding and
caring so deeply*

Acknowledgement

Through two long Adirondack winters, encouraged by a loving husband who patiently accepted my needed hours of seclusion, I labored with the mechanics of setting this story on paper. Not only did he supply wit and wisdom when it was crucial, but he also shouldered many of my business and household chores. I cannot possibly acknowledge all that he has done and continues to do for me. Without him, this project might have remained forever in my heart and mind, but never on paper for others to read.

In addition, I wish to thank a small but very important group of family, friends, and associates who believed in me and what I was doing. Their love, their advice, their opinions have been invaluable to me and remain a very real part of this book. To each of you - my deep appreciation.

"How could an actual person fit into the covers of a book? The book is not a continent, not a definite geographical measure. It cannot contain so huge a thing as an actual full-size person. Any person has to be scaled by eliminations to fit the book world."

From ADVICE TO UNBORN NOVELISTS
by Pearl S. Buck

CONTENTS

Pearl S. Buck

The Final Chapter

Raison d'etre

Pearl S. Buck was one of the world's most beloved and most translated authors during her lifetime. When she died in March of 1973 at the age of eighty she left nearly one hundred published books as well as scores of stories and articles. It is a rare public library that does not list THE GOOD EARTH, PAVILION OF WOMEN, or at least one of her dozens of other book titles.

Many people at many times before and since her death have written about this extraordinary woman, speculating on events concerning both her private and professional life. She was the recipient of the Nobel Prize for Literature, the Pulitzer Prize, and numerous other major literary awards. She established a foundation bearing her name on behalf of Amerasian children. She was dedicated to bettering the care and environment of the mentally retarded, and she was continually involved in a variety of business ventures. She was inevitably a very public personality, complicated and challenging and controversial. As a private person, she was no less complicated or challenging or controversial. She guarded her privacy by reserving the right to reveal her inner self to very few human beings.

How do I know this to be true? Because poignant circumstances thrust me into an unusual and privileged role - first as her personal secretary and ultimately as her companion and confidante. Within the context of the time I was privileged to be a part of her temporal life, we progressed far beyond the boundaries of an ordinary employer-employee relationship. I was delicately, but deliberately, led step-by-step to the very essence of a lovely soul - old, wise, still brilliant, and incredibly brave.

It is with conviction and pride that I state that I knew and understood this person called Pearl S. Buck; or rather, she allowed me to know and understand her, an honor she chose to bestow on very few.

It has taken over ten years for me to break a self-imposed silence concerning my intimate association with this individual at the end of her life. Mine was an uneasy silence - a relentless tug-of-war between my deep desire to do what I know she wanted and expected me to do, and my wish to leave the past in the past, thereby ensuring (or so I selfishly thought) my own privacy and peace of mind.

However, my knowledge and understanding of the complex person who was Pearl S. Buck, as she so carefully and purposefully revealed herself to me, relentlessly taunted me, and peace of mind eluded me. The tug-of-war finally ended. There is too much to say that has never been said. I gave up, gave in, and decided I had to share my rich legacy.

For me to remain silent any longer would be doing a grave injustice to a great lady who gave up so much of her own privacy and peace of mind for the sake of others during her long lifetime. For me to remain silent would he forgetting the many readers of this prolific author and the admirers who wrote to her from all over the world, seeking her advice, sharing encouragement and love. And what about the new generations of readers who need to be introduced to her wonderful world of books and way of thought? Her books span continents and generations and speak a universal language. It is for all these reasons and more that I must share this legacy she left me. Why me? I will tell you....

The beginning, how I met Pearl Buck and went to work for her - is deceptively simple. What happened after that, the end time with her final personal struggle and the ensuing complications surrounding her "several worlds," as she called them - is not simple at all.

When I first met this remarkable woman in 1970, I had no idea that I would become intricately involved with the final dramatic chapters of her life. In fact I had no idea that I would become involved with her at all. Nor could I anticipate or easily accept the torrent of emotions which have engulfed me and so deeply affected my own life.

Miss Buck thought of herself first and foremost as a story teller and she felt compelled to write. This story I now share is *her* story and *she* should tell it - but when her life ended, her pen was silenced forever.

Contrary to the old Chinese way which accepts death as an integral part of life for which one has properly prepared and to which one can proceed in a calm and orderly fashion, Pearl S. Buck was not properly prepared for her own death, and the proceeding was far from calm and orderly.

How could this have happened in one as Oriental in thought as she appeared to be? Why did it happen? And how do I know about these things? Because I was there. It is not for me to question why I was there. I only know I was invited. I was welcomed. And I was there with her.   Now it is I who feel compelled to write, and I am convinced that she knew this would happen. You will be looking over my shoulder while I tell you this special story. Look and listen carefully, for this is a true story which unfolded page by page as I sat in the presence of a master story teller who would want it to begin this way:

Once upon a time....

Chapter 1

Prelude

It was spring, the year was 1970, and the place was a small village in southern Vermont. Home for me at that time was a rambling old white farmhouse where I was living with my retired Air Force officer husband, now a school teacher, and our two adolescent sons. We were enthusiastic country converts, having moved several years before to Vermont by way of a city background and a wandering military life, where a tour of duty in the English countryside had hooked us on rural life in general and set us on a determined road to New England in particular.

Spring in Vermont is a wondrous time of exaggerated anticipation and fulfillment. Arriving slowly and hesitantly after the long, wearisome Winter, the new season seems to assume the image of a fresh young Golden Gloves contender hoping to outclass the fight-savvy old timer with hard white knuckles. Historically, the youngster always wins, and the Spring of 1970 was no exception.

Spotting the first migrant robin early in the season is a rite of Spring that coincides with the ritual of making maple syrup when the days are warming and the nights are still cold. It usually takes at least two people to play the game of spot the robin - one to spot and one to verify: and the earliest verified report generally appears in the local papers with glowing details. It's big news - that's how welcome the robin is as a sign of spring's return to the North.

Around our farmhouse and its cluster of red barns, the stiff icy blankets were being rolled up and replaced with plush golden-green carpets. Looking out the window one fine day to admire the picture created by the big green and gold field to the west set off by the hazy blue Adirondack Mountains in the distance, I was amazed to see not one, not two, but dozens and dozens - maybe hundreds - of robins. They were in the new grass, on the fence posts, on top of the barn roof, even in the road. They were everywhere, more robins then I had ever seen at one time. But there was no one around to play the robin game with me - no verifier. Who would ever believe this scene before my eyes. In my excitement I opened wide the door and shouted. "Robins, robins, we're being invaded by robins!" Our Golden Retriever, Big Red, who did not know the rules of this crazy people game, reacted instantly to my excitement and dashed out into the field, barking furiously and scattering the beautiful invaders.

My true but unverified robin story gave a very special flavor to the spring of 1970, and I repeat it here only to emphasize the already heady sense of wonder and urgency that sent each of us scurrying to fulfill our own Winter promises. There were rooms to clean, fences to mend, new calves to welcome, gardens to till, and seeds to plant. We rushed about our assorted seasonal chores with the added anticipation of a visit from a dear friend from England who had never been to America and whom we had not seen in over ten years. She was to arrive towards the end of April just in time to help our older son Tom celebrate his first teenage birthday on April twenty-second.

Prelude

During a lunch break one day during this extra busy time of preparation, Tom and his brother Jim (eleven years old) handed me a copy of *Boys' Life* magazine and told me they had just read a story about some teenage brothers who had come to Vermont one summer and helped to build a stone house in the mountains, where they had lived pretty much on their own with hardly any adult supervision. It was, they said, a really good story and I should read it; and they wanted to know whether I thought it was a true story about real people.

It always pleased me when Tom and Jim asked me to read something special they had read so we could talk about it together. This kind of sharing was an old habit that had developed from their earliest reading days, and I looked forward to reading the story in *Boys' Life* and reporting back to them about it. It certainly sounded like a story we could all relate to in our own way of life.

They didn't say and I didn't ask who the author was, and I remember thinking to myself that probably a man had written it, based no doubt on one of his own boyhood experiences in the country.

To my surprise, the author was not a man, but the famous lady Pearl Buck whose photograph I had been surprised to see recently in a local newspaper. I had, in fact, cut out and filed the photo and accompanying article. Pearl Buck, it explained, had moved to Danby, Vermont, where she was restoring a number of old buildings and was planning to establish an antiques center, or something of that nature.

Tom and Jim and I discussed the story about the boys who built the house in the mountains, and I agreed that it was indeed really good. I showed them the newspaper article and the picture of the author. They had never heard of her.

Then I mentioned that, strangely, until I read about her Danby venture, I had actually thought she had died some years ago. I knew of her, of course, as a very famous writer, mostly of books about the Orient; but for some unknown reason I had never read any of her books, not even the one she seemed best known for called THE GOOD EARTH. This was a book about China, and I knew it had been made into a movie in the late 1930's when I was a little girl. Later on in high school and in the big city library I frequently visited, I remember seeing many Pearl Buck books lined up side-by-side on the shelves with faded red bindings and old fashioned gold lettering.

How mistaken I was, I told the boys, to think this lady was dead. She certainly looked very much alive and handsome in the newspaper picture. Asked why I was saving the article about Danby, I casually explained that Pearl Buck was a very famous person who apparently had come to Vermont to live and work and I was interested in her because I had been collecting information about prominent women in Vermont. I had, in fact, started to write a series of articles and had already interviewed several other well known ladies: author Melissa Mather, marble sculptor Jane B. Armstrong, and prima ballerina Marina Svetlova. All this was part of my free-lance writing projects I had been pursuing for some years, with enough published successes in newspapers and magazines to keep me going. *Yankee* magazine had recently published an article of mine about our historic local church and its intriguing painted window. Tom and Jim knew about my scribbling and often teased me about it, especially when I wrote something about them and their activities, which was quite often.

Anyway, we talked some more about the story of the boys in Vermont, and I said that probably the best way to find out for sure whether or not the story was true would be to ask the author directly. And since she lives in Danby right near us, I said, I'll write her a letter. They didn't think she'd take the time to answer a letter from me. After all, who was I? And maybe, they said, it was a "not so good idea that I had just better forget." Then they wanted to know if I was going to write an article some day about Pearl Buck. I answered immediately that I was much too busy at present to even consider such an important matter as approaching this famous lady, who must be very busy herself. And besides, I teased them as they had teased me, who was I that she would take the time to talk to me, and maybe it was a "not so good idea that I just better forget."

The idea of talking to her I did forget, but I didn't forget the letter, even though this one from me might end up in her trash basket; at least I could welcome Pearl Buck as a new neighbor.

I don't think I ever really expected a reply to my simple message, which went like this:

April 5, 1970

Dear Pearl S. Buck:

Welcome to Vermont! I wish you success in your new business in Danby, which I read about recently in the "Rutland Herald." We live over the mountain from you in the village of Wells. My two sons, 11 and almost 13, just read and thoroughly enjoyed your story in "Boys' Life" about the brothers who built the stone house in Vermont one summer. At their suggestion, I, too, read and enjoyed it, and now we are wondering whether or not it is a true story about real people. Either way, thanks for some very fine reading. Vermont is a beautiful state, and we hope you find much pleasure in your life here.

Sincerely,

Once written and mailed, the letter was all but forgotten in my busy routine of those April days. I was astonished, therefore, when I received a phone call some days later. The friendly voice identified herself as Pearl Buck's secretary in Danby. Miss Buck, she said, had received my nice letter and would I like to come to Danby to meet Miss Buck in person? A few such appointments for local people were arranged from time to time.

It took, as I recall, a long moment or two before this invitation fully registered with me. Pearl Buck's secretary calling me in my country kitchen was totally, delightfully unexpected and definitely something I had not anticipated. When I recovered and a definite day and hour was suggested, I accepted and said I'd be there with great pleasure.

In my hasty acceptance, I had altogether forgotten that my English friend Marge would be in Vermont visiting us on the appointed date, which was the day before Tom's birthday. Maybe it would be all right, I thought to myself, to take her along. But I didn't worry about it right then.

When I told Tom and Jim that I would be getting the answer to our question from Pearl Buck in person, they were impressed. So impressed, in fact, that my celebrity date became a local news item. Word got around, as word always gets around in a country village. Some further complications set in when two very special elderly friends of mine excitedly heard about where I was going and what I was doing.

Ruth and Gertrude were both retired librarians, and I worked closely with them on activities at our little village library. I had assisted them in setting up a new card catalog system and starting a weekly library information program and story hour for the local school children. We shared a love of reading and talking about books and authors, so it was natural that they were enthusiastic and understandably a little envious concerning my unexpected opportunity to meet our famous Danby neighbor. They both had read many of Pearl Buck's books and were also aware of her involvement with retarded children and her more recent work for the half-American children in Asia.

Caught up in my own enthusiasm and the accelerated tempo of that whole month and without stopping to seriously consider what I was suggesting, I generously said that maybe it would be all right to share my appointment and expand it to include Marge and Ruth and Gertrude. Looking back on my spur-of-the-moment idea, it seems pushy for me, a total stranger, to ask for a change of plans and request what amounted to a group meeting. My innocent intention was to share my good fortune with good friends, and I had no discourteous or complicated ulterior motives. At least I had the good sense to make a polite phone call back to Danby. When I explained my dilemma of the extra ladies I would like to bring with me, the still friendly-sounding secretary, who said her name was Wendy, graciously assured me that if we did not take up too much of Miss Buck's time - maybe an hour or so - it would be perfectly all right for the four of us to chat with her. And that, somewhat incredibly, was how my first meeting with the author was arranged.

It was a lovely, mild sunny afternoon when I, driving our two-tone Volkswagen bus, set off from the farm with Marge beside me. We had been in giggling high spirits all day, chattering like a couple of school girls about what we would wear. We finally decided that to dress conservatively would be proper no matter what. I chose a plain dark green linen-like dress with high neck and long sleeves, high-heeled dark pumps and - one of those ridiculous bits of trivia I vividly remember about that particular day was that it was the first time I had worn a pair of pantyhose - a gift from fashion-conscious Marge from Marks and Spencer in England. That was the store, she reminded me, where it was said the Queen purchased her "smalls," that term being the delightful and ever-so-British name for underwear. The laughter continued as Marge divulged my fashion secret to Ruth and Gertrude when we picked them up and settled them in the back seat of the bus for the winding trek over the back road to Danby.

With another one of my spur-of-the-moment decisions, I had wrapped a loaf of homemade wholewheat bread, one of eight or ten loaves I had baked that morning. And as an afterthought I had hurriedly fixed - and Marge was carefully holding - a little crystal glass bursting with just-picked purple violets which were blooming everywhere among the ferns around the house. Now that I think of it, I hardly ever visited anyone anywhere without taking along a loaf of homemade bread or just-baked cake, some vegetables or a bunch of flowers - whatever was in season. It was a nice neighborly gesture, a country kindness which had been extended to me many times, and I found it natural to repeat the custom whenever I could. At the time it never occurred to me to consider that the simple significance of my simple country gifts might be lost or even ridiculed by so worldly and sophisticated a lady as Pearl Buck obviously must be.

But it was with genuine high good humor and eager anticipation that we rode the twenty or so miles over the scenic back roads, commenting about the old working farms and the newly renovated homes of rich city folk. At Danby Four Corners (which is really only three corners because the fourth road finally disappeared as a private driveway), we had to stop by the old general store and wait while half a dozen geese plodded purposefully from one side of the road to the other. As we paused, we talked about the fact that Vermont scenery in general is an almost continuous panorama of snug green villages and rounded mountains rising and falling in gentle perspectives. But every so often the scene shifts dramatically and becomes nothing short of spectacular. Danby Four Corners is one of those wind-swept high plateaus where the usually easy undulations of the Green Mountains give way to a wider and wilder vista of more grandiose peaks. It was a pleasant quiet moment there as we waited for the geese to cross, and we speculated with some seriousness now about what Pearl Buck would be like, what she would be wearing, and what we would talk ahout. And please don't anybody let me forget to ask her about the *Boys' Life* story, I said; after all, that's the reason I wrote to her in the first place.

The final few miles down into the lower village of Danby is, for the most part, a narrow, twisting, wooded way, paralleling the brook in some places and criss-crossing over it in other places. The old houses, with an occasional trailer or modern home here and there, get closer together; and on the final steep hill the houses hug the road. On the right side there's not much land between the road and the brook which widens out and tumbles along in stair-step waterfalls. Here and there at the edge of the deep-shadowed woods are big chunks of white marble, remnants of the once important industry that flourished in the area, and still exists on a smaller scale today.

We passed a large three-story house on the right with its

flat front freshly painted white and a door that opened directly onto the road. (We did not know at the time that this plain looking building was being renovated as a home for Pearl Buck). Three or four buildings, including one little derelict with a sagging front porch, and then we slowed down to make a right-hand turn at the bottom of the hill where there was yet another big building being torn apart and put back together. I had driven through Danby several times before in past years and always this corner building and others we were now passing along the main street had been boarded up and pasted with For Sale signs. Out west such a sight might have been called a ghost town. For me, Danby had always had the air of a very sad town - a lonely place waiting for people who had left to come back again and fill the empty houses with lights and laughter and open up the stores for buying and selling. Today there was a noticeable "up" air about the place - people moving about, no obvious For Sale signs, and the appearance and sound of busy activity.

We knew from the newspaper article and the directions of Wendy the secretary that Pearl Buck's office was in the main building of a complex of shops and houses in the center of town. We knew too that the main building was painted bright red and newly christened The Vermont Village Square. It seemed, at a glance, that the entire village was in need of restoring and repairing. We commented on what a lot of work it would be to put everything in beautiful condition again. "She has herself quite a job," one of us remarked about the silver-haired lady who had, for reasons of her own, taken it upon herself to revitalize this interesting little mountain town.

I pulled head on into a parking space directly in front of The Vermont Village Square, helped the ladies out one by one, with Marge still carrying the loaf of bread and the tiny vase of violets.

Suddenly we were all quiet and subdued. There really is something a little special about meeting someone whose name and words are familiar to people all over the world - people in England and China and India.... A sort of stage fright hit me momentarily, and all I could think of to murmur shyly was "Well, here we go - we're about to meet Pearl Buck."

Chapter 2

First Impressions

The room we entered was a colorful version of what I believed an old country store should be. At least that was my quick first impression. A heavy, not unpleasant scent of old wood, wax, and coffee hung in the air. There to greet us with a big smile and the appearance of efficiency was Wendy of the cheerful telephone voice. The name and the voice matched the person now standing in front of us. She was clutching what appeared to be a bulging black leather notebook and a stenographer's pad.

Before lengthy greetings could be exchanged, a phone rang nearby and Wendy excused herself to answer it. I was aware of a subdued hum of activity all around us. A young man behind the counter next to the cash register was stacking boxes. Another man walked in the front door with cans of paint and a ladder. Standing in the doorway to an adjoining room (probably the coffee shop from the sound of it) was a dark-haired woman wearing an over-sized denim apron. She held a coffee pot in her hand.

Wendy herself was tiny and pert - a stylish Pixie in spike-heeled pumps and tailored dark dress topped off with a carefully made-up face and a cap of very short white-blonde hair. She looked like a high fashion model posing for far-out photographs in an unlikely rustic setting - some ad man's dream of the off-beat but workable contrast of satin and sawdust.

The satin and sawdust dream, however, became the reality as Wendy the secretary again turned her smiling attention back to us and assured us that Miss Buck would be with us shortly. As she briskly propelled us to a table by the window in the coffee shop where Miss Buck would meet us, she made small talk about the Spring weather and our drive over the mountain. Once again we were interrupted by the ringing of the telephone. Wendy seemed poised to run, but someone else answered this time, and I took the opportunity to ask a direct question. "In general conversation, is *Miss* Buck, rather than *Mrs*. Buck, the title we should use?" I wanted to know. "I hear you saying Miss, so I assume that is what she prefers." Wendy replied that Miss Buck did indeed prefer to be called Miss Buck, in private as well as in business. As an aside, she added that hardly anyone ever called her Pearl.

Another phone call, and yet another called Wendy away, leaving me and my companions with a few short moments to wait by ourselves.

The tiny vase of violets and the fat loaf of brown bread looked rather forlorn in the middle of the empty table. I was beginning to feel embarrassed about my simple country gifts and debated about taking them back out to the car, when Miss Buck herself walked slowly through the doorway from the country store. She paused serenely, turned to speak briefly to someone out of our sight, then smiled and walked over to us. No mistaking who she was, for she looked just like her pictures. Only in person she presented an extraordinarily vivid image: bright blue penetrating eyes accented with dark mascara, red lipstick and rouge, and silver hair swept up and pulled neatly into a chignon. She was dressed in a green - dark but not dull - tailored wool suit. Handsome and theatrical are descriptive words that leaped to mind. She appeared large without actually being heavy or overly tall. An elegant Queen-motherly air of class and authority was apparent. In a word, she seemed impressive.

It wasn't until we had introduced ourselves and rearranged chairs so that Miss Buck sat facing all four of us that I noticed she was wearing a lot of jewelry - gold earrings, beads, a brooch, bracelets, and a number of large ornate rings. On most women the combination would have been flashy and overdone. The same could be said for her bright make-up. But on Pearl Buck the gaudy jewelry and make-up in contrast to her unmistakably aristocratic bearing was somehow highly individual and attractive.

With quiet grace and courtesy, this unusual looking lady in her bright plumage put us at ease immediately and quickly dispelled any doubts we might have had about finding her difficult to talk to. She admired the violets, picked up the loaf of bread and hefted it appreciatively, and seemed surprised and delighted that they were gifts for her. Good wholewheat bread, she said, was a special treat, a favorite of hers, and she didn't get to enjoy it often enough. There was no doubt that her generous thanks were genuine.

Coffee, tea and a plate of vanilla wafers were brought to us, and we settled down comfortably for what promised to be a very pleasant conversation.

Without any prompting whatsoever, Miss Buck said that in answer to the question in my kind letter that the story about the boys building the house in Vermont was based on the very real experiences of her own adopted sons one summer near Stratton Mountain.

Pearl S. Buck
by Bruce Curtis

Most of her stories, she went on to explain, were from her own life experiences. And her books, her novels, she continued, could be described as autobiographical. She said she was somewhere in each of her books speaking her own thoughts through one of the characters - not always a woman, interestingly enough. The character might be a man, but always it was a strong character through whom she spoke.

For the next hour or so - the minutes slipped by easily and quickly - I found myself more and more intrigued by this unusual personality. As I observed her, my one word description - impressive - seemed applicable, but there were notable contrasts about her which defied immediate categorization. Authoritative, yet shy. Gaudy, yet chic. Perplexing, but oh! so interesting....She, in turn, appeared to be as interested in us as we were in her. She asked each of us all sorts of questions about our own lives, what we did, where we came from, where we'd been, and so on. With gentle good humor, she insisted on details about us - I even found myself repeating my robin story and Marge related the pantyhose episode, amid much laughter.

We sipped our drinks and the conversation flowed lightly. Suddenly shifting moods, at one point Miss Buck looked pensively out the window to where a group of children were running around a monument (a gun-carrying figure of a Civil War soldier up on a pedestal) on the grassy area by the white church across the street. The youngsters were throwing what looked like stones and trash at the figure. Miss Buck shook her head sadly as she reflected on the fact that all too often American children seem to grow up with a lack of responsibility towards the property of others. There is a lack of civic responsibility - an indifference towards public property here as compared, for example, to China as she remembers it. I was surprised to learn that she had been born in West Virginia and then taken to China at an early age by her Presbyterian missionary parents. Wrong again, I had assumed that she had been born in China or somewhere else in the Orient.

After the observations about the children, who continued to run around the monument, Miss Buck then quickly and eloquently outlined to us her plans for an antiques center and the rejuvenation of the old village.

"I have a dream for Danby," she stated emphatically. She was working, she said, with a small group of close business associates and it was obvious from her description that the young people of the village would be - in fact many already were - involved in actual restoration work underway. "The Danby project," as she called the actual face-lifting going on, would bring out the real beauty once again in the area. She pointed to the range of magnificent mountains off in the distance and said that their awesome beauty reminded her of mountains she had known and loved in China.

"I have a dream for Danby," she repeated quietly with a smile. And smiling back at her, I thought that here was a lady who had the power to make dreams come true. Although I had just met her, I had already decided that Pearl Buck had a touch of magic about her - a grandmother who would not be content just to sit and knit, although very likely she could do that too, if she so desired.

Never once during our meeting did Miss Buck seem hurried or eager to get away from us to some other appointment or activity. I never saw her glance at a watch or clock. But I had looked surreptitiously at my own watch from time to time, and towards the end of our hour I noticed that her expressive eyes strayed towards the coffee shop door behind me. Aware of conversation in the background, I turned and saw several people I had not noticed before.

One man in particular, with burnished red hair, left the group and started towards us. He was smiling broadly - a bemused smile, I thought, and I had the feeling he had been observing us for some time. Miss Buck rose to greet him, giving us a silent cue that our meeting with her had come to an end. We all stood then as she introduced that newcomer as "Mr. Harris, my Business Manager, come no doubt, to take me away to some pressing business matter." She smiled warmly as she said this, as if pleasantly resigned to his expected interruption. They bantered lightly back and forth for a brief moment. As Mr. Harris exchanged pleasantries with each of us, when my turn came I found that his very intense dark brown eyes met mine head on which meant, I calculated automatically, that he was about my height (5'7" with my high heels) and a little shorter than Miss Buck (I noticed for the first time that she too was wearing heels). With his wavy red hair, a clipped mustache and goatee to match and a polite but very self-assured and almost haughty manner, Mr. Harris the Business Manager created his own instant, flamboyant image. A deep, resonant voice and a regal bearing made this man appear much taller than he actually was. Standing side by side, Miss Buck and Mr. Harris made quite a picture. Theatrical - there was that word again. I quickly judged Mr. Harris to be forty or forty-five. With interest and growing curiosity, I observed them standing there; easily they could have been actress and actor. An aging, still elegant and proud leading lady teamed up with a vibrant, stylish younger leading man.

As we expressed our thanks and said our good-byes, Marge asked if she might take one photograph with her small pocket camera - a tourist souvenir to take back to England to show her husband and children. Miss Buck readily agreed.

It was right here at this point, as we prepared to leave, that I suddenly found myself asking spontaneously whether Miss Buck would object if I perhaps wrote down a few impressions of our meeting and talking about her Danby project. With her permission (I rushed ahead now with my unrehearsed proposal) I would perhaps be able to use my impromptu comments in a little article - part of my free lance "prominent women in Vermont project." Incredibly and without hesitation, she said she would be pleased to see what I might write, and we could talk about it some more at a later date.

Had we seen the rooms on the second floor being filled with antiques, she wanted to know. We hadn't, and so we trooped behind the author and her business manager, up the narrow old wooden stairs. While she proceeded alone to the third floor where her office was, we were given a tour by Mr. Harris and one of the antiques dealers through an organized clutter of quilts, crocks, tables and chairs, brass and woodenware and high-priced bric-a-brac. Cabinets full of dazzling glassware claimed the most attention, since art glass, as Mr. Harris explained, was his major interest. He mentioned many of Miss Buck's likes and dislikes, where and how some of the rare pieces had been acquired, and what a good investment they were. Talking about him later on the way home, the ladies and I decided that he was a charming super-salesman who could sell snowballs to Eskimos. He was a personality not to be ignored; in fact, he appeared indispensable to the Danby project, and to Miss Buck, if my intuition was correct. But all this was supposition on my part, and would remain supposition for some time to come.

Totally unprepared as I had been for an interview, with no written notes, no tape recorder, no camera, and no specific questions in mind, I had absolutely no idea that my first

37

meeting with Pearl Buck was going to be anything but a lovely shared experience with three good friends - a kind of very special country tea party on a beautiful Spring afternoon.

As I said good-bye that day, I was not yet aware that destiny was casting a new drama, and I was to be one of the performers.

Chapter 3

New Dream for an Old Village

"....a few impressions of our meeting and talking about her Danby project...."

These words kept nagging me during the next few weeks as I set about the task of putting my impressions of Pearl Buck and Danby into workable proportions. How and what I wanted to write did not immediately become clear. In fact, I had to figure out the "why" before I could go on to the "how and what." Why indeed did I want to write about Pearl Buck?

Prior to my actually meeting her, I would probably have said that given the lucky chance for an interview, I would have written about her in much the same way I had already written about other famous women living and working in Vermont. An interview with Pearl Buck would have been any free lance writer's dream assignment. It certainly would have been a scoop if I had requested and been granted an interview. Stories of Pearl Buck in Danby had already been in at least one local newspaper and I assumed she was hounded for interviews at every level, from the local school journalism classes to the features scribes of international publications.

The more I pondered, however, the more I realized that the way in which I had met this celebrity author - she had invited me to meet her and not the other way around - could open the door to an unusual writing opportunity. I came to the conclusion that the manner in which we were introduced would and should affect the manner in which I wrote about her. Opportunity was certainly knocking. Did I really want to open the door? There were persistent feelings that cautioned me that there was more behind that door than just a simple writer's assignment.

My feelings, however strong and persistent, seemed frustratingly devoid of positive factors to help give me direction. Something was tapping me vigorously on the shoulder to get my attention, but when I looked around, there was no one and nothing there and no explanation forthcoming.

I shrugged off the elusive feelings as best I could, kept them to myself, and tried to stick with the facts - facts in this case being my own observations during the Danby tea party. It was also a fact worth mentioning that my observations were not colored by pre-conceived ideas about what should or should not be, and my personal knowledge of Pearl Buck was practically nil. It was embarrassing to admit that not only had I never read one of her books, but I had thought her long dead and gone. Until Danby, that is. So I stuck to the facts about what Miss Buck told me concerning her Danby project; for here, I believed, was a real human interest story which would find a receptive audience.

If I went ahead with a full-fledged article, I would have to proceed quickly, writing in the few remaining weeks before the end of school. After that my treasured solitary hours for concentrated writing were all but non-existent. I was what could he called a "closet writer" - or a more accurate description would be "kitchen writer" - sneaking time from baking, cleaning, washing, and all the other necessary household chores. I did not feel comfortable about writing until or unless everything else was in order.

Many days during the school year, after everybody was out of the house, I rushed through essential chores, even preparing the evening meal ahead of time, so I could justify to myself what I considered the luxury of writing. My old standard typewriter and stacks of writing paraphernalia were brought out of the closet into the kitchen; and there, at the tiny cluttered built-in table, I happily indulged and tried everything from children's stories to Haiku poems to profiles of people. Some days, totally involved in what I was doing, I was still writing as I heard the Volkswagen drive into the driveway and only then did I frantically gather up the writing things for their hasty trip back to the closet. Anyway, rightly or wrongly, such was my guilty regimen, and any writing I was to do about Danby would have to coincide with the school calendar...and the Spring semester was fast coming to a close.

I finally decided what I wanted to do. I'd do a little more careful research on the Danby project, write it up in the next few weeks, and seek Miss Buck's approval. (It was my practice to submit for clarification and accuracy anything I wrote about a specific individual). I would send what I wrote with no advance query to the *Christian Science Monitor,* where several dozen of my pieces had already been published, including two articles on other famous women in Vermont.

So to Danby I went, unannounced and alone, one bright beautiful June day, when the outside flea market and antiques show was in full swing. The "T" intersection leading up to the Vermont Village Square main building was jammed with vehicles, most with out-of-state license plates. The area was alive with groups of people walking, talking, eating, and carrying everything from balloons and stuffed animals to antique clocks and desks. A kind of high-class carnival atmosphere prevailed.

I wandered in and out of the country store seeing no one I recognized, and wove my way through the throngs dickering at the flea market tables and ogling the offerings of what seemed to me to be a very large number of dealers. The wares ran from the serious to the frivolous and the entire scene was a stunning study in contrasts all set in a grassy field with a backdrop of mountains so dramatic they looked unreal, painted, theatrical. Yes, theatrical described the whole bursting, boisterous drama before me and I wished for a window seat on the top floor of one of the old adjacent buildings. Looking down on such a scene, I imagined, would be like observing and enjoying a colorful Medieval pageant.

That day, on my second visit to Danby, I spent perhaps two hours wandering as a stranger in the crowd. I spoke to no one and no one spoke to me. Miss Buck was not in sight, nor were any of the staff members I had met before. I returned home, vivid images fresh in my mind, and wrote down some more observations. Then, a few days later, I called Danby and asked if I might come once again, this time specifically to talk with some of the young people about their involvement with Miss Buck.

Miss Buck herself was away, but I was met by the effervescent Mr. Harris and introduced to several of the teenagers who willingly and proudly showed me various jobs they were working on. Without prompting on my part, many offered candid opinions about Miss Buck, Mr. Harris, and their effect on the village in general. Their over-all attitude was positive and complimentary.

Once more I returned to my kitchen, assembled my

thoughts and notes, and drafted a final version for Miss Buck's perusal. It was gratifying to me that her approval was swift and forthright, and I immediately forwarded my written efforts to the "Monitor." Again, approval was swift. Gordon Converse, the "Monitor's" chief photographer, was dispatched to Danby to take accompanying photographs for my article.

I was in Danby on the day Mr. Converse was there for his picture-taking session. He seemed enchanted with Miss Buck as a photographic subject and, as I recall, delighted with the whole Danby scene and its riot of color and activity

My article, with the Converse photographs, appeared in the "Monitor" of Friday, July l7th, just about three months after my initial introduction to Pearl Buck. I believe my original title for the article was something like "New Dream for Old Village" and I wondered why some editor changed that to "A Pearl Buck project - Young Vermont volunteers rebuild village." But editors like to change titles, even good ones, as I found out from Miss Buck, who should know about such things. However, the article itself remained as I submitted it and stands as a fair and accurate description of my impressions of The Danby project:

A Pearl Buck Project

Young Vermont Volunteers Rebuild Village

This tiny mountain town is putting itself on the map in a big way. Although marble has been quarried here for more than 100 years (the U. S. Supreme Court Building in Washington is constructed of Danby marble), the local youngsters will tell you in Yankee understatement that "things have always been pretty quiet." Settled in 1765, Danby has taken a new lease on life in 1970, and is bursting with civic pride and enthusiasm.

Rumors flew a few months ago about "big developers" who had pounced on the area and bought up the derelict village center with its depressing boarded-up buildings.

To find out what was going to happen, the village youngsters kept watch on the old country store. Instead of being dismissed or told to move on, a handsome silver-haired lady and a group of friendly people surrounding her actually encouraged the youths to "hang around."

The woman turned out to be author Pearl Buck, whose deep concern and genuine affection for young people follow her wherever she goes.

If Pearl Buck and Danby seem an unlikely combination, Miss Buck is quick to point out that her interest in Vermont goes back many years. As often as her busy schedule allows, she comes to enjoy the home she designed and built near Stratton Mountain, not far away.

The boys and girls who formed an early bond of friendship with Miss Buck are still happily "hanging around," and it could be said that they are Danby's "secret weapon."

"Without the young people, this Danby project would not be progressing as it is, they are magnificent," Miss Buck said in a recent interview here.

It took imagination and foresight for Miss Buck and her business partners to see what might be done in Danby. The restoration plans call for repairing and refurbishing buildings (stores and houses), bridges, gardens, lawns, brook, a waterfall, and woodland to beauty and usefulness. Few would doubt that the arrival of these good neighbors is the biggest and best thing to happen in Danby.

How does one go about restoring a village?

Slowly, step by slow step, the author indicated. It takes painstaking and loving care to do it properly.

"Aren't you just going to tear everything down and bulldoze it away and start all over?" a boy asked Theodore Harris, Miss Buck's biographer and dynamic associate at Danby.

"That's exactly what we're not going to do." Mr. Harris replied. And he has repeated this answer many times.

Thus far, the old general store, now called the Vermont Village Square (painted a barn red and decorated with hanging flower baskets, and selling everything from farm-fresh eggs to original paintings) is the only building which has been completed and is open for business.

"I enjoy being here in this small country community," Miss Buck explained to a recent visitor. "I can observe the people, but I also feel that I am a part of them."

"You know," she added, "when I was in China, I was always 'somebody special' because I really was an American; when I came back to America, I was always 'somebody special' because I had spent so much time in China."

In Danby, Pearl Buck is putting down roots, and she likes the day-to-day stimulation of watching the community grow in beauty and spirit. She plans to build or restore a home of her own nearby.

Miss Buck chats freely with visitors as she sits at her corner table in the Maple Skillet, a coffee shop adjoining the store. The talk comes back again and again to praising the young people.

"The kids can't do enough for Miss Buck," says Wendy Conklin, Miss Buck's pert secretary, "they're fantastic."

"Sure they work, and work hard, but it's all volunteer," explained her husband Alan.

"We were warned about possible vandalism, but the kids are so loyal to us and take what they're doing so seriously that they won't even let a visitor throw a bottle or can on the ground in front of the store," said Tom Laypoldt, the young man who "tends store."

"They run the admissions booth for the antiques show and sale each weekend," he continued. "Half the admission goes to them, and if we get extra busy in the shop, the kids help wait tables; all their tips they put with the admissions in a 'general fund' they have to finance their own project, the Danby Youth Center."

(Mr. Laypoldt's wife, Phyllis, runs the Maple Skillet.)

Miss Buck has promised the young people part of one of the buildings as "their thing." They have meantime decorated for their after-hours' recreation a room in a deserted house at the crossroads. Here, brightly colored paper cut-outs contrast oddly with the gray boards of a building which probably hasn't heard a young voice inside in decades.

How about the parents of the young people? Do they approve of all this sudden busyness and activity?

Said one girl, "Oh yes, as long as I'm down in the village working, or with Miss Buck, it's all right."

A recent evening found a group of the young people helping Miss Buck to box up some of her manuscripts for shipment to the city.

Mr. Harris is a handsome, articulate man who seems to have boundless energy and good humor. He is as much at home tramping over the rocky fields and introducing visitors to Connie, Keith, Bruce, Doug, Terry, Arnold, Mary, Annie, or Steve, the grinning teens (there are about 30 of them) who are doing the lion's share of the outdoor cleanup work ("Sixteen-year-old Keith is the best bulldozer operator we have") as he is describing the valuable antiques which area dealers have on display and for sale in rooms over the store.

Miss Buck maintains an office upstairs in the store and writes there regularly; Mr. Harris is working on a novel, as well as on the third volume of his biography of Miss Buck. The two literary figures consider themselves "just folks," who are proud to be known as good Vermont neighbors. As one boy said grinning broadly, "Groovy."

* * *

Having a subscription to the *Christian Science Monitor* meant that the paper was delivered daily to our rural mailbox. Aside from not liking the changed title, I was pleased with the article in print, and as soon as I saw it I had a photostat made and took it proudly to Danby, along with a promise that I would request that several tear sheets be sent directly to Miss Buck. The article and I were greeted with warm thanks and comments and for months thereafter the copy appeared prominently on the bulletin board in the country store. Of all the many stories written subsequently about the Danby project, Miss Buck told me many times that mine stood as an honest, down-to-earth account of what was actually going on, but even more important, what she intended the spirit of the project to be.

I valued her praise and vowed to follow the progress of her

venture. Would I consider writing more articles? Only time would tell. I still had the feeling that if I kept opening doors, what I might encounter would become more and more complicated.

Anyway, it was mid-summer and I shoved aside any writing possibilities that might be building in my mind. More contact with Miss Buck? Ever cordial, ever courteous, I was aware of a gentle, subtle probing each time we met, as if she were somehow exploring future probabilities as yet undefined. She left a door temptingly ajar when she invited me to "come back any time." I didn't know then that it was no idle invitation, because Pearl Buck didn't issue idle invitations or say things she didn't mean.

Summer slipped into Fall and I slipped easily back into my kitchen writing routine. I read and re-read my Danby article and my old notes and decided to query *Vermont-Life,* the State's beautiful, prestigious magazine. I sent them a copy of the "Monitor" article and was optimistic about their response. Back came the editor's surprising and disappointing response:

> 5 October 1970
>
> Dear Mrs. Drake:
>
> Mainly what we would be interested to cover in a story here would be the physical and economic restoration of the community - and not in progress, but when it is almost fully accomplished. This would lend itself better to story interest for our readers we feel than the activity of the youth group, as a main focus that is. So we would rather wait a while and see what develops.

Sincerely.

/s/ Walter Hard, Jr.

But not content to wait a while and wishing to focus on the "now" aspect of Pearl Buck in Danby, I next telephoned *Yankee* magazine and talked with Associate Editor Esther Fitts. It had been just about a year ago that my first *Yankee* article about the Wells church had been published and maybe they would be interested in what I thought was another very feasible idea. Back came this reply:

October 10, 1970

Dear Mrs. Drake:

Referring to our recent pleasant conversation, the editors were sufficiently intrigued by the Danby project to want to know a bit more. Could you 1) send a copy of your "Monitor" article for us to read, and 2) let us know just what ways the teenagers are becoming involved.

We would be interested to know a bit more too about the significant differences in this project from some of the others: somehow a restored country store and imported antiques shop isn't enough to go on, without knowing the proposed plans for the other buildings around the square.

In other words, we are on the fence about the article but far from being "turned off" by it.

Cordially.

/s/ Esther Fitts, Associate Editor

Armed with that encouragement, I dropped in on Danby one cool rainy October morning. Gone were the summer throngs of visitors and busy young people, the colorful outside market and the heady atmosphere that had been so obvious before. Nevertheless, at least three of the renovated buildings were brightly lighted and open for business. Wendy, I was told, had driven Miss Buck to her Foundation in Philadelphia and they would be gone for several days. I found Ted Harris with several assistants in the corner shop directing a paper-hanging project which apparently had hit some snags; simultaneously, he seemed to be over-seeing the arrangement of some newly-arrived antique furniture. He welcomed me heartily and immediately sent someone for coffee.

The room he was re-doing was tasteful and elegant - a sort of Victorian parlor and I fell in love instantly with a round mahogany pedestal table and four little matching chairs with plush blue velvet seats. Without thinking, I said the set would be perfect in my farmhouse parlor which was slowly getting a face-lift. "But of course you should have it, "he suggested, half in jest and half serious as the true salesman who never misses an opportunity for a sale. I laughingly protested that I was not a buying customer but was certainly enjoying looking. Off to one side was an unusual Victorian sofa whose flowing lines suggested luxurious lolling, all in very prim and very proper Victorian style, of course. We all laughed as the definitely formal looking Mr. Harris (in dark conservative business suit) demonstrated how a proper Victorian gentleman might loll. The actor part of him, I decided appreciatively - even his voice sounds like that actor among actors, Richard Burton.

New Dream for an Old Village

Before coffee arrived and before I got around to explaining my reason for being in Danby this quiet gray day, Ted (he had suggested I drop the unnecessarily formal Mr. Harris) steered me expertly around the furnishings explaining with interesting rapid-fire details about where this or that item came from, what Miss Buck had said about this or that piece, and so on.

He seemed totally and happily engrossed in what he was doing, and very optimistic in spite of the present lack of customers. I could understand why Miss Buck had him as a Business Manager, for if intelligent enthusiasm and energy were necessary ingredients for a successful business, the Danby venture was off to a good start. I told him that, for what it was worth, and then briefed him on the letters I had received — the disappointing one from *Vermont Life* and the encouraging one from *Yankee*, which I would really like to pursue.

Did he think, I wanted to know, whether Miss Buck would be pleased if I took a theme similar to my "Monitor" article and expanded it for a longer *Yankee* piece? His reaction was an immediate Go - do it - what are you waiting for? His light-heartedness was contagious and we bantered back and forth about the proposed article. It was the same kind of easy repartee that I had noticed bouncing back and forth between him and Miss Buck. She must really enjoy talking to him, I mused. I certainly did.

Just before I left, the merriment in his talk and his eyes suddenly shifted to a gravity as he quietly asked me, "Do you know anything about the Philadelphia story?"

"You mean the movie by the same name starring Katherine Hepburn?" I replied lightly, even though I knew instantly that the movie was not what was behind his pointed question.

He laughed in spite of himself, and the subject was dropped, at least for the moment. In a back drawer of my mind, I automatically filed away "Philadelphia Story." For now it was just a shadowy question mark.

Chapter 4

A Corner of Her World

I sent a copy of the "Monitor" article to *Yankee* magazine, to give them background for my proposal, along with a brief cover letter promising a detailed outline or draft in the near future.

That near future, however, stretched into lengthy weeks as the busyness of first Thanksgiving and then Christmas claimed more and more of my writing time. My thoughts of Danby and just how I would approach the *Yankee* story were suddenly given a welcome impetus by an unexpected phone call from Ted asking me whether or not I would be interested in interviewing Phyllis Maguire (one of the singing Maguire sisters of Arthur Godfrey program fame) who lived nearby and would be in Danby to discuss a proposed Christmas choral concert involving the local young people.

I liked the idea and thought it would add yet another interesting facet to my story. This time I arrived for the interview prepared with notebook and some tentative questions. But Phyllis Maguire never appeared. While I waited for over an hour, I chatted with Wendy and Ted in the third floor office where Miss Buck and Ted had large matching flat desks facing each other. The room was as yet unfinished and sparsely furnished, but Pearl Buck's unseen presence was there in the books lining the shelves on the outside wall.

"Does Miss Buck know I'm here?" I wanted to know.

"Of course", Wendy and Ted chorused. "she knows everything." Putting that another way was Jimmy Pauls, an everpresent dark shaggy bear of a man whom I had seen before and who always seemed to be hovering in the background. This time he was more in evidence during our conversation, and he announced that "Miss Buck doesn't miss anything that goes on around here."

Their remarks weren't critical - they were good-natured, even affectionate. Just what was the relationship between Pearl Buck and these three, I wondered - were they friends, just business associates, or what? My more intimate glimpse of them today left me more than curious about them but with little doubt that whatever they were doing was for Miss Buck, apparently with her complete approval and knowledge. They seemed to be working as a trio with a singular purpose - to do the bidding of one very determined and dynamic lady who wanted everything done not today or tomorrow, but yesterday.

In the gathering dusk of that cold afternoon, we all left the office together to go to other places and to other responsibilities. I went away with colorful visions of having been surrounded by the Three Bears, for red-headed Ted, blonde Wendy, and black Jim were each swathed for the outdoors in enormous and identical dark furry long coats. Mama Bear, Papa Bear, and Baby Bear, of course. But then, I elaborated, Miss Buck would have to be Goldilocks! I really did not mean any disrespect to any of them, but the comparison was too obvious to ignore. I wondered if Miss Buck would be amused by my frivolity. I rather suspected she might be, but I wouldn't have a chance to find out for sure unless my association with Danby deepened, as it continued to do so slowly in curious fashion.

In a letter to Wendy and Ted while a draft of the *Yankee* article was slowly proceeding, I mentioned the possibility of getting to Danby one December weekend, the occasion being the Christmas songfest involving the young people and Phyllis Maguire. Miss Buck herself was scheduled to make a little speech. At the last minute, I found it was possible to attend with my family, and I spoke glowingly beforehand to Bill and the boys about seeing Miss Buck and enjoying what I knew would be a lovely, old-fashioned musical evening. Alas, the school auditorium was virtually empty. Only a handful of people turned out to listen to the seasonal renderings of the little group and Miss Buck's gentle comments about her feelings for the village and her hopes for the future.

I felt sorry for Miss Buck and the others involved and was more than a little puzzled at the poor showing. How unfair, I thought. It was such a simple, lovely idea. Just what is it the people want? Or is it that they don't want anything.

What should have been a joyous occasion turned out instead to be a sad affair, brought to a premature conclusion. Miss Buck, accompanied by an exhausted looking Wendy, left the auditorium immediately, as did Ted and Jim and Wendy's husband Alan, whom I had caught a glimpse of briefly. The evening had been disappointing; but I was, perhaps, being a little too hasty and too harsh in my judgment. Having lived over seven years among Vermont natives, I well knew that they could be taciturn and unpredictable concerning someone "from away" or "down country" as they were apt to describe newcomers. On the other hand, these same qualities were to be admired, for they were the stiff-upper-lip strengths that the first Vermont settlers had to have in order to contend with the severity of the northern environment. Then, as now, the young people tended to be the first to embrace change and give new people a chance. It might take their elders a bit longer, but I knew from experience that they could be staunch supporters and loyal friends. I had no way of knowing yet how well Miss Buck understood the Vermont character when confronted with it on a day-to-day basis and not merely part time, and I just hoped she would not grow discouraged too soon, though I already knew she had considerable strengths of her own to draw upon.

Back home I picked up *Good Housekeeping* magazine and read Miss Buck's latest annual Christmas story. It was an uncomplicated story about a young married couple and how the possession of a large glass vase had solved a problem for them. The story, called "Two in Love," was sweet and sad, but it had a happy ending and I had no trouble putting Pearl Buck in the role of the spunky young wife.

The holidays became history, and it was early in 1971 before I finally settled down to a final version of the article for *Yankee*. Miss Buck liked it, and it was subsequently sent off to the magazine. I called it "A Corner of Her World."

She read Dickens at age four, and her childhood chums were Chinese scholars. Her birthplace in West Virginia will soon be open to the public as a national monument. Pearl S. Buck belongs to the world as one of its most famous women. She is a prolific writer whose literary genius defies classification.

As if to prove this last point, even after years of turning out best sellers on a variety of subjects, Miss Buck's published books in 1970 included a novel about India, a look at the Kennedy women, and a study of China.

Never content to remain aloof from the problems of

human beings, America's Nobel and Pulitzer Prize winning author has refused to remain perched on a pedestal or isolated in an ivory tower. She has written and spoken about many of the major issues of the twentieth century. Declining to sweep under the carpet the unlovely or unpopular topics, she has knowingly exposed herself and those close to her to the build-em-up, tear-em-down games that people often play with public figures.

Now in her seventy-ninth year, she continues to write with determination and vigor. In her biography by Theodore F. Harris, she speaks of an "endless and growing curiosity about life and people, and I cannot keep my discoveries to myself. I put them into books and thus share them." She has shared herself with us through dozens of fictional characters, some of them strongly autobiographical.

Miss Buck exists between book covers in many disguises. In actual life, she has had many different homes in many different geographical locations. This year, Vermont is "where she's at." She is not a stranger in Vermont, and her introduction to the mountain state occurred several years ago when she and her family observed a "sugaring off," that magical time between Winter and Spring when the maple trees wake up, the sap begins to run, and folks stand around waiting to sample the first syrup.

"Where she's at" is a youngster's description, and it was the local young people who came to her first when she moved into their quiet New England village. Danby, Vermont, hunches in the shadows of the Green Mountains, off to one side of a main tourist path linking ski and shopping centers. It's been there since about 1765, when settlers came to farm and later to quarry marble in the surrounding hills. In a village of about a thousand people, any outsider is fair game for rumor, gossip, and speculation.

Restorations of one sort of another and the re-opening of derelict country stores in Vermont are not exactly a dime-a-dozen,but they are common enough to prompt genuine curiosity when one comes along that seems to be different.

At the old Danby country store, long vacant and boarded up, rumors began circulating among the youths who congregated to observe and size up the "famous people" who, they heard, had plans for the tumble-down emporium.

If the youngsters expected to hear "move it, cool it, or beat it," they were in for a big surprise, for the password became "welcome"; and they were encouraged to hang around and help if they wanted to. Did they want to? Miss Buck and her small group of colleagues involved in the Danby adventure say that the surprise volunteer working force (now formally called the Danby Youth Center) has been nothing short of fantastic.

It should be emphasized that there never has been a master plan for this restoration project. Like Topsy, it just grew, from a small enthusiastic beginning to an increasing awareness of what might be done and how worthwhile it could become.

Seven buildings have already been acquired around the village square, there is an eighth one to come, and a ninth one under consideration, as well as a meadow (cleaned up, reseeded and planted with spring bulbs by the young people), a waterfall and brook. The right of way between the old country store and the building now housing a tasteful array of antiques had been in dispute for many years. It was decided to buy the driveway and the other building, thereby ending the controversy once and for all. One is reminded of a lady who went shopping for a dress, found it, and then decided that she just had to have a hat, gloves, and purse to match.

The Danby Youth Center, graduating from its original function of broom, mop, and bucket brigade, is playing a growing role as a community cultural force. The Vermont Village Square (as Miss Buck and her associates officially call the business)has given the group a building of its own. Sparked by this group and its success, other youth activities have quietly sprung up in Danby and nearby villages. Community pride is replacing apathy.

Last summer the youngsters prepared and presented a pageant based on the history of Danby. They are probably the only organized youth group anywhere to be sponsoring a State Symphony Orchestra (the oldest in the United States, it is claimed). Alan Carter, long-time director of the state's musical aggregation and deeply concerned about its continuing financial crises, has been working enthusiastically with the Danby group. A series of concerts was arranged throughout the past year, and last December a special appearance by the symphony highlighted an old-fashioned Christmas carole fest. Christine Maguire (well-known as a member of the popular singing Maguire Sisters, and in private life Mrs. Robert Spain of Manchester, Vermont) volunteered to help the youngsters with choral arrangements and programming.

Skeptics scoff that Danby will inevitably lose its momentum, but friends of the project predict that it will continue to grow, guided by Miss Buck's genuine concern and affection for all young people and the need to bolster their sense of community spirit.

An ad for the weekend Danby Antiques Show (where New England dealers display quality merchandise) asks: "Ever had the thought that things today just aren't built like they used to be? Plan today to visit the Danby Antiques Show and take a trip back into the pre-plastic days. Beauty, workmanship AND utility...built into every item."

There is a growing hope that Danby will one day be a place where a family may spend an entire day and find something to interest everyone - from picnics in a naturally rural setting along the brook to browsing among an array of handmade gifts and crafts from all over the world.

The Vermont Village Square has already become an integral part of the life of the community. The oldsters, as well as the youngsters, accept Miss Buck as the quiet, moving force behind it all. Danby admires its newest and most famous resident, now "at home" on the hill road near the country store.

Pearl S. Buck is keenly interested in each aspect of the Vermont Village Square. Never far from her mind and heart is the necessity of continuing the flow of funds needed for her Pearl S. Buck Foundation, which works on behalf of needy Amerasian children.

On the third floor over the store is Miss Buck's spacious office. It is here that she writes and reads. It is said that she reads as many as 1,000 books a year, peruses dozens of popular magazines each month, and absorbs all of the major daily newspapers of the world (subscriptions to these newspapers were a recent gift from a friend). Personal outpourings of feelings from all over the world reach her here in huge piles of letters each week. The overwhelming majority of these letters contain words of praise and admiration for Miss Buck, the author, and Miss Buck, the person.

Danby is a combination of old and new, of tradition and innovation. It is here that Pearl S. Buck is presently at home, and it is here that she will continue to write about things as she sees them, from this corner of her world.

Chapter 5

A By-Pass

About the time I mailed my manuscript to *Yankee* and was anticipating what I was sure would be a favorable reply (surely the Pearl Buck in Danby story would attract readers), I happened to mention to a friend something of my own interest in the Vermont Village Square. Being in a skiing crowd and social set that I was not, she said she had heard some unsavory gossip about Miss Buck concerning her personal life and her business dealings. The area business community, my friend suggested, was not taking kindly to what she called "those people." I instantly visualized "those people" in the form of gracious Pearl Buck, the friendly "Three Bears"called Ted, Wendy, and Jimmy, and the little band of young people who had voluntarily rallied 'round. I could not think of them as "those people"; that sounded derogatory and somehow degrading.

I bristled with defensive questions. Have you been to Danby? Have you seen for yourself what's going on? Have you met Miss Buck? Have you met any of "those people"? The answer, on all counts, was "no" and my friend admitted that her gossipy information was second-hand and strictly hearsay. Nonetheless, she maintained a "where there's smoke there's fire attitude" and cautioned me that there might be more to Danby than the pleasant little story I was so enthused about.

My own nagging feelings along these lines floated to the surface of my consciousness, and I remembered The Philadelphia Story still filed away in the back drawer. Although I had some unanswered questions, I kept a neutral wait and see attitude and discussed the gossip as just that - gossip - and the inevitable consequence of what Miss Buck herself had called the build-em-up, tear-em-down games people in this country love to play with their celebrities.

From my few conversations with Miss Buck thus far, it was my understanding that Danby had not yet received much attention of any kind, good or bad. And with the exception of my "Monitor" article, the publicity so far had been pretty much of the local variety. It seemed to me that if *Yankee* published my article, it might be the start of a national focus and a much needed boost for the future of the project.

Although it may seem that I was looking for recognition for myself, I truly was not. If *Yankee* published my article, naturally I would be pleased and proud, but I did not consider what I had done to be a big deal. By a lucky coincidence, I had been around when opportunity knocked, and I had merely acted on impulse and opened the door. Yes, Pearl Buck and Danby intrigued me, but realistically I had no illusions about my importance. What was important, I thought, was to put Danby on the map fairly and squarely. In some small way, I was trying to do that and I had already caught *Yankee's* attention. Why, I wondered, was it taking so long for them to reply?

I found out why on a late Winter Sunday afternoon. Returning home from a Wells Library meeting, I had a message that Ted Harris had called and wanted me to get back to him as soon as possible.

He was calling for Miss Buck, he explained, and had I heard anything from *Yankee?*

No, I had not, and I was surprised when he said Miss Buck had been contacted by the editor in a rather strange turn of events.

I then talked directly to Miss Buck, my first phone conversation with her. Her voice was soft, but high-pitched with a hint of child-like hesitancy. She sounded like Britain's Queen Elizabeth but without the British accent.

It seemed, she told me, that the editors of *Yankee* liked my story very much indeed. So much so, in fact, that the executive editor himself was coming to Danby to talk to her. Because of my article he was interested in doing a story himself; or, as he had already suggested, in having Miss Buck write the Danby story herself.

She made it very clear that she was distressed at their method of by-passing me and my article. It was not at all what she would have expected of them. But she allowed the ways of editors were indeed strange sometimes. She asked me to come to Danby in the next few days - she herself would be away at the Foundation - but Mr. Harris would speak for her and discuss with me some other writing ideas and arrange some sort of compensation of one kind or another. I did not expect any compensation for anything I had done and couldn't imagine what she meant.

These unexpected circumstances gave me a golden opportunity to test my "I don't care about myself-just good publicity for Danby" attitude. Yes, I was disappointed and miffed because if they liked my article so much, why couldn't they have used it somehow, even incorporated it as an installment in a series of articles, or something. On the other hand, given the opportunity, wouldn't any editor bounce an unknown free-lancer in favor of Pearl Buck?

I came away from that next meeting with Ted convinced that Miss Buck had been put in an awkward position by *Yankee,* who in turn had put me in an awkward position. Ted assured me - and I had no reason to doubt him - that when next a writing opportunity presented itself, Miss Buck would call on me to conduct an interview, suggest another Danby article for another publication, or whatever.

As for some sort of compensation Miss Buck had alluded to, I was taken aback when Ted said she wished to give me the little Victorian parlor set I had so admired. I accepted the gift in the manner I thought Miss Buck had given it - as a simple "thank you and I'm sorry for the way things turned out." Another writing opportunity arrived in due time. Miss Buck invited me - via a telephone call from Ted - to conduct a luncheon interview with her and three visiting dignitaries she was expecting from Japan. I accepted the invitation.

Chapter 6

A Dream for Danby

The innuendos and snide remarks persisted locally and became more strident - everything from "I hear Pearl Buck lives high, wide and handsome," to "she surrounds herself with queers," to "her money comes from the Mafia." I viewed this as offensive muck-raking, and my stock retort was "Do you know that for a fact?" No one could ever substantiate the crude remarks which circled relentlessly like waiting vultures. What a price to pay for fame, I fumed.

But what really set my defense mechanism in high gear was the icy cold shoulder I got from the *Christian Science Monitor* when I telephoned to inquire about a follow-up story to my first enthusiastically received Danby article. Their response stunned me. Had they known, they curtly informed me, what kind of people I was writing about, they never would have condoned the first article. "What kind of people?" I repeated incredulously. Everything I wrote about Pearl Buck *and* Danby was absolutely true. What could be wrong with that?

I was told coldly without further explanation never to contact the "Monitor" again about Pearl Buck *or* Danby. I was hurt and furious at the same time. I felt strongly that if I had confronted Miss Buck then and there with my unanswered questions, she could have put an end once and for all to shadowy doubts. I just couldn't imagine her being embroiled in some sleazy or sinister dealings. I had already become pro-Danby and so I decided to bide my time. If I ever wrote any more about Pearl Buck and Danby, I would continue to write about what I saw and heard - no digging and delving into what I *thought* I saw and heard.

But before the time came for me to write anything further, Miss Buck's own efforts appeared in July, 1971. Here, in *Yankee*, she speaks for herself:

"I happen to be a great believer in the village in any country," says author Pearl Buck. For the last year, with the help of an enthusiastic group of young people, among others, she has been proving her point in the village of Danby, Vermont. Here, and especially for Yankee, she describes what it's all about....

A DREAM FOR DANBY
by Pearl S. Buck

The village of Danby, Vermont! Population 950, clustering around a beautiful clear brook, flowing down a steep mountainside. It was once on the main highway of Route 7, but now it is bypassed, though barely, for it is only a quarter of a mile away, in a curve of its own. Postoffice? Yes, in a rather beautiful old building of the classic New England style. A village green? Yes, with a modest white church and a surprisingly well done statue of the Civil War.

But Danby is fortunate in its buildings for it is fortunate in its history. Not that I knew anything about Danby or its history until a shamefully short time ago - I say shameful, for though I have been coming to Vermont for some twenty years, I am a stay-at-home when I like a place and my house in Vermont was thirty miles from Danby on a mountainside of its own and facing the now famous ski resort of Stratton Mountain. My house there was an odd but huge and comfortable one of my own design, based on a Chinese inner structure, its view from three walls of glass magnificent enough to occupy me and keep me from much wandering. That house I have finished with and, its purposes fulfilled, I have passed on to others, complete with its vast eternal view. One's life with a house ends, I have discovered, when the purpose for which it was built is fulfilled.

But Danby? Well, it was by chance I came upon Danby - or by that seeming accidental occurrence that we call chance. By a fortuitous incident, let us say, a friend, who is also my business manager, sold at a considerable profit a small country store he had once bought for a very modest sum in the days when property in Vermont was modest. The storekeeper, a young man with a young family, wished to stay in Vermont and asked that another job be found for him in Vermont rather than returning to the state from which he had come. The business manager looked at the *for sale* signs in the local newspapers and saw a notice of a store, long closed, at Danby, at a modest price. He went to see it, I went along for the ride through beautiful mountain scenery over excellent roads and that was how I came to Danby.

Danby? What I saw was a lovely old village, but it was dying. I could see that at a glance. I had seen many a dead and dying village in many places in our beloved country. North and South, East and West, but especially in the West. I had seen dying and dead villages. I know the signs - the closed and decaying houses and stores, the broken windows, the paintless walls, a handful of people still clinging to the only home they know - a sad and heartbreaking sight. Since I must always know the why of all I see and experience, I stopped often at these villages to ask where nearly everyone was gone and why were they gone - and would they never come back? The answers were always the same. Once upon a time the village had been a small prosperous center of an industry, centered at a crossroads of a natural resource. But time passes as it will and must, industries opened elsewhere, the natural resource was exhausted, there was nothing to keep the young people in the village, and with the youth goes the life of any village. One cannot blame them for going, since to stay is death, but they take life with them.

Now I happen to be a great believer in the village in any country. Great cities a nation must have and great industries, too, but they need the villages to draw upon. At least this has been so in the enduring old nations of Asia. I grew up among the villages of China, and knew them to be strongholds of life, not only in agriculture but also in the raw materials of industries. The villagers fed the cities and their industries. The fine rugs and carpets of Peking were usually woven on city looms but the wool of sheep and camels came from the villages. Every morning anywhere in China the village roads to the cities were busy with farmers carrying loads of grain and vegetables and fuel to the city. When the huge and ancient city of Nanking, where I lived for seventeen years of my adult life, was encircled, six thousand years ago, by an enormous city wall, high and wide and as solid as the day it was built - unless the Communists have torn it down - that wall enclosed within its limits enough land so that if the city were besieged, as it was many times during the centuries, villages within the land area could feed and clothe the city proper for an indefinite length of time. And the villages, I am told, still exist.

And do not remind me that I speak of ancient times, either, for modern Japan is still a country of villages, solid family villages, and it is those villages, my Japanese friends tell me - and they are learned men in modern matters as well as ancient history - they tell me that it is the Japanese villages which have been able to make their country recover so quickly from the world war. The cities were bombed and destroyed but the villages worked and went on working, families holding together and working together, so that as soon as the war ended, the villages were the foundation for new Japan, a country today so strong, so rich, so modern, that she ranks next to the United States. I have many times in recent years visited in those Japanese villages, lived in their modest inns and with their kindly folk, and I know whereof I speak.

And so I was sad when I came upon the village of Danby and saw its dying plight. Most of the center of the village was dead - houses without paint, for sale signs everywhere, one small grocery store still alive, a struggling church, a postoffice in a room in a building that had once been fine.

That was what struck my first attention. Danby had once been a beautiful village. It was dying, but it was still beautiful. The country store was unusual in its structure and design. The houses had not been built originally for poor people. We bought the store and searched the region for books about Danby. There was no doubt about its decline. So evident was it that an aged resident, who had spent his life here, said that the villagers had been trying to collect enough money to burn down the country store and all surrounding houses and persuade some modern shopping center to buy the land! We shuddered as we read our old town history books. For Danby was never an ordinary village. No wonder the houses, dilapidated though most of them were, are fine houses, well built by people who had worked and received good pay - once upon a time. The country store itself, empty for nearly two decades, is so well built that we have had to do little to bring it back to its original style and structure.

I say *we,* for by now I was into it, too. I read the books myself, and discovered that the country store - today in full life again, let me here interject - was built well over a hundred years ago by Silas Griffith, Vermont's first millionaire, who made his fortune in lumber. A marble quarry is still in production up on the mountain - Danby Mountain I call it - and it is the second largest marble quarry in the State of Vermont. Many of the buildings in Washington D.C. are made of Danby marble. So is the monument at the tomb of John F. Kennedy.

The country store, now named The Village Square Country Store, was, when it was built, the highest building in southern Vermont. Its vast cellar is paved with slabs of solid marble. The store rooms were there and are again. The store, original floors, windows, shelves, is on the first floor, cleaned and painted; it is once more a busy village center, filled with country foods, crafts and delicacies.

In the old days, the storekeeping family - there were only two of them in the century - lived on the second floor. Today it is the Village Square Antique Shop. The visitor will see lovely old glass, furniture, silver, jewelry, oddities, a book store - anything you could want. The old floors are sound and clean, the wide old boards the same, bare because they are too beautiful to cover, the walls painted or burlapped if paint was not enough. Altogether that second floor is a place to browse in, to enjoy, to buy in if something catches the fancy. The variety is exciting, the quality is high, the prices reasonable. I love beautiful things myself and I like people to own them. Beautiful things, large or small, add their beauty to life.

On the third floor the attic floors are sanded and clean, too - the old wide boards as they were. It is now the company offices. A large square desk stands in the middle of the room, a huge room it is and needs to be, for big dreams are being made there and being brought to reality. A grandfather clock stands between two doors that lead to store room and secretarial rooms. Opposite to the wall facing the village square are four high windows with book shelves crowded mainly with books on antiques. At one end of the room is a long old conference table and Windsor chairs, where nowadays we hold staff meetings, and at the other end is a conversation place, a rug, a small table, two chairs, a couch. These and a few treasures make up the work room for the executives.

Danby today? Ah, it is not dead or dying. Many dreams are waiting to come true, but they are coming true. Next to the store on the first floor is The Maple Skillet. You can get sandwiches - any you wish - freshly made soup every day, ice cream and hot drinks, a daily special for a meal. That is only the beginning of the dream, too. Soon there will be a dining room serving a good country meal, The Fish and Fowl. In summer perhaps a terrace, facing the brook, where tables will be set? Anyway, a wide green lawn with trees and the sound of the waterfalls, and there is our rain-or-shine flea market, with everything you have seen and not seen. And on the other side of the driveway are three houses - one, The 1836 House, restored and used by the Antiques Fair, every room a treasure of antiques for sale by dealers from all over New England. The next, The 1850 House, in process of restoration, and in a matter of weeks, the other, connected by a covered bridge over the brook.

It has been fun, it will be more fun as dreams come true, but what gives me joy is to see a dying old village coming to life again and with its own effort. It brought me a rare happiness, too, when the teenagers, telling us there was nothing for them in Danby, asked us what we could do for them. Otherwise they would drift away.

"We will do nothing *for* you," was the reply, "but we will give you the chance to do something for yourselves. We will give you half of our admissions if you take charge of the admissions booth. You can elect your officers, set up your own bank account. We will give you a room as your center. All we ask is that you choose two pair of parents to be your chaperones at your parties, and so on, because your behavior affects our business!"

All this has happened. What did they do with their first money? Some twenty of them, with chaperones, went to see The Ice Capades in Boston, spending two nights in a motel. All but about two had never been out of Vermont. Next spring they plan to hire a bus and go to Washington to see the capitol of their country. They have earned the money: it is theirs to spend. Meanwhile the older ones are working on the restoration of the old buildings. We want it that way. It would be easy to bring in a construc-

Old Silas Griffith Store, which became the Country Store and focal point of the Village Square Complex

tion company and get it all done fast. Instead we have incorporated the Danby Construction and Decorating Company. It is made up of Danby young men. Some of them, with the kind help of our dealers, are learning how to finish fine furniture. Others are acting as sellers when a dealer is absent. This means they must learn antiques. It is not only to their benefit but ours. The Danby Antiques Fair may some day be the largest antiques center in New England. Ah, but some day we will have beautiful things from all over the world - The House of Japan, The House of Korea, The House of India, The House of Europe - you see how dreams grow? But the foundations of all these Houses have already been laid; connections are firming all over the world.

Yet what makes me happiest is still Danby itself. Danby lives again. Danby and its people are *with us*.

* * *

Surely, I thought, the Pearl Buck in Danby story would attract readers. It did. Written by the author herself, it attracted a great number of readers; all that summer and for many months beyond, visitors came to Danby from all over, many clutching the *Yankee* article and some of them hoping perhaps for an autograph or a glimpse of the famous lady. More than that, though, all of them came with dreams of their own and ideas and impressions, and they went away having at least satisfied their own curiosity about what was happening to somebody else's dreams.

Chapter 7

A Seemingly Accidental Occurrence

My stepping into a prominent role in Pearl Buck's life occurred as she herself might have described it, "by that seemingly accidental occurrence that we call chance." In retrospect, random accidental occurrences do seem to emerge as inevitable stepping stones towards a specific goal. Some last big personal steps had to be negotiated before I found myself face to face with not just an interesting and famous lady but the real person behind the name and face. The drama continued off-stage this way:

The school year had gotten off to a difficult start for my husband. Perhaps, having taught for some seven years now, he was headed for what is sometimes described as teacher burn-out. I cannot say for sure, but what I *am* sure of is that by the end of September he was in what he himself called the "blue funks."

While it would be tedious and unnecessary to chronicle all the harrowing hours and days that followed while I searched my bag of tricks to dispel my husband's doom and gloom, this episode is essential in understanding the next fast train of events that took place.

Aware that some sort of career crisis was occurring, I

spilled out an alternative plan. The plan called for my husband to take time off - a sabbatical from teaching for an unspecified length of time; he could stay home on the farm and immerse himself in a more leisurely routine. I, in turn, would sharpen up my once-excellent secretarial skills and go after an office job in the area, one which would bring in enough to off-set his salary loss and adequately supplement his military retirement check. Again, while it is not necessary to detail the pulling and pushing and the many arguments and counter-arguments that ensued, it was finally agreed that if I could find a job paying $5,000 a year (it was 1971), Bill would reluctantly consider the sabbatical idea.

I outlined what talents and skills I possessed: Katharine Gibbs graduate, art and music background, and considerable experience working for executives in New York and Louisiana, plus Civil Service jobs with the Air Force. I had also typed manuscripts for Vermont author Sam Ogden and had dabbled with some success in free-lance writing.

Hand-delivering my credentials to a local attorney, the president of a wood-working business, and Ted Harris at Danby, I explained that personal problems had compelled me to rearrange some of my priorities and I was seeking a $5,000-a-year job so my husband could take a much needed break from teaching. What I was doing would be, I believed, in my family's best interest. To Ted Harris I added that I was a good public relations person and perhaps the rapidly expanding Danby complex could find some use for a person like me. Pearl Buck was never mentioned.

I said my piece, then went home and waited, hopeful but not overly optimistic that anybody would want an over-the-hill, rusty 40-year-old demanding $5,000.

I didn't have long to wait, for it was Ted Harris who called

Beverly Drake

back almost immediately, saying that Miss Buck wanted to see me right away. She was offering me a job as her personal secretary. Wendy, it seemed, had been just filling in, there were other duties she should be attending to, and Miss Buck had for some time been looking for someone with my qualifications. Was I interested?

More to the point, I was flabbergasted. My flabbergastedness reached new heights when Ted told me to be in Danby the next day and that Miss Buck had already decided that she wanted me for her secretary. And that's the way it will be, he laughed - a *fait accompli!*

Chapter 8

"Damn the Torpedoes, Full Steam Ahead"

"When can you start?" was literally the way Pearl Buck greeted me, her smiling but penetrating blue eyes cutting through my maze of doubts and confusion. She knew me, she said, better than I thought she knew me. She needed help and she needed it now and she needed *my* help. I would be responsible for typing her manuscripts and personal correspondence and organizing her Vermont appointments calendar. She wasn't worried at all about my being over the hill - a rusty has-been. "You are half my age," she commented dryly in mild chastisement. She had everything decided, just like that, a snap of the fingers.

"Damn the torpedoes, full steam ahead!" Suddenly I laughed and so did she. Serious as the situation was, at least to me, there was also a marvelous comic aspect to this whole incredible *fait accompli.* One queenly old lady striking with her velvet sledgehammer and everyone in its wake scurrying madly about picking up pieces and trying to bring order out of chaos.

While she didn't want to hear about the nitty-gritty logistics or the follow-through mechanics of what she had set in motion, this she dismissed with a wave of her hand and "of course you'll find a way to do it," she was far from unsympathetic to my plight. There was kindness and concern in her soft voice when she said she realized she would be interrupting my entire way of life and that I would have to find ways of placating a disgruntled husband and upset children. What could she do to help?

For starters, she proceeded to answer my shadowy unasked questions which had been filed in the back drawer of my mind. Her answers were brief but to the point, all the information I needed to know now, with an unmistakable promise of more detailed accounts in the future. One by one with uncanny preciseness she ticked them off:

1. The Philadelphia Story - a most unfortunate, complicated and misunderstood situation involving her Foundation in Philadelphia; or rather, involving Mr. Harris who had been her chosen Executive Director of the Foundation, that is until recently when she had reluctantly accepted his resignation. Mr. Harris, she explained, is a man of the highest integrity and ability and he had and has her complete trust and confidence. His motives and methods had been unfairly suspected, and speculation was still erupting in the press in a most nasty manner. (Now I understood for the first time where the "Monitor" had been coming from when they refused to talk to me about Pearl Buck and Danby; of course, they had been reading the tainted grist of the gossip monger mills and they could not risk offending their discriminating readers). She had had a choice, to stay and fight along with Mr. Harris; to spend years maybe to right the wrongs, or be done with it, leaving the fighting to others if fight they must. They chose to leave together, and move forward to a different location, where she could devote more and more time to her writing. Yes, others were carrying on the day-to-day operation of her Foundation and she was still in control, but from a distance and only occasionally now in person. Here in

Vermont she felt free - safe. There was much yet for her to do, much she had to say. "I hope," she said, "there is enough time left to do all that I have to do."

2. She chose to live the way she lived, demanding of herself and demanding of those chosen few around her. Her own writing had afforded her a more than comfortable life style - luxurious even, and she insisted that everything around her be of the highest quality. She could not create in other surroundings.

3. Back to the Philadelphia Story. Mr. Harris, she said, is a most unusual man and has led a most unusual life. She knew everything there was to know about him. They had no secrets from one another. And she lamented the fact that his often flamboyant past and his choice of personal friends made him a constant target for jealous and vindicative finger-pointing. She trusted him utterly.

4. Her own personal lifestyle, the support of her retarded daughter (her only birth child), and the endless funds needed to keep the work of the Foundation going put tremendous burdens on her financially. She depended upon her writing to keep the funds flowing. And most assuredly she had no link to the Mafia! She was her own Mafia!

It was clear that she was aware of and resigned to the gossip mongers. She lived the way she wanted to live and she did what she felt compelled to do, whether anybody liked it or not. She felt at ease and comfortable with the small inner circle of associates surrounding her, and they were allowing her to do what she wanted to do most, which was to write.

She explained that as her personal secretary I would be joining that small inner group she now had with her: Ted, Wendy and Jimmy, and to a lesser degree Wendy's husband Alan; their close ties went back many years.

Pearl S. Buck and Ted Harris with astronauts while on tour to raise funds for the Foundation

They had developed their own unique ways of working and getting along together. She did not think they would overwhelmingly take to my presence, but would accept me because it was her wish. I would have to find my own place among them and my own ways of dealing with them. The important thing for me to know and to have no doubts about was the fact that I would be working directly for Pearl Buck and would be responsible to no one else.

"You can tell your military husband," she said mischievously, "that you will be taking orders from me and no one else." Better yet, she told him herself in my presence during another hastily arranged meeting designed to allay the fears and anxieties of the troubled husband whose household was being turned upside down by some old lady author who didn't have sense enough to sit in her rocking chair and leave other people alone.

Chapter 9

A Command Personality

As a means to an end in understanding Pearl Buck, it is imperative to point out at this juncture the imperious way in which she was going about this entire episode. It beautifully illustrates a basic quality of her personality which she had honed to a razor sharpness and which she had learned to use cunningly when it served her carefully calculated purposes. I am talking about her command presence, a charismatic pot pourri of intellect, intuition, verbal ability, animal magnetism, compassion, and single-mindedness. In all this mixture, and I have named but a few of the essential ingredients, perhaps it is single-mindedness that emerges as the most devastating characteristic. Consider, further, that it was with devastating single-mindedness that Pearl Buck, as one woman in her seventies, observed, contemplated, and ultimately fought to set up a Foundation to help remedy the bitter circumstances of the thousands of half-American children in Asia, forgotten fruits of the wars. Had she been less than single-minded, she would have given up before she even started.

Anyone who has been in the presence of a command personality is instantly aware of it; he may not like it; in fact he may not like it at all, but he is aware of it. It is said that Louisiana's feisty legendary Governor Huey Long, who never doffed his hat in deference to any man, took one look at President Franklin D. Roosevelt during an interview in the Oval Office and reached up to quietly remove his hat. That's command presence.

Pearl Buck was not God or some extraordinary super-human being. But she had command presence and it was not to be ignored.

A fair description of that first encounter between Miss Buck and my husband was that the Colonel entered the scene reluctantly but formally prepared for battle with the enemy. Actually, I had assumed he was prepared for battle with her. In truth, his battle was not against her but me, for he had reversed himself completely and had decided he did not want me to go to work for Pearl Buck or anybody. He was not giving up his teaching position and of course he expected me to be at home where I should be, instead of pursuing this crazy idea of mine. While conceding that Pearl Buck was a person of some renown, he still considered her just another person; in his own words, he blustered that he "wouldn't go across the street to greet the Queen of England."

She wasn't the Queen of England exactly, but Miss Buck had become my willing ally in a plot to win over this man who in my own words "does not walk easily through life." I was the one who wrongly anticipated a battle royal. No bombs were dropped. No bombs were needed. I had also failed to comprehend that the war had already been won.

Outwardly I was a silent observer. Inwardly I was charged with a growing anxiety. I fidgeted nervously and felt, rather than heard, the conversation between Bill and Miss Buck, waiting for the explosive anger and logic without reason that Bill used with me. I kept thinking that in working for Miss Buck I would be facing a supreme personal challenge, for it was obvious that I was not merely some insignificant part-time liaison officer. I would actually be working intimately now for both sides, so to speak. My time, talents, confidence, and loyalty would be demanded and expected on two demanding fronts - home and work.

A little game of wits was underway, and with cool, competent strategy, the "General" quickly proceeded to pull her rank on the Colonel. We sat at the small gate-leg table in one of the upstairs rooms over the country store. And we went through the ritual of sipping coffee and making polite small talk. It didn't take Miss Buck long to first measure and then appreciate and even enjoy the Colonel's keen mind and sharp wit. She artfully verbalized her appreciation, saying something direct and flattering. "You are obviously a man of considerable intellect and sensitivity; I like that."

And she appealed to all the altruistic things he espoused:greater understanding between human beings; helping one another in the teaching and learning process; working towards peace and harmony and away from war. On the subject of war she said she had seen too much of it and "it never works." She suggested to him that, as a former military man, he would be interested in her two-volume Chinese to English translation of ALL MEN ARE BROTHERS, a sort of primer on Asian guerilla warfare. "Had our own military leaders but heeded the warnings and lessons therein..." she said with great sadness. Bill went away from that first meeting with Miss Buck with the two volumes of ALL MEN ARE BROTHERS. He *was* interested and he *did* read the long and difficult treatise; many months later she was to write these words in the frontpiece:

To Lieutenant Colonel William Henry Drake, as a small reward for being the only military official ever to have read this book, I hereby inscribe my effort, four years of translation, of this classic of Asian guerilla warfare.

/s/ Pearl S. Buck

Danby House

January 26, 1973.

The avoidance of war became the topic of many involved conversations between the General and the Colonel. It was, in addition to me and my services, another interest they shared and she capitalized on this as a way of drawing him to her. In doing so, she made my position a little easier, and I was grateful for her maneuvering.

When she sweetly purred, "I am not taking your wife away from you; I am asking you to let me borrow her for a while...," bear in mind that the war was already won as far as she was concerned; indeed she had *avoided* a war, and the words were just a pleasant formality. There was nothing particularly powerful or extraordinary about what she said, though the actual words were carefully measured. They found their mark. Pearl Buck had quickly and easily succeeded, as I was to see her do many times, in disarming a wary and wiley adversary. While not surrendering unconditionally, the Colonel at least was now willing to sit down and negotiate in the enemy camp.

It was agreed that I could be borrowed - on a temporary basis, of course - for $5,000 and with a few strings attached

"Mr. Harris will work out all the details," Miss Buck airily delegated this authority to her Business Manager. Right from the start, an uneasy cordiality prevailed between Bill and Ted Harris and the others of the inner circle. The Colonel did not capitulate to their charm as he had to Miss Buck's. They were not "Generals" and he considered them, most especially Ted Harris, too smooth, too fast-talking, too sure of himself to be completely trusted. "They're not going to snow me with their fancy footwork," he declared. With frosty sternness, the terms under which I was to be borrowed were enumerated:

1. I was to be working for no one but Pearl Buck.

2. I was to be paid at least $5,000 - although he thought I was worth much more.

3. I was to work in Danby only - there would be no traveling to Philadelphia or anywhere else.

4. I would work Monday-Friday only, no weekends or overtime — and my hours would be arranged so that I could leave Danby at what was termed a decent hour, say not later than 4 p.m.

5. I would not be involved in any way in the business part of Danby. As Miss Buck's private secretary, I would be in a protected position, away from the public eye behind the scenes.

As I sat uneasily listening to that last final condition of my employment being pronounced, I had a wonderful and hilarious vision of a meek, mousy me chained to a desk in a dimly lit room and valiantly struggling at a typewriter to keep up with a monstrous pile of manuscripts growing beside me. At four every afternoon a great gong sounded, my shackles fell away and I stumbled through a bamboo curtain, free at last to go home....

My vision was a great inner tension breaker and I had all I could do to keep from exploding with outrageous laughter.

For Ted's part, acting on behalf of Miss Buck and not for himself, he accepted the pompous declarations with what seemed to be easy good humor and tolerance.

So it was agreed that I was to be borrowed, on a temporary basis, of course.

There was a brief and frantic four days in which to work out all those logistics and mechanics leading up to my first day of work. I knew not what I was getting into, only that I *was* indeed getting into it and that I wanted to get into it.

In the background, I could still hear Ted's knowing laughter - this time with a great gong going off somewhere in the distance.

Chapter 10

Closing the Gap Between Fantasy and Reality

Back on the homefront, the emotional situation grew hot, so hot that I knew I was in great danger of backing out of my Danby commitment with scared cold feet. For the first time ever, it occurred to me with a bittersweet stab of comprehension that I had always been trying to change my husband, never accepting him the way he was. As a wife I had thought it my duty and responsibility to constantly try to smooth out his ups and downs. I was forever trying to replace the bumps and potholes with smiles and soft cushions.

Wrong - wrong - wrong I was now shouting to myself. Wrong for him, wrong for our intelligent perceptive sons, and wrong for me.

In retrospect, I think if it had been any other boss but the very determined Pearl Buck beckoning to me out there, I might likely have given up and given in and stayed stoically in my accustomed role at home, down-playing and down-grading my own needs and desires. I could always flourish in a fantasy world, which to some extent was exactly what I had been doing with my kitchen writing. Faced now with the very real opportunity of closing the gap between fantasy and reality, I had unknowingly (or was it knowingly?) come up against the whole feminine mystique of the early 1970's. In my own singularly naive way, I was crashing the gates of the women's movement. Strong feminine intuition told me that Pearl Buck had already crashed these same gates long ago and she wouldn't expect me to hide behind unnecessary feminine frailties, not even scared cold feet.

She was right, of course. Ultimately, I didn't hide behind anything. I made up my mind to do what I had to do. I plowed my way through the emotional turmoil like a farmer plowing his way through rocky fields, slowing down now and then to throw the rocks out of the way but never stopping completely.

With a sigh of relief and pride, I discovered that Tom and Jim were secretly proud of the fact that I would actually be working for the lady whose story they had read. I teased them that it was all their fault I was going to work outside the home. If they hadn't read the Pearl Buck story in the first place, none of this would be happening now. They sensed tension and dissension between their parents, something they had unfortunately grown used to over the years, but were probably no more apprehensive than they had ever been that things would work out. Busy with school, sports, and friends, they were removed from the adult in-fighting. I figured the actual time I was with them would be about the same as it had always been, but the quality should be enhanced by my new experiences.

The complicated logistics and mechanics which were miraculously worked out read like some stripped down offbeat shopping list: car, clothes, meals, meetings, and so on. In spite of a continuous barrage of verbal stumbling blocks from Bill, I was determined to exit from my old identity.

Closing the Gap Between Fantasy and Reality

My first cover to cover reading of Miss Buck's MY SEVERAL WORLDS, her early autobiographical account published in 1954, not only helped to calm my own jitters but provided picturesque background bits and pieces, adding to the preliminary underpainting for the full portrait of this multi-faceted woman who would soon be my employer.

Chapter 11

"Fresh Paper
Lies On My Desk
Waiting for the Book"

Now, in the Autumn of 1971, as I stepped into yet another
of Pearl Buck's worlds, it was natural that I found her comments about Vermont of particular interest.

With time to spare early on that first morning of work, I
drove slowly towards Danby along Route 7, the wide highway linking Manchester and Rutland, finally pulling off and
stopping for a few quiet moments by the side of the road.
Gazing at the mountains all around, those magnificent sen-
tinels which Miss Buck had said reminded her of mountains
she had known and loved in China, I thought of my first
simple meeting with her and the story behind the story my
own sons had read about her sons. Here, from Part III of MY
SEVERAL WORLDS written at the place she called Forest
Haunt, Vermont, are the origins of that story:

The landscape outside my big window this morning is a
forest clearing and beyond the pines and the maples at
its edge green mountains rise in rounded peaks. Our
simple house is the result of a plan and the plan is the
result of a mild revolt on my part. These American
children of mine were growing up without knowing how

94

to use their hands. On the farm the boys rode tractors and fastened the milking machine to the cows. They sat on a combine and harvested the grain and called it farming. It is farming of course, the American way, but I was dissatisfied with it. They had no touch with the earth directly, and I feel that there must be the direct touch, hands upon stones and earth and wood, in order that life may have stability. My own life has been spent in many places, but it has not lacked continuity or stability because everywhere I have made gardens and lived on farms and planted and harvested in the unchangeable turn of the seasons.

And the houses people build nowadays! The old strong farm-houses in our Pennsylvania community still stand, but I see bulldozers sweep them down as though bombs had fallen, and in their place upon the raw and bleeding earth machines have built little metal boxes a few feet apart, and they are called homes and twenty thousand families crowd into them. When I saw them I knew that I wanted my children to know how to build a real house.

We went to Vermont one spring to see maple sugaring by helping to make it, and while we were there my revolt took sensible shape in a plan. Land covered with forest was cheap on the mountainside, a little more than two dollars an acre. We bought some high acres far from the road, and the next summer upon an old clearing where a farmhouse had stood a century ago, the boys began housebuilding under the direction of a Vermonter who knew how to do his job well. Thereafter each summer the boys went to the mountain and worked. Foundation, walls of stones mortised in cement, a beamed roof, two big fireplaces, windows and doors, a well-laid stone floor, these slowly came into being. The work was finished by a fine German workman whose passion for perfection was irritant and stimulus to the young Americans but joy to me, for I despise shoddiness of handwork, believing it to be accompanied always by shoddiness of mind and soul.

Slowly, slowly the learning went on, and at last the house was done, and here we are in our mountain house. Water has to be carried from the brook, lamps have to be cleaned and filled with oil, there will never be a telephone. I cook our meals on the fireplace and think it the best way of cooking in the world. Around us the forest folk come and go, squirrels and deer and sometimes bear, and we always watch for Brother Porcupine who will eat his way through anything, especially enjoying rubber tires. The house has cost us a third of what the new metal boxes in Pennsylvania cost, and the boys now know how to build for themselves and the girls know how to keep house anywhere and still be civilized. As for me, I have this big window, the fir trees and the mountains....

That first Vermont house was now a part of Pearl Buck's past. I never saw it and, to my knowledge during the time I knew her, she never returned to it.

Once she had decided to move on to Danby, Forest Haunt became for her "that house I have finished with and, its purposes fulfilled, I have passed on to others, complete with its vast eternal view. One's life with a house ends, I have discovered, when the purpose for which it was built is fulfilled."

It was time for me to go to work now and I moved on to meet Pearl Buck at Danby House, her home here which I was soon to see for the first time, her home where new purposes were being fulfilled. I recalled her exact words in the closing sentences of MY SEVERAL WORLDS:

> "In this mood of faith and hope my work goes on. A ream
> of fresh paper lies on my desk waiting for the next book.
> I am a writer and I take up my pen to write."

Written nearly twenty years ago as an appropriate ending, it
now seemed an appropriate beginning....

Chapter 12

So Much to Do, So Little Time to Do It

Danby House was on the hill around the corner from the main square - the large three-story plain looking house with its flat front and a door that opened directly onto the road. It was neither pretty nor special looking, and its disappointing exterior seemed a puzzling contradiction to the elegant highest quality surroundings Miss Buck said she needed in order to create.

My knock on the street door was answered by Mr. Choi (pronounced Chay), the small unsmiling Korean man I had seen once before serving luncheon to Miss Buck and some Japanese visitors. Jimmy hovered close behind him but immediately disappeared somewhere. I heard Ted's welcoming Good morning, you're early, come in and sit down, Miss Buck will join us shortly. A strong smell of cigarette smoke and frying bacon mingled oddly with an elusive scent of roses.

There was nothing plain about the luxurious and comfortable looking room I stepped into. I took a seat at the end of a long dark sofa, in front of which was a long low polished table. Two gold velvet chairs sat side by side opposite the sofa. Ted sat in one chair smoking and quietly watching the morning news on a large color television centered against the wall to my right. My first glimpse into this private world of Pearl Buck revealed the elegance I had anticipated: soft drapes drawn against the outside world, an off-white plush carpet underfoot, subtle light from a Jade lamp in one corner, tiny crystal globes in another, a grand piano, and everywhere a profusion of what can best be described as exquisite objects of art, from the paintings on the walls to clusters of tiny lacquered boxes to the large sculptured Goddess presiding over the entire scene. Time and money and good taste had gone into the making of this room, creating an atmosphere of order and serenity which was at once more Oriental than American or European.

At a few minutes after 8 A.M. into this stylish and eminently suitable setting walked my new lady boss, smiling and serene, bright make-up and jewelry complementing her royal blue Chinese robe. (I had been briefed before that her private living quarters were on the second floor of Danby House and that Ted and Jimmy had an apartment on the third floor; Mr. Choi served as house man, drifting silently from task to task like some minor character actor, until a future day arrived when he was to drift back to his native Korea.)

Woman to woman, I admired the blue outfit and heard her say that she allowed no one to see her - day or night - unless her hair was carefully coiffed and her make-up and jewelry in place to complete whatever outfit she had chosen. "Vanity, thy name is woman," Ted quipped with obvious admiration and affection. To which Miss Buck replied, with that same warm tone of affection I had heard before, "Mr. Harris quite spoils me, for you see," she said, referring to her clothes, "he has had these lovely robes made for me and now I must wear them or risk hurting his feelings." She laughed delightedly and Ted responded, for

Pearl S. Buck
by Bruce Curtis

my benefit, that he had finally succeeded in pursuading her, she could be very stubborn indeed, that at her age she should be able to wear whatever she wanted to wear, not just what other people thought she should wear. "You see," she confided, "I am basically a very shy person."

This personal shyness (could it be vulnerability I wondered?) was not evident in public, and in sharp contrast to her decisiveness and single-mindedness. I sensed that there was much more to be revealed.

So there we were early in the morning talking of all things about clothes, and already one of the dozens of curious questions I had about Pearl Buck had been nicely answered. Only on one or two occasions was I ever to see Miss Buck in American-style clothes, and even the Danby residents grew accustomed to the sight of her striding rapidly along on her customary daily walk, accompanied by little Mr. Choi who was almost running to keep up with her.

I knew I had endless details to learn all at once. Behind the scenes, I was an eager student taking a crash course in what might be scholastically called something like "Pearl S. Buck as Revealed in her Writing"; starting with MY SEVERAL WORLDS, I was working my way through dozens of books and stories and articles jumping from past to present to past again, absorbing and forming strong opinions of my own. I was reading to learn and absorb, all the while enjoying and wondering why I had never discovered her books before.

To do the best job I could for this lively lady, I knew I had to learn things quickly, big things and little things, not the least of which was to discover that Mr. Choi was not the only one who had to run to keep up with her. It's no wonder she surrounded herself with vigorous younger workers. Behind the calm exterior of the smooth satin robes lived a veritable powerhouse of energy, who often sat at her writing desk (upstairs at Danby House now) for eight hours straight, turning out page after page of careful manuscript written in longhand with a black felt-tip pen. Ted had warned me that Lady Peasbee (for P. S. B., of course, an apt name coined by him but never used in her presence, for in person he spoke to her always as "Miss Buck" or "my dear"). Lady Peasbee wanted everything done yesterday and did not tolerate shoddy or tardy work.

As the new member of her select inner sanctum, I was ushered swiftly into the routine she had established to her liking. She assumed right from the beginning, for I was given a minimum of direct instructions, that I would be quick enough and perceptive enough to catch on and keep up. If not, it would probably be "chop-chop, off with her head" - I later laughed to Ted and Wendy. This became a catch-all phrase when the going got rough (as it frequently did) and we were all pressed to the limit to do her bidding.

Does it really matter, one might pause and ask here, is it really important to know that Ted Harris convinced Pearl Buck that it was all right for her to wear Chinese robes, or that Ted and Jimmy lived upstairs? And does anyone really care what Pearl Buck ate for breakfast, or that she ate breakfast at all? Of themselves, these or similar tidbits certainly do not set Pearl Buck apart and make her worthy of study and speculation, but they do help to form a real image of the person behind the Nobel and Pulitzer Prizes for Literature, the dozens of book titles, the Foundation for the half-

American children, and so on from documented deed to documented deed. These accomplishments of Pearl Buck undeniably set her apart and do make her worthy of study and speculation. Whether or not what she accomplished can be considered great can be clinically debated by scholars and scoundrels as well. Distilling the deeds and accomplishments into the essence of a real person requires just the right touch; too heavy and the person emerges as godly or ghastly; too light and the person is wispy or without life altogether. Just right, and the subtle essence is there, unmistakable as the special perfumed scent of a woman which lingers long after the woman is gone.

"How could an actual person fit into the covers of a book?" Pearl Buck asked. And I answer her question, which is also my question, and some justification of the way I am trying to fit Pearl Buck between these pages by reminding myself that "she guarded her privacy by reserving the right to reveal her inner self to a very few human beings" and once again reminding the reader that "you will be looking over my shoulder while I tell you this special story. Look and listen carefully, for this is a true story which unfolded page by page as I sat in the presence of a master story teller...."

"Arpege," that beautiful well-known fragrance, together with the scent of fresh roses will always be, for me, the beautiful perfumed essence reminding me of Pearl Buck. Trivia? A certain amount is necessary. I must not stop my story now, and I shall try to choose the trivia carefully. Yes, I believe it is important to relate that the scent of fresh roses surrounded the private world of Pearl Buck. While no day in the life of Pearl Buck could accurately be called routine in the full sense of the word, traveling through that first day with her in Danby provided a sort of pattern which was applicable, with variations, for the first eight months I worked for her.

So return with me to the breakfast table, for breakfast was an important part of Miss Buck's day, she at one end of the table and Ted at the other finishing with enjoyment a hearty breakfast of orange juice (always freshly squeezed), scrambled eggs, bacon, toast and coffee served by Mr. Choi over the raucous and ridiculous accompaniment of a parrot in the kitchen. Rowdy and unpredictable at times, the old green bird was a source of much amusement to Miss Buck, who loved to repeat this story. She insisted it was true and absolutely unrehearsed, bird experts notwithstanding. It seems that Wendy (who usually was at Danby House for the early morning staff meeting) has a tiny poodle named Sam who apparently infuriates the parrot. On one of Sam's infrequent visits to the Danby House kitchen, the parrot looked down disdainfully from his cage and said distinctly these untaught words, "Oh no, here comes that damned dog again!"

This story punctuates the light, quick and playful conversation that bounced around the table, balancing the very serious subjects that also were constantly under discussion. To be with Pearl Buck was to know that this playfulness was very much a part of her personality and her humor surfaced frequently and spontaneously. She expected the person or persons with her to be "tuned in" or her impatience was just as quick to surface. Impatience and disappointment. Tentatively at first, I began tossing the conversational ball around when it was tossed to me, and soon I was a regular in the verbal gymnastics, puns on puns, rhymes and hilarious relevant one-liners by Miss Buck which those of us with her never could top. Ted and Miss Buck were the star performers and they would have made a wonderful vaudeville act; not too surprisingly, I soon discovered that they frequently fantasized about this themselves, laughing about their "Buck and Wing" act. The whole breakfast scene - from very serious to very slapstick touched on Danby and business topics, as well as current world news, art, music, fashion.... The interest and curiosity of Pearl Buck seemed virtually endless.

Decision making and pressing details of the day also got under way over coffee at the breakfast table. It was Wendy (now called an Administrative Assistant) who was in charge of the business correspondence and financial information, working directly with Ted, with Miss Buck first approving the grand plan of everything. She insisted on being informed concerning every aspect of the Danby business—every aspect of every business that involved her and she would not tolerate being kept in the dark by those of us whom she trusted to keep her informed. In this sense, she was unrelenting and demanding.

My real work with Miss Buck and my intimate understanding of her began after breakfast when Ted and Wendy left for their appointed duties at the office. I was involved with the most personal side of her affairs and there was no subject of interest to her which was not ultimately and openly discussed between us, even my own view on my own marriage, which I had vowed to leave behind me during the work day. I was early initiated into her most intimate concerns. First, she carefully dictated thoughtful answers to the current batch of family and fan letters. She received dozens and dozens of fan letters from all over the world, answered them all, and the files were crammed with the correspondence covering every conceivable subject. Never, in the time that I knew her, did she ever cast aside a letter unread by her, ignoring it or refusing to acknowledge it. Each letter was read by her and sometimes, but not always, discussed with me. I did not edit or alter her letters in any way, not even her own individual punctuation, which I sometimes disagreed with.

If she didn't like the finished typed letter, which rarely happened, she herself changed it and it was retyped to her satisfaction. She was a perfectionist and I learned soon enough that even her hand-written manuscripts were carefully crafted, rarely needing another draft. The first draft was the finished draft - no scratching out, scribbling over, or starting again.

When the dictation of that first day was completed and some of the details out of the way I started an appointments calendar and a telephone directory which grew to read like a crazy mixed-up Who's Who - everybody from the youngest family member to Chou-En-Lai in China to Elizabeth Taylor and Richard Burton in Rome. After the necessary affairs of the day were dispensed with and I knew what secretarial work I would be expected to complete for her, Pearl Buck fell silent and stared deeply at me for a long moment. I waited expectantly, not knowing what was coming and finally I dropped my own gaze from her probing eyes. At last, as if satisfied with what she had been probing for, she smiled and spoke gently in measured words. Simply said, her words assumed complete understanding (on my part), complete confidence (on her part) and formed a mutual bond of trust between us and established the basis for my entire relationship with Pearl Buck.

"You must be my eyes and ears," she said, "for I must be about my writing. There is so much I must do and so little time in which to do it...."

The objective observer might well interject a question here. Was this some Mafia-like tactic cleverly designed to elicit blind trust in the new, capable but naive female flunky? Wouldn't certain ongoing events give credence to the suspicion that Pearl Buck and those other people with her were engaged in sneaky shenanigans which required, when things grew hot, a "respectable" person who could "front" for them and whose credentials could not be faulted? I early warned the reader that Pearl Buck was her own best character and that the truth of her own story might sound more like fiction. I am constantly aware that if I tell it like it is - was - there are those who will still say it's fiction. Without attempting any complicated analysis or dissection of her simple words, I state simply that I accepted my new role and the challenge of doing it well. I accepted as truth the fact that author Pearl Buck was in her seventy-ninth year with books and articles yet to write (I already had been given a book manuscript to work on). I accepted as truth the fact that humanitarian Pearl Buck, in her seventy-ninth year, was determinded to prevent the disintegration of her Foundation. And I accepted as truth the fact that the woman Pearl Buck was determined to prevent the disintegration of a man half her age who was so important to her at this period of her long life. It hurt her deeply, she said, that the Foundation and the man had been victims of scurrilous attacks. As the one person who had carried through her hard-fought plans for the Foundation, Ted Harris remained, till her death, the object of her grateful devotion and number one on her long list of concerns and worries. This fact cannot be glossed over or brushed aside as insignificant if one is to understand with any depth the real Pearl Buck behind the headlines.

I learned early that Pearl Buck could be demanding, even dictatorial but those tactics were designed to cut through red tape and speed up whatever it was she wanted done. Never once in my association with her was I aware of activities of hers being sinister or illegal. Yes, she could maneuver and manipulate and persuade people to bend the rules. She could be selfish and impatient. Her cloak and dagger tactics (velvet sledgehammer?) could be all of these things, but sinister or illegal? Nothing could be further from the truth. And although I frequently acted as her "front" - that is, speaking and acting on her behalf following her instructions, I was no flunky, and neither was Ted Harris. But so misunderstood and misrepresented were so many of her tactics that in exasperation even we laughed about "Pearl Buck and her evil ways."

"You must observe and tell me everything that goes on in Danby." Miss Buck commanded. Her immediate concern that day was what Halloween pranksters in the village might do. Did I think there would be any danger to the antiques shops or to the people, especially to Mr. Harris? "I can't believe," she fussed, "that at certain hours of the day there is only one Vermont State Trooper on duty in this part of the state." This remained a very real worry to her and if there had been enough hours in her day, was a problem which she would likely have taken upon herself to solve.

As it turned out, Halloween in Danby was uneventful, except for some minor egg throwing and window soaping. She was fascinated, however, when I related our Wells Halloween incident and I suspect it would eventually have found its way into one of her fictional stories. The incident was this: that a big pile of pumpkins - perhaps 50 or more that the boys had raised in their garden - and which they had been selling, had been stolen from under our very noses while we ate supper in the kitchen. It must have been somebody with a truck to be able to carry so many away, and a quiet truck at that, not to warn our ever-alert Big Red retriever. She liked that story and fussed anew about the lack of troopers around.

"Mrs. Drake," she said (and here let me say that she always called me Mrs. Drake, an odd formality which she herself could not explain but with which she felt comfortable.) "Mrs. Drake," she said, "you must get to know and understand Mr. Harris (again, her preferred formality and she rarely called him Ted), for it is important to me." I was to hear from her over and over the story of how she and Ted had first met in 1963 - he an Arthur Murray dance instructor and she a restless widow. Of immediate concern to her, however, was how to combat the so-called infamous Philadelphia Story. "A full written explanation is somewhere in our files - pay no attention to newspaper or magazine accounts." I took this (correctly) as an oblique suggestion that I should find and read this explanation and any other pertinent information in order that I might more fully understand and have no unanswered questions.

With that, I left Miss Buck for the rest of my fast-paced first day which, summarized from my own shorthand notes (which incidentally became a secret storehouse of all sorts of information and a much-needed outlet for my inner thoughts) reads like this:

Wow! My two worlds - home and hers. Running all day; don't like sharing IBM typewriter with Wendy; Ted in constant motion; he needs more and better helpers; unreal workload for three people; found the Philadelphia Story. I really like and trust Miss Buck and Ted; keep eyes and ears open at all times; everyone friendly. Home at 4:30; Mrs. Thomson's chicken dinner ready and waiting; so thankful she can work part time each day. Boys interested, Bill wary; says he's lost a wife, now he has a mistress; things will never be the same. Try try try to keep my two worlds separate.

Chapter 13

The Philadelphia Story

It is imperative to stop and clear away the gossip that swirled around Danby like chill Autumn winds. I knew that I would need the ultimate weapon — truth — to help combat the snide remarks that already were being directed at me. And for the truth about the Philadelphia Story and Ted Harris, always at the center of public controversy about Pearl Buck, I dropped my own velvet sledgehammer, by-passed everyone and everything and sought direct answers from Miss Buck. I never knew her to hide the truth from me, even when it hurt. Searching for the most direct and most accurate way to present what was behind the Philadelphia Story, I believe there is no better way than to repeat the full written account which she had directed me to in the files. This account, corroborated verbally over and over by Miss Buck, was actually written by Ted Harris as a speech to be delivered by him to the Board of Directors of the Pearl S. Buck Foundation from which he had resigned in a cloud of controversy. The written speech ends somewhat abruptly, as if the writer intended to summarize or end it with extemporaneous remarks. Here is the speech, then on to the man behind the speech, as told to me by Miss Buck:

I have asked to come here this evening to meet with you as a group in order that I may do what I have refused to do for seventeen months, and that is speak for myself.

I have not talked to anyone regarding my association with this Foundation except my own attorneys who are Gale Raphael and Louis Nizer. I have had numerous reporters and other parties, including criminal investigators from Internal Revenue try to get me to speak in my own behalf and I have not done so, not because of any guilt but because of one simple fear. I fear that to defend myself would do more damage to Pearl Buck and to the Foundation we set up together than has already boon dono. I opcak now bccauoc I vowed that during Pearl Buck's lifetime I would put the entire story into the minutes of a Board meeting of this Foundation in order that it become a permanent part of a public record, and during her life time because if there is any part of what I have to say that is not true I wish her to so state as a part of that same record.

After sixteen months of careful scrutiny Internal Revenue has dropped their criminal investigation of me and has finally decided that there is no evidence of fraud, a fact I could have told them and did in fact tell them through my attorneys, but I wished them to find out for themselves. As a matter of fact I told my attorney to tell them to charge me if they could and that then I would speak in my defense but until they could find the evidence to charge me I would not even talk to them.

I do not wish the newspapers or anyone else to know what I have to say because it does not concern anyone other than those present here tonight and I'm not sure that it's any of your business except that it is your Foundation and I feel that you have a right to know its master plan, how it was laid out and to understand why.

When I met Pearl Buck I was a salesman and today, I

am still a salesman and I shall always remain a salesman, and it is a perfectly honorable profession. In training sales people in the past, and I have done a great deal of that, the very first point I make is that a salesman must be absolutely honest in everything he says, for when he lies he becomes a con man and there are laws to put con men in jail. I have no wish to go to jail, ladies and gentlemen, so I can assure you that I am not now and will never become a con man. I am a salesman and a very good one, and I have never claimed to be anything else; and if it was of any importance I could give you a long list of famous salesmen in whose classes I have learned my profession but since none of you is a salesman you probably would not be familiar with any but Dale Carnegie. I have also sent several members of this organization to Dale Carnegie and some at my own expense.

When Pearl Buck asked me to head her Foundation it was, according to her, because of my salesmanship that she wished me to accept. I reminded her at that time that as one of the world's greatest literary figures she should choose a man with a degree or at least a retired military officer as the head of her organization and not a man such as I, highly trained in my chosen profession, but with only eight years of formal schooling. Her argument to me at that time and still is that I have more than adequate formal schooling in my chosen profession to do the job she wished done, a sales job. She wished me to sell to the American public the bastard children of their sons and to persuade them to do something to help them. She specifically told me at that time that she wished *none* of her money used to directly benefit *any* child but that she wished her money used to set up a tool that would

provide a way by which responsible Americans could fulfill at least a part of their responsibility for these
children. She further told me that she was no longer
young, that she wished to see this done during her
lifetime so that she would know that indeed it was done.
She informed me that since 1960 she had tried to get the
Board of Welcome House to do the job and that they had
promised they would do so and that in four years they
had done nothing and she said to me, "I have no time
now to crawl, we must run, we must do everything at
once."

She also said she would prefer not to ask the general
public for support but would prefer to go to a small number of important persons who have control of vast sums
of money and interest them in undertaking this project.
I told her then that I could not see that anyone would
give us vast sums of money for a project not yet in existence and that I felt we should appeal to the public for
small sums and get something started and show what
could be done and then go for large contributions to expand already successful work but in this instance, as in
all others, I deferred to her judgement. To the long list
that once appeared on our Board of Governors, all of
whom control vast sums of money, we went personally
and talked of what we wished done. After several months
of driving and talking, Mamie Dowd Eisenhower sent us
five dollars and that represents the total of all of their
contributions except a humorous article by Art Buch-
wald, which I practically forced him through embarrassment to write and spasmodic support of a child by Arlene
Frances until Paul Robeling, a personal friend of Pearl
Buck, gave a contribution, after she asked him to become
a Governor. This organization was founded on January

25, 1964, and its first office was in the kitchen of my apartment in Jenkintown, where it remained until March 13, 1964, when it moved to a small and certainly not deluxe apartment in the Drake Hotel where I worked alone until April 20, 1964, when Mrs. Wolfson joined me. On March 12th, 1964, Miss Buck and I were in her car going to New York to see another important and wealthy man, Joseph Levine, and I told her at that time that I would have to see some facts and figures so that I could see what I had to work with in order to proceed. Miss Buck closed the window separating the driver's compartment from ours, and as we have many times since, we mapped out our plans. That is the main reason we have always had a chauffeur, not because I want one because I prefer to drive myself, but because with someone to drive we can work, which we always do. Two Foundation books, FOR SPACIOUS SKIES which was actually written in the back of a car and THE NEW YEAR which was laid out and planned in the back of a car, among other works we have accomplished while being driven.

She informed me that her income was between $125,000.00 and $150,000.00 per year of which she needed $50,000,00 per year to maintain her standard of living and about $50,000,00 for taxes and other expenses and could give $50,000.00 to the Foundation. At that time she also asked me if I would undertake a job no one had ever undertaken and look into her personal financial affairs and help her to straighten them out for she felt that in spite of paying lawyers and accountants and having had two husbands, she had never found anyone who could help her. She told me that her husband's seven-year-long illness had put her deeply in debt, as indeed it had, and that she had no help from anyone, though his own son, her step-son, was then president of The John Day Company, the stock of which he holds today because Pearl Buck insisted she not inherit from her husband's estate even though their entire living expenses up to and including all of his medical expenses came from her income alone for his income was totally committed elsewhere.

I told her that that was not the way Foundations were set up, that usually a person wanting to start a Foundation founded it with a lump sum, usually large, and then contributed to it each year, and that then a budget could be worked out. She told me she had no time to work this out, that there were still books she wished to write, that if she knew how to do what she wished done she would not need me, and again she emphasized she wished all of this done during her lifetime. As a matter of fact, at that time, she made an entry in her personal journal, the book from which I quoted in my later biography of her and referred to as The Treasure Book in which she began, "Today I have set up my Foundation..." and which she ended saying, "Ted Harris is a brilliant young man with energy, a keen mind and is capable of great dedication. I have about ten years left...let that be enough." She told me she was willing to give everything she had to the Foundation except for a trust that would provide a small income for her children, and she emphasized small. She told me to do what she wanted done and to do it quickly. She told me of her dreams of a Townhouse to be centrally located which could eventually house the awards from her literary career and where future generations could come to learn of her and through her could learn of these children at the same time. I listened as she talked of a library of all of her books in foreign languages with reading rooms where foreign students could come for study. She told me also that above all everything that bore her name must be of the finest quality and in the very best of taste. She emphasized that the money she herself gave was to be used for these purposes and that only public funds were to be used for direct aid to children. Before the office moved from Jenkintown, we contacted a realtor whom I knew and asked him to find a large old estate that someone might give us as a place to work. He took us to the Paley Estate in Chestnut Hill and told us he thought this perhaps could be worked out if Pearl Buck knew someone in the Paley family. She did, and he made further inquiry and told us we would have to apply directly to the Paley Foundation and then go to the family, and we did so apply. In the meantime, we moved to the Drake Hotel, whereupon Pearl Buck decided she did not wish her Foundation in Chestnut Hill but in Center City where anyone could get to it easily. We called the Paley Foundation and withdrew our request because this was her wish and it was to be her Foundation, down to the last detail. She asked me to go into her financial situation and figure out how to do what she wished done. While we were still working with the original one thousand dollars from the Gimble award, I sat down with her and looked. During all of this, only she and I were present for she has never wished anyone, including her children, to know anything of her affairs, but she knew if I was to do what she wished, I had to know. I am still the only person alive to have seen much of the material we went over together, including her personal journal.

What I found was not good and gave little to hope for in the way of improvement. Her total indebtedness at that time perhaps balanced her total assets but if they did, it was by a very slim margin and her indebtedness was added to by many many thousands of dollars shortly after that by a situation of which she was totally unaware which made her completely responsible for the heavy business loss of a member of her family.

I told her, after careful study, and after consultation with two different legal firms that in my opinion the following moves would accomplish her goals in seven years - remembering that she had said during her lifetime and had expressed her feeling that that was at least ten years and this would give her at least three years to enjoy the work.

1. I told her that in my opinion she had never traveled enough in this country to keep alive the image of the only American woman to win the Nobel prize for literature. When I spoke of her to persons of my generation the response was too frequently, "Pearl who?" or "Oh, you mean that Chinese woman who wrote THE GOOD EARTH." If she wished, in my opinion, to undertake such a big work because she was American, as she told me, then she had to have the definite image of being American, a very great American, and very much alive.

She asked how this was to be done, stating she loathed speaking engagements, hated all forms of publicity and wished only to write though travel appealed to her but cautioned me she did not know for how many more years she would be able to travel so we had better get busy. I believe my exact words to her were, "We have to somehow get out and beat the bushes and let people know you are still around."

She told me she would go but that she did not wish to

make speeches except briefly to tell of the children. She explained she had in the past agreed to make one tour of speaking engagements and had cancelled after the first speech because she hated it so much - that she had felt she had to give so much of herself because people were paying to hear her and that she was not a performer but a writer and someone else would have to sell her books.

2. I told her I felt I could walk over the boundaries of all of her property with the right realtors and sell the idea of eventual development thereby substantially increasing the appraisals and that then with these higher appraisals that were realistic based on our plans, she could then convey her real estate to the Foundation, subject to her lifetime residency in her homes in Pennsylvania and Vermont and subject to her daughter Jean's residency in her home in Bucks County and subject to her children's use of the home in Vermont which they themselves built for the lifetime of her youngest child, and subject to all of her indebtedness including that represented by the substantial business loss by one of her children, all of which I was assured was absolutely legitimate because of the increased evaluations I felt I could get.

3. I told her I felt we had to substantially increase her own personal income which I felt could be accomplished in two ways - increasing the sale of her books while traveling, by increasing the demand for her titles, and by selling them ourselves with the proceeds going to the Foundation. She agreed as long as she did not have to sell her books herself, which she had never done, as long as she did not have to give or attend autograph parties, and as long as she did not have to give long lectures.

4. I told her that because of my educational background and because of my health - I suffered a very severe attack of hepatitis (which I contracted from impure water) in 1957 and had only very recently recovered my full energy, that I did not feel that I could maintain the pace needed to fulfill all of her dreams in a short time. That I felt all of this could be accomplished in seven years and be set up with work being done in all seven countries and on a permanent basis, but that in the event that my health did give out I would have to have the security of some sort of medical retirement beginning after ten years and automatic retirement at my wish after twenty-five years, and I expressed to her that my desire to eventually develop other resources and become the unpaid president of her Foundation, an idea to which she emphatically objected but a dream to which I clung.

5. I told her I wished to bring to help me certain persons I knew would help me upon whom I knew I could depend and who would perform their duties to the utmost of their abilities and who would be completely honest and whom I knew would work long hours for next to no money to get us started. That we would need Lillian Wolfson as a secretary, a highly competent woman who worked with me on a fund raising benefit in the past year. Wendy and Alan Conklin would be needed and while I knew, and told Pearl Buck in the beginning, that I did not feel they were the highly qualified individuals that would be needed to fill the positions, they were and are fully qualified to create those positions. Wendy was keeping a set of books at that time and had previous experience in bookkeeping. Alan had sales experience, fund raising experience of a minor sort, and direct mail experience. Another person I wished to bring was James

Pauls, a man of varied and valuable experience as a Production Planner in Lockheed and Douglas aircraft companies, as a cabinet maker and construction supervisor in several firms on both the East and West Coasts, and three years as professional photographer on Tom Brennaman's Breakfast in Hollywood, a job which ended with the death of Tom Brennaman, and also as an excellent promotion man for me for ten years prior to that time. Jim was involved in an unfortunate experience in Jenkintown in 1962 in an entrapment situation. His mother was very ill and his only wish was to avoid any publicity which might bring harm to her and, good or bad advice, his attorney suggested that one way to avoid any possible mention was to plead guilty, pay his fine, and that he had state connections to obtain a full pardon for Jim at a later time. Jim followed his advice and the attorney died before obtaining that pardon and so the record still remains. I have known the man for more than twenty years and I have never known him to be capable of a single evil or dishonest deed nor will I believe he is now capable. Pearl Buck knew of all of this and everything that I knew of all of these persons several months before any of them came to work for the Foundation because I told her myself long before anyone else had the opportunity to do so. I also told her I was sure that none of us had ever had any experience in setting up any kind of charity or Foundation and to this she replied, "No, but this is a new work to be done and for an entirely new group of persons. No one has any experience in this work and I have had a lot of experience with people who have strings of degrees and they sit in offices behind desks and they don't get anything done."

I also sat down with Pearl Buck and told her my entire

life story from the very first moment I could remember, leaving out nothing not even some of the most intimate and personal details in order that anything anyone might ever tell her about me, if it were true, she would already know it from me and if it were not she would know it was a lie. There is nothing I concealed from her nor do I now conceal anything.

I have taken a very long time so far and I am sorry but I want you to see how very much took place in the first couple of months of 1964 and now I will go over briefly what has taken place since then, and I shall attempt to be very brief. I have only told you all of this in order that you know I was fully aware of Pearl Buck's full financial condition, which was indeed very bleak, even before I became head of the Foundation, I knew the full and complete background of how it got that way - and she in turn knew everything about me and my associates.

In the years that followed I will tell only the things that I feel have not been told by anyone else. I will tell you in advance that I am not and have never been a nice guy. I have never wanted to be a nice guy because as the saying goes, "Nice guys finish last." I have never in my life been interested in finishing in any position but on top and if you help me or if I think you can, you can enjoy the benefit of my professional charm - which I have and know that I have because it has been my business to be charming. I made it my business to acquire the know-how of personal charm. But do not be deceived; I am not a nice guy. If you can help me to do what I have made up my mind I am going to accomplish, I will like you and you will like me and we will get along fine. But if it appears you will hinder me in any way, I can and will be ruthless in removing you as quickly as possible from my life. In 1964 I pledged all of my efforts toward accomplishing the aims Pearl Buck outlined for me. It has been said many times by a member of your present staff that "Ted Harris is demanding but fair."

6. I outlined the Arthur Murray tours of benefit balls because Miss Buck needed to travel, had no money to do so, the Foundation had no money and the balls would at least pay all the costs for thousands of column inches of publicity about Pearl Buck and the Amerasians. It was all done for publicity and to enable us to meet with important persons in every city in the country. It was standard procedure to get the key to the city, hold a press conference, meet for a time with important persons, rest for a while, attend the ball, go to bed, then the next day move on to another city and do the same things all over again for thirty to sixty days in a row. On the first tour Miss Buck's chauffeur drove and he was rude, crude and unattractive - not just to me but often to strangers. I believe his tour ended the day Miss Buck wished to continue and push through to home in one day because we were tired after forty motels and he pulled up to a motel and refused to go on after eight hours. He was nearly fired outright, but instead he was relegated to painting while we went on tour. He hates painting so ask him what a nice guy I am. I hired a young man to wear a uniform and drive. Why young? Because you can get a young man to travel cheap for a couple of years and you can't get a mature man cheap for anything. We paid our average chauffeur (house man when not driving) fifty dollars a week and bought them nothing but uniforms. The balls produced more than expenses ranging from $500 to $5000 per stop. After the Arthur Murray balls became no longer news, I asked Miss Buck if she would

accept speaking engagements if she only gave the same speech she delivered at the balls, and she agreed. It was after she had been accused of Communist tendencies several times that she told me she wished to discuss only the Foundation with the press, and you can take my word for it there were many times I was not a nice guy when reporters wished to talk about other things - *she* never refused - *I* always did because I felt it would be bad public relations for her to refuse, and I made many enemies in our press corps. At any rate, the tours were a success bringing $30,000 to $50,000 in funds to the Foundation for each tour and we took one in the spring and one in the fall from 1964 to 1968 and all of the fees, from $2000 to $3000 per engagement, except for a few special ones, went to the Foundation - plus all of the publicity and the resulting very large contributions. Hawkins and Wilson resulted from these tours, and Wilson from a ball. On the final tours I drove myself because it was easier to do so than to hire someone to do so at the salary we were prepared to pay. At times Miss Buck and I were on the road for as many as eighteen hours a day.

7. Alan and Wendy came to the Foundation after the first tour and regardless of any personal problems they may have had Alan put out 100,000 pieces of mail for me every month for one entire year, mailing to the phone books of the cities we visited and showed a profit on first contributions and built a donors list of 8600 that year and he was paid by the grand sum total of fifty dollars per week for that year. I can tell you I didn't feel like a nice guy when I fired that man at the insistence of the Philadelphia Volunteer Chapter because the pressure I had applied on him sent him back to drinking - a problem he had had in the past. As far as bookkeeping is con-

cerned, Wendy did no worse for $50 per week for the year 1965 than her followers have done and they get a damn sight more money and string of degrees, if I am to judge by the fact that $24,000 dollars that Miss Buck spent February 28, 1966, as a down payment on the Spruce Street building was not entered on any book anywhere until December 31, 1969, even though accountants, attorneys and bookkeepers and directors were told to set it up on the books as a loan by Miss Buck to the Foundation and not a gift. I didn't feel very much like a nice guy when Wendy had to go also, but it was said by others that she threatened the success of the work so she too had to go..."

And of the man behind the speech, which ends so abruptly as if he had said all he wanted to say and enough is enough is enough —

Chapter 14

TFH

Of that man behind the speech, Pearl Buck wrote these words in 1966; taken from her Treasure Book of private poetry and prose, they remained the definitive essence of her feelings for Ted Harris until the day she died.

To TFH
What are you to me?
You are my faith renewed.
Lost through the years.
Yet now by faith imbued,
I cease my fears.

What are you to me?
A heart so quick and true,
That my own heart,
Inured, is stirred anew
To do its part.

What are you to me?
A strong young source of power,
Who, with no strife,
But bringing seed to flower.
Infuses life.

And it should be further noted that on May 21, 1971, she wrote this dedication in the front of the Treasure Book:

This book I give, will, bequeath to Theodore S. Harris, to be his own, forever, in recognition of all he has done on my behalf and for me.

/s/ Pearl S. Buck

It was inevitable that Ted Harris' position in Pearl Buck's business affairs and his personal relationship with her should come under constant scrutiny by family, friends, and foes. A flamboyant forty-year-old dancer with a hazy past living under the same roof with a seventy-nine-year-old world famous writer? Surely, but surely, Ted Harris could be up to no good with Pearl Buck and she was being duped by a flattering fake - a fraud, a fancy gigolo who really was a homosexual (this last bit, when I heard it in 1971, was usually repeated in an embarrassed whisper).

It is of the utmost importance to realize that Americans had just emerged from the militant upheavals and loud protests of the 60's, and we were standing uneasily on the threshhold of yet another history-shattering and history-making decade which would find us floundering uncomfortably through the Vietnam War, Women's Lib, Watergate, and a frightening epidemic of new attitudes and life styles. We were being fed a rich diet which spawned all kinds of ailments, for which it seemed there was no cure except time and hopefully, understanding and tolerance which comes with maturity. Even the media (except for the scandal sheets) worried about their reputations and ratings and tiptoed around such scary topics as living together without marriage, black and white problems, the joys of sex for women, pornography, and babies out of wedlock. Abortion

was a hot issue and homosexual and lesbian were unacceptable four-letter words, replaced in polite conversation by
queer and fruitcake. Gay hadn't entered our vocabularies
yet, except in the old-fashioned sense of being light-hearted
and merry. Queers and fruitcakes were members of some
mysterious and nefarious underground made up mostly of
artists, writers, musicians, and dancers - the Bohemians of
an earlier era. They were the out-of-step members of our
Puritan society to be pitied, ridiculed, scorned, to be kept at
a distance by "nice" folks. We had to move through a dark age
of suspicion and embarrassment to reach a new age of enlightenment and freedom and reason. A later generation
would have it easier, but in 1971 speculation simmered behind closed doors, amid much tsk-tsking, eyebrow raising
and off-color hearsay. We were going through public puber-
ty, and we were definitely not comfortable with the exploding times which challenged our old conservatism and forced
us to think about a new liberalism.

Pearl Buck settling into Danby, in the very heart of shel-
tered Yankee conservatism, can be likened to an exotic bird
of paradise dropping into a flock of nesting hens - peaceful
coexistence might be possible but not without plenty of ruffled feathers and critical cluckings.

Of the critical cluckings, Miss Buck offered one of her
droll one-liners. I have already directed Mr. Harris to write
a complete expose called *Pearl Buck, Her Evil Ways* - said so
very seriously with an evil twinkle in her eyes. And I understood why Archie Bunker in the new television program "All
in the Family" was a favorite of hers. She saw the pathos and
the humor behind the exaggerated prejudice and bigotry.
This ability was a saving grace in her own life, for if she
was to continue with her own creativity she would have to
continue to rise above the barbs of those who could not see

and could not understand yet.

There was nothing coarse, or crass, or cheap about conversation with Miss Buck, and I cannot imagine anyone confronting her directly with the street talk I was hearing. Things like "Hey Pearl Baby, who's keepin' yer feet warm these days?' or "Who ya kidding callin' that fruitcake yer Business Manager?" or "Ted Harris ain't even his real name - what's he doin' hidin' behind an old lady's skirts?" Maybe, maybe not, she would laugh at this insulting low-brow language, so I carefully rephrased the street talk I heard so she would know the basic questions circulating about Ted.

1. How would you describe your relationship with Ted Harris?

"Ours is an unusual relationship, based upon mutual confidence and understanding. He knows me better than anyone else does, and because of that I chose him personally to write my biography, something I have never allowed anyone else to do. Mr. Harris is a man of extraordinary intellectual powers and innate business ability."

2. But no relationship between a man and a woman can be all intellectual, without the physical, can it?

"That is a delicate question, one I have spent much time pondering. I think you will find the answer in THE GODDESS ABIDES, my latest novel, soon to be published, for I am there as the central character exploring a relationship with a younger man and a much older man as well. I will be interested in your own reaction..."

3. Is Ted Harris a pen name or stage name?

"Theodore F. Harris is his legal name, but not the name he was born with. Ted Harris was born Frederick Hair - an impossible name, as you can see, for it became F. Red Hair and the object of much ridicule. He comes of an old, quite distinguished Carolina family that fell on hard times, and he is a direct descendant of Robert E. Lee. They are strikingly similar in appearance."

4. Is, or was, Ted more attracted to men than women?

"Perhaps, at some time, he has been more attracted to men, though he tells me that is over and in the past. It worries me that he has a tendency to be attracted to the wrong kind of people especially women of lesser intellect. It is not important to me except that people do not understand him and he is hurt by their lack of understanding. He has been married three times - he is still married today, to a woman older than he is - an old friend whom I have met. They are married in name only, for she lives on the West Coast and he, of course, lives here on the East Coast. Some of these things I am writing about in what I call THE GENIUS BOOK, another manuscript you will be typing..."

It did not matter one bit to me whether Ted was or was not a homosexual; as long as Miss Buck was satisfied with his business capabilities and his friendship, who was I to waste valuable time in idle speculation. I did not then, nor do I now, have all the answers as to why Pearl Buck was so intensely devoted to Ted Harris. They were friends of a very special kind. They had been together for many years now. What is it, anyway, that sustains a deep and lasting relationship between one human being and another human being, be it woman-man, woman-woman, or man-man. In her Treasure Book of September 20, 1968 Miss Buck must also have been wondering as she wrote:

Question

You are not brave,

I am not brave,

Love's debt unpaid

We are afraid

Lest we destroy

Our present joy.

I born too soon,

You born too late,

We two still wait.

Our times not matched,

Our hearts are latched.

Yet comes that day

I go, you stay.

I gone, you here -

What then, my dear?"

Chapter 15

The Goddess Abides

Love is a questing spirit,

Seeking where to find

A human frame to live in,

A human heart to bind.

A human heart to bind, dear love,

And so I offer mine.

Accept this heart and, if you will,

Use it as bread and wine.

THE GODDESS ABIDES was released in 1972, and a pre-publication announcement stated, "The author has long wished to write a novel based upon the many ways it is possible for one human being to love another. This is the book that has been growing in her mind for many years. It is the story of a woman and her involvement with two men - one younger and one older - and the goddess abides."

As a preface to her own novel, Miss Buck used the following from THE WHITE GODDESS by author Robert Graves:

A Muse-poet falls in love, absolutely, and his true love is for him the embodiment of the Muse. In many cases the power of absolutely falling in love soon vanishes; if only because the woman takes no trouble to preserve whatever glory she gets from the knowledge of her beauty and the power she exercises over her poet-lover. She grows embarrassed by this glory, repudiates it, and ends up either as a housewife or a tramp; he, in disillusion, turns to Apollo who, at any rate, can provide him with a livelihood and intelligent entertainment - and goes out of circulation before his middle-twenties. But the real, perpetually obsessed Muse-poet makes a distinction between the Goddess as revealed in the supreme power, glory, wisdom and love of woman, and the individual woman in whom the Goddess may take up residence for a month, a year, seven years, or even longer. The Goddess abides.

* * *

In no other novel has Pearl Buck revealed herself as intimately as she does through a woman called Edith in THE GODDESS ABIDES. In revealing herself, she gently touches the universal needs and desires in each of us - man or woman. THE GODDESS ABIDES has a pleasant setting and is a lightly written story for enjoyable reading. Its power lies in the deft handling of delicate involvements and the reasoning leading into and away from the involvements.

Miss Buck was keenly interested in my reaction to this

Pearl S. Buck

newest novel of hers, and I sensed a worry and concern about just what my reaction would be. She need not have worried, for I related instantly to what I knew was writer and woman rolled into one. Further, she had touched me deeply and personally as I sought to unravel my own intimate thoughts about personal relationships.

"THE GODDESS ABIDES is pure and beautiful reading," I enthused, "and I believe I'm right in saying that it is pure and beautiful Pearl Buck. But I fear it will not be understood by everyone, especially men. Men should read it but I doubt many will..."

Relieved at my comments, she said, "You are quite right, my dear, in all you say, and I thank you for calling the book pure and beautiful. There will be many, I dare say, who do not understand the story at all...."

The Edith in the book is a recent widow, searching for herself at mid-life. She is involved with Edwin, a philosopher-professor years her senior and Jared, an engineer-inventor years her junior. Both men had real-life counterparts in the author's life. Ernest Hocking was the old and revered philosopher, now gone. Ted Harris, for the most part, was the younger man Jared. I say for the most part, for Jared contained some elements of another younger man during an earlier interlude in Miss Buck's career. She spoke very little about that other younger man, and it is safe to say that Jared is very much Ted Harris.

Relative to my delicately-phrased question about whether or not it is possible for a woman to have just an intellectual relationship with a man without the physical side, I never could and I never would ask Pearl Buck outright whether she had slept with Ted Harris. It was none of my business in the first place, and in the second place, even if I had asked the direct question, she would not have replied with a direct answer. It was too crude and not her way in such matters, either as a woman or as a writer. As both, she handled the most intimate dimension of love and desire with perfumed subtleties and petal-soft finesse.

From the pages of what she called her very sophisticated love story, here is how she handled a poignant scene with the older man. Edwin, the old philosopher, is speaking:

"We inhabit these bodies, my darling. They are our only means of conveying love. We speak, of course, but words are only words. We kiss, yes, but a kiss is only a touch of the lips. There is the whole body through which the sacred message can be exchanged. And for what do we nurture the body with food and drink and sleep and exercise except for the conveyance of love?"

When she hesitated, transfixed by sudden shyness, he laughed, but gently.

"Don't be afraid, my child." I have been quite impotent these ten years. I wish only to lie quietly at your side in the darkness of the night, and know that finally we are one, never again to be separate, however far apart we may be."

She was able to speak at last. She heard herself say words as unbelievable as those he had spoken. Yet she spoke them. "Why not?" she said, "Why not?"

....They parted as usual after the usual late dinner. In the presence of Henry the butler they said good night formally and so wholly as usual that she half wondered whether she had not imagined the sunset scene. And knew she had not, for with an instinct, long dead, now in her own room she searched among her garments until she found a lace-trimmed nightgown. She wore plain suits by day, their simplicity becoming her classic face, but secretly, at night, ever since she had been alone, she bought and wore, now that Arnold was dead, those fragile exquisite confections that he had disliked. Pajamas suited her better, he had said, and so she had worn them until he was gone. Then, and who could possibly understand this, the very day after his funeral she had gone to the finest shop in the city, and had bought a dozen nightgowns, wisps of lace and silk and, quite alone, she decked herself nightly for sleep.

Thus she decked herself now, after her scented bath, and standing before the mirror she brushed her long fair hair and braided it as usual and climbed into the high old bed as though nothing were about to happen, and lay there, her heart beating in expectant alarm that was also reluctantly pleasurable. Should she sleep - could she sleep? Debating it, she fell into a light slumber without being aware that she did so. She was wakened by his voice. He was bending over her, a lit candle in his hand.

"I knocked, you know, darling, but there was no answer. And so I came in, hoping to see you beautiful in sleep as I have been doing these last five minutes. Now I know what sleep does to your dear face. You were almost smiling."

He put the candlestick on the bedside table. He lay down beside her as though it were already habit and, slipping his right arm beneath her head, he lifted her to his shoulder.

"Now then, we're comfortable, aren't we? And we are as it should be, man and woman lying side by side in mutual trust. I shan't ask you to marry me, my love. It wouldn't be fair to you. I'm too old."

"What if I ask you?" she inquired. Comfort, sweet and profound, flowed into her blood.

"Ah, that would be a question," he replied.

But no, she thought, she would never ask it. Marriage? She had no wish for it. Marriage would make her think of Arnold. Let her explore this relationship with Edwin quite free of memories!

Suddenly he threw back the covers and sat up to survey her. "What's this lovely thing you have on, this gossamer garment, this silver cobweb?"

She lay smiling in enjoyment of his pleasure. "You like it?"

"Very much, but - "

He broke off and she felt his hands dexterously slipping the lace from her shoulders, from her breasts, her waist and thighs, until the garment that had covered her lay in a soft heap at her feet.

"Blessed be our bodies, for they are the means of love!"

She did not reply, choosing to allow him to lead where he would, watchful only for distaste in herself. But there was no distaste. Nothing she had ever known prepared her now for his grace, his delicacy, the sureness of his touch. The philosophy of love! The phrase sprang into her mind. This was more than physical, whatever it was. Then he put aside the robe he wore and lay beside her again.

"Now we know each other," he said. "We can never be strange to each other from this hour on."

There in the night they lay in each other's arms, passionate and passionless. The moon rose high and shone through the wide window and she saw his body, beautiful even in age, the shoulders straight, the chest smooth, the legs slender and strong. He had given his body respectful care, and was rewarded even now. And how many women had loved this body? Impossible that so powerful a beauty of mind and body had not combined often in the act of love! But she felt no jealousy. This was her hour, her night. And it was true that, knowing themselves as they were, they could never again be far apart.

"Yes," she said clearly and aloud.

"Yes, what, my sweet?"

"Yes, I love you."

He gave a long sigh and drew her again to him. "I thank God," he said. "Whom I have not seen, I thank. Once more, before the end, to love and be loved! What more can I ask!"

* * *

Farther on in the book, as farther on in the life of Pearl Buck, comes this scene involving the younger man. The woman's mood and the setting are described before the man speaks:

"The air had been golden with sunlight through the afternoon, turning at sunset to rose and crimson. Evening star and a crescent moon hung over the trees and beneficent calm pervaded her - and him, too, she felt, a relaxed mood which was in itself communication between them. She was happy in his presence, she now realized, happier than she had been for a long time, happier perhaps than she had ever been. Certainly with no one had she felt this conviction of life and its goodness, this ease of presence with another human being. She turned to him impulsively and found him looking at her, dark eyes questioning.

"Shall we stop here? Dine and then walk on the beach?"

"Yes," she said. "In this air - what is that scent? Pines, I think. It is too late in the year for flowers, though it's still warm in this climate."

"Pines warmed by the day's sun," he said. "And shall we stay here for the night? At this season the inn will be nearly empty. I dare say - people at home for Christmas, but you and I are making our own Christmas."

"Let us stay," she said.

He gave her a look, passionate and deep, and for an instant she wondered what it meant. There could be no question, surely there could be no question about rooms, separate rooms. She was startled to discover in herself the question answered, hidden in her own being a reluctant yearning to forget her years and her reserves. She was no longer any man's wife. She was free to be what she wished to be, to do what she wanted to do. There was no need to refuse herself - or him - anything that pleased them. She had fulfilled all duties to others.

"Then I will engage our rooms." he said.

He left her in the car while he entered the office of the inn and she sat alone, a sweet intoxication pervading her. She recognized it without ever having felt it before, a powerful attraction to this man, an attraction of mind first, but so complete that it flowed through her body in a warm current. She tried to stay it, control it, to analyze it. Let her remember herself. Let her ask herself what she truly wanted - no complications, she told herself, no foolish complications of emotion. Above all, no heartbreak at this time of her life.

He came back in a moment, very cheerful, very composed.

"I got adjoining rooms," he said. "If you want anything you can call me."

....She woke in the night as usual after five hours of sleep. That was her habit - five hours of deep dreamless sleep and then she woke absolutely, her mind clear and aware. Moonlight streamed through the open window and the air was crisply chill. She pulled the covers ahout her shoulders and breathed deeply. There was a smell of the sea, the softly rushing sound of distant surf. This was how it would be in her house on the cliff when she slept there alone. Only now she was not alone. That is to say, Jared was on the other side of the closed door, not locked, only closed. She was suddenly acutely aware that it was not locked, only closed.

"There's no telephone between rooms in an old inn like this." Jared had said. "I'll not lock the door in case of anything."

She had not replied. Instead she had stood quite still in the center of this big square room with its four-poster double bed.   "I hate to say good night," Jared said.

"It was a delightful dinner," she said. "I didn't know how hungry I was."

"Oh, I'm always a hungry beast," he twisted his handsome mouth in a wry smile as he spoke.

"You should be to cover that big skeleton of yours," she

said.

He had not replied to this. Instead, after an instant of looking at her intently, he had put his arms about her and kissed her full on the lips.

"Good night, you darling" he said, and opening the door between the rooms, he closed it firmly.

....Now, lying in the big bed, she thought of the kiss. He had simply given it, taken it, without asking and without comment. She felt again the young warmth of his lips against hers as she remembered the moment. But was she not being ridiculous? What was a kiss nowadays? Women kissed men, men kissed women, with no feeling beyond a cheerful friendliness. Ah, but not she! She had never been one to give kisses easily or to welcome them. Even with Arnold they had seemed - unnecessary. As for Edwin,his kisses had been those of a child - or an old, old man, tender but pure. So what had this kiss been, this kiss which she still felt upon her lips? Then she rebuked herself again. The truth was that no one kissed her nowadays and she kissed no one. This one kiss lingered in her memory now merely because it was unaccustomed.

Then at this moment, as though to refute this self-deception, her body rose to defy her. She was suddenly seized by a surge of physical longing such as she had not known for years. No, let her be honest with herself. She had never known such longing, perhaps because she had always before this had the means of satisfaction. Now a door stood between and it was only closed, not locked. Suppose the impossible, suppose she got up from this alien bed, suppose she wrapped her rose silk negligee about her - it lay there on the chair - and suppose that she opened the door softly into that other room and then went in, even if it were only to stand and look at him as he slept. And if he woke and saw her standing there —

No, it could not be done. Perhaps, if she could be sure that he would not wake? But how could she be sure? And suppose his eyes opened, how could she know what she would see there. She did not know him well enough. She could not risk the possible rejection. She was too proud. Of course there were women who could cast away all pride, women who would count on physical response whatever the cost, but she knew herself. She could not escape herself, shamed. She would walk on shame, thereafter, and then whom would she have? She had only herself.

She lay rigid with desire, refusing to move, refusing to rise, refusing to walk across the floor, refusing the very imagination of what it would be to open the door and see him lying there, even sleeping. She forbade it to herself, until at last the throbbing of her body subsided and she slept."

* * *

Edith did not sleep with Jared that night or any subsequent night. In the last few pages of the book the woman, laughing inside herself and alone now, has this to say: "Only a goddess could fulfill all that she was demanding of herself. This, then, was her first task, to make of herself a goddess, the first task and the most difficult. She must set herself apart if she was to fulfill the monumental task, which in itself must be perfection."

Yes, I had the answer to my delicately posed question. Nothing, during my increasingly intimate association with both Miss Buck and Ted Harris, ever caused me to change my mind. Whatever it was they shared set them apart - this shared love affair of the mind which was all-consuming, passionate and passionless. I marveled at the extraordinary sensitivity and total understanding which flowed between them.

....."the real, perpetually obsessed Muse-poet makes a distinction between the Goddess as revealed in the supreme power, glory, wisdom and love of woman, and the individual woman in whom the Goddess may take up residence for a month, a year, seven years, or even longer." The goddess abides.

Chapter 16

People Yes, Machines No

As a secretary, my first experience with another aspect of Miss Buck's impatience came soon enough the morning she handed me the draft of a lengthy magazine article and said, "Please type this as soon as possible. And I shall want to read it, of course, before it is mailed off to the editor."

The manuscript was given top priority in my folder of never-ending work to accomplish: the daily stacks of correspondence, telephone calls to answer and initiate, memos, reminders, and always waiting when everything else was done (an impossibility) the big current manuscript Miss Buck was working on with the tentative title of THE GENIUS BOOK. Without saying anything to anyone, that morning I had lugged my old standard Royal typewriter from home, and one of the young men helping in the store downstairs had positioned it in the office next to Wendy's IBM Electric machine which we were to share for the time being. There was no money yet to buy a second expensive electric typewriter and besides, Ted told me, "the IBM Executive creates the kind of image Miss Buck's manuscripts and letters should have." Not for me, I stubbornly decided, was that monstrous machine with its keys that typed with the slightest touch and its individual spacing which made correcting and repositioning a mathematical nightmare. I considered that it was in control of me, and not the other way

Beverly Drake in Pearl S. Buck's gold velvet chair at Darby House, 1972 - photo by Linda Richardson

around, and for me this was not conducive to turning out my best work in the least amount of time.

I was just starting on page two, working rapidly and confidently with my old Royal, when Miss Buck called on her private phone from Danby House. "Mrs. Drake," she said. "Have you finished typing the article yet?" I stared incredulously into the phone, then at my watch. Only a few minutes had elapsed since I had left Miss Buck and I hadn't been sitting around drinking coffee or drying my nail polish. I'm fast, but not *that* fast, I worried to myself. I typed faster. Ted came in and stared incredulously. "Is the IBM broken?" he asked. I shook my head and kept typing. "I don't like it - it's got a mind of its own."

Minutes later Miss Buck called again to see if the article was ready yet. "I'm on my way to the office to read it," she added.

I was still typing as fast as I could. This time I didn't even look at my watch or the number of pages left. Next thing I knew Ted appeared smiling broadly and said Miss Buck was sitting downstairs on the second floor waiting for the finished manuscript. "Don't I even have time to proof it?" I inquired. "No time" - he was laughing now. "Miss Buck, by the way, shares your feelings about machines," he gestured to the silent IBM.

The humor of this whole little episode suddenly hit me when I rushed downstairs to find Miss Buck sitting imperiously on an antique chair surrounded by a bevy of dealers and customers. The caption under a picture taken at that moment could read "The Queen Holding Court." There she was, as I was to see her so often, charming a group of people with her personal mixture of command authority, cool serenity, and underlying merriment. She succeeded in looking imperious and sheepish at the same time. She was chuckling when she said to me, "Now you know how impatient I can be. And of course," she looked at Ted knowingly, "of course Mr. Harris will have to get you a typewriter of your choice..." I saw the resigned look on Ted's face in response to the fait accompli tone in her voice. "You are too much," he laughed, knowing she would not leave him alone until somehow a suitable typewriter had been purchased for the new secretary, who was not enamored of fancy machines.

Some further observations about Miss Buck and machines. She did not share Ted's fascination with man-made gadgets designed to make man's work easier and more efficient and was never surprised when the newest model trash compactor in the Danby House kitchen whined to a stop, or the washer and dryer in the Danby House basement refused to wash and dry anything, and the chores were relegated to man - or woman. "I confess," she writes in MY SEVERAL WORLDS, "that sometimes I find myself nostalgic for a house where the servants are humans and not machines, the while I know and hate the poverty that makes human labor cheap. And yet the servants in our Chinese home enjoyed their life, and they respected themselves and their work and us. They would not work for masters they did not like, and they expected and received respect from us. The relationship was irreproachable, and a decent servant would give up his livelihood immediately if he felt a lack of due regard from the master and his family. If he did stay on, he took some secret reward which compensated him for what he suffered - certainly machines are not so companionable.... And at home in Pennsylvania I went not long ago to call upon a neighbor, a young farmer's wife. It was the early afternoon, and I had perhaps half an hour to spare. I entered the kitchen door, for she would have been astonished otherwise, and encircling her big kitchen I saw monumental machines, washing machine, drier, mangle,two freezers, refrigerator, electric stove, sink. With such help her daily work was soon done, and we went into the neat living room where there was no book, but where a television was carrying on. She paid no heed to it, and inviting me to sit down, she took her fat baby on her knee, immaculate and well fed, and we talked small stuff while minutes passed, and then I had to leave. Said she, real disappointment in her voice and look, "Oh, can't you stay? I thought you'd spend the afternoon. I get so bored after dinner - I haven't a thing to do."

Miss Buck tolerated machines - was pleased when they performed perfectly - but much preferred a human being over a metal monster. But her impatience could be quickly directed at either when performance was not to her liking. By nature an impatient person who wanted everything done yesterday, under certain circumstances Miss Buck's impatience escalated to very personal and sometimes unreasonable demands. There seemed to be a direct correlation between this kind of personalized impatience and her own creative writing and thinking. Writing at best is a lonely and exacting task, mentally and emotionally exhausting. When the creative process was not progressing smoothly, Miss Buck was not only very impatient with herself, but with the whole world. Starting with herself, this impatience grew out in concentric circles, touching first those of us who were closest to her. It was, for her, part of the mysterious ebb and flow of creativity - a temporary frustration which needed an outlet. Never far behind though was her ability to laugh at herself and the exasperating situation. The more I observed this ebbing and flowing, the more I understood its direct tie to her creativity. Understanding this was one thing; coping with it was another. Just as Miss Buck had directed me to find my own place among Ted and Wendy and the others, she expected me to find my own way of coping with her personal impatience. I coped, drawing on my own patience and sense of humor and reminding myself that I agreed with Ted the many times I was to hear him chide her good-naturedly. "You are too much..."

Searching, perhaps, for his own way of coping during a particularly demanding period, Ted questioned me thus, "Do you sense an over-all speeding up in what Miss Buck is working on, what she hopes to accomplish?" To which I replied succinctly, "Yes." A large part of my job was to ease the demands put upon her by other people. She, however, burdened herself with greater and greater demands, as if time itself were running out. From the Treasure Book:

Ask me no questions.

For I do not know

How into so many books

My lively dreams must grow.

Mine are dream-folk maybe -

Yet somehow they continue

In their own way, through me

To wake and come alive.

Ask me no questions, pray

There is no more to say.

Chapter 17

Comfort Wasn't Her Name

And she worried - oh, how she worried about ways and means to make the Danby Project a success as soon as possible. The beautification and renovation program never proceeded fast enough for her high expectations. And oh, how she worried about Ted, charged by her with the responsibility of making Danby the instant success she wanted it to be. "And all," he said wryly, "without money, but then, anybody can do it with money..." As to how to do it without the vast sums of money which rightfully should have been poured into it from the beginning to quickly achieve her dream, her unflinching retort to Ted was always. "Of course you can do it..."

But to me, in private and in confidence, she admitted to being deeply troubled about this undertaking she had set in motion - anxious and fretful that she was expecting too much of this man who had already accomplished for her what no other person had been able to do. "He has already done the impossible," she told me, "he has seen to it that my dream of a Foundation on behalf of the Amerasian children became a reality; I care not what others think, for I know what Mr. Harris has done for me and the children."

But the dream of the Foundation was in the past - accomplished - and it was to her present unfulfilled dream that she directed her anxiety. "Once again I seem to be upsetting a great many lives," she mused. "You see, when Mr. Harris was working on the first volume of the biography, he suggested a title, 'And Her Name Shall Be Comfort,' Comfort is my middle name, to which I have always objected and I objected to this title of his, for I fear I have never been much of a comfort to anyone. I think in my own quiet way I've upset many lives and made many people very uncomfortable." (I was soon to read these exact words of hers in the just-published Biography). And in her own quiet way she proceeded to clarify her thoughts so that I might fully comprehend. A great sadness filled her eyes. I felt - yes - uncomfortable, like she was coaxing me to peer deep inside of her, pleading with me to understand. "I want this house," she said very carefully, "this whole Danby Project to be a home and a means of livelihood for Mr. Harris for the rest of his life. I must know that in my lifetime this is accomplished. But I must have *your* help, my dear, if Mr. Harris is to remain strong enough to carry through with my plan. I must know that he has a home and a business here after I'm gone and no matter where in the world he may wander from time to time, for there is a certain restlessness in him as there is in me..." She was asking, she said, the impossible of me; not only did she charge me with helping Mr. Harris in every way possible, acting always on her behalf, she also wanted me to find ways to protect him from the public hurt and humiliation he had already suffered.

"I am not blind," she said, "though some people would have me so; I am fully aware that Mr. Harris is not perfect; he has weaknesses. Physically, he is not strong for he has suffered some serious illnesses; he smokes too much and at times he drinks too much, and I doubt that his excessive consumption of vitamins is beneficial. In addition to all this, he is troubled by what is called a manic depression. I am told this is an unfortunate dilemma not uncommon to persons of high intellect..."

Elaborating no further on this revelation, here Miss Buck veered off with a personal apology to me. She realized, she said, that she was interrupting my own life by taking me away from my own family and my own problems with what she called my "brilliant but difficult husband." Now she was directing me, for her own selfish motives, to find ways of daily dealing with not one but two brilliant and difficult men. Having made up her mind, apparently, that I could do this impossible thing, all that remained to assuage her lonely anxiety was my answer to her direct question "Will you do everything you can to help Mr. Harris carry out my wishes?" My answer satisfied her that she was no longer alone in her mission. But I? I had never felt lonelier in my life as I replied quietly, "I shall do everything I can to help Mr. Harris carry out your wishes."

I was already walking a personal tightrope between home and work - trying to keep one from interfering with the other and doing a good job in both places. Now I would be walking a professional tightrope between my employer and what could well be the rest of the world. I felt like the rest of the world was resting on my shoulders.

"What do you and Lady Peasbee discuss for so long, just the two of you?" queried Ted with a puzzled expression which left no doubt that he was feeling left out of our intimate tete-a-tetes. What Miss Buck told him, I do not know. That was between her and him. My reply to him was simply "Woman talk." When he pressed for details, I hid behind the mounds of work waiting at my desk, unwilling to break the confidences I now shared with my employer, who was also *his* employer. As time went on, I found a multitude of subtle ways to help Ted carry out Miss Buck's wishes, some of which he may or may not have suspected, for he knew well her manipulative ways behind the scene.

Up front, my direct help was needed all the time. I was required, for example, to take a long deposition in shorthand from one of the young employees at the Vermont Village Square who was being harassed by a snooping reporter determined to substantiate the gossip which, if nothing else, seemed to sell newspapers. Frustrated at not getting an interview with either Miss Buck or Ted, the snooper was working her way through first one and then another of the local employees, apparently hoping to embarrass them and catch them off guard so they might reveal some juicy indiscretions about their famous employer. Miss Buck knew all too well that even her velvet sledgehammer could not prevent the prying and poking into her affairs. She read through the deposition, shaking her head sorrowfully at the insistent questions: "She (the reporter) asked me did I know whether Mr. Harris was - or is - (I don't remember whether she said was or is) - a homosexual?" And did I know that this had been proven. And I told her that I guess people can go to the library and read about anything they want about anybody. And as far as I was concerned you can't believe everything you read in newspapers and magazines. What is in somebody's past is in the past and it is the future that counts for a person, not what is in his past. And then she said, "But you do know that he is - or was - a homosexual?" And I said that I wouldn't know one way or another. So then I said I would tell her something about Danby. I told her that if he is one, then there are two others in Danby and I know who they are... The young employee, angry now and hoping to silence the reporter by dishing up some tasty local stories did a bit of village name-dropping, having absolutely nothing to do with Miss Buck or Mr. Harris. The reporter, however, wasn't interested in the locals. "And she said does Mr. Harris mess around with the kids in Danby? And I looked at her and I said absolutely, definitely NO!"

The deposition drones on relentlessly, but that last question proved too much for Miss Buck. "A despicable accusation" she fumed, "and deplorable that one of our fine young women employees should have to answer such trash." Not wishing to dignify this situation by involving herself personally ("That is exactly what the reporter and the newspaper want," she said), she was nevertheless unwilling to ignore it without doing something. "Mr. Harris and I must continue with our own work - yet I must do something..."

The something, she sighed, would no doubt be an exercise in futility, but she dispatched Wendy and me to personally voice her displeasure and disappointment with the office of the weekly newspaper that had sent out the snooping reporter. We were coolly received, coolly dismissed by the editor who had not met either Miss Buck or Mr. Harris and could care less about her "Dream for Danby," the real story that even Miss Buck admitted "nobody will believe it if you tell it like it is." The editor wanted to tell it like it wasn't - a case of "don't bother me with the facts, I've already made up my mind."

But at least we had done something and we all had too much work to do in Danby to waste time on hate and hurt. When Miss Buck wanted to know the name of the individual Wendy and I had talked to, laughter had the last word as we tried rhyming endings to "His name was Gall, as we recall, a name that suits him well. . . "

Chapter 18

The Pearl S. Buck Book Club

The arrival of the first copies of Volume I of the Biography was a cause for jubilation. The proud satisfaction Miss Buck expressed about what she considered a difficult job well done("difficult because the subject is difficult," she explained), is evident in the Preface she wrote:

It is impossible to judge a biography of one's self excepting the area of accuracy. I told Mr. Harris before he began writing that I made only one stipulation, namely, that whatever was put between quotation marks, as having been said by me, had really been said by me. We provided for this by the use of tapes. As to his qualifications for the task of writing the biography, I can only say that he knows me better than anyone else does. Ours is an unusual relationship, based on mutual confidence and understanding. The result is that I have been able to talk with him freely and at length and to answer his questions with complete frankness. I cannot be responsible, of course, for his personal opinions about me and these we have not discussed. But he has presented the facts of my life accurately and, I feel, with perceptive comprehension. He has researched my books thoroughly and with intuitive insight that is satisfying at least to a writer."

The book is dedicated "To P.S.B.: Thank you for giving so much of yourself to the world and to me. - T.F.H."

I was pleased when Copy No. 24 of the first edition was presented to me with this inscription: "For The Drake Family with deep appreciation for sharing your wife and mother. Theodore F. Harris, Danby, Vermont, November 3, 1971." Nicely put, I thought, for it reiterated the sensitivity voiced by Miss Buck when she had been explaining to my husband why she needed me as her secretary and apologizing for the upheaval it might cause in our family life.

The Biography was a valuable learning tool for me, for as I read it from cover to cover, it provided me with additional background information and gave me further insight into the lady whose present concerns were now my concerns. I came into her life where the Biography went out of her life.

As the days and weeks went by, the background information chronicled in the Biography came to me slowly and beautifully in Miss Buck's own words as I sat and talked with her. She had already told me that the Biography was factually accurate, but it is worth noting that never was I to discover major differences of past events as she told them to me or as they were written in the Biography. "I insisted on the accurate presentation of facts," Miss Buck told me on many occasions.

Early in my relationship with her I discovered that she and Ted both possessed what she called "almost total recall" the ability to recall and repeat, after deep concentration, conversations and written passages heard and seen long ago (or minutes before for that matter). This facility, whether natural or learned or a combination of both, Miss Buck put to good use in her writing and in real life circumstances. Many times I was to hear her repeat word for word an intricate conversation which I had taken down in shorthand - any discrepancies (if absolute accuracy was essential) were usually on my part, not hers. Whenever she asked me about my conversation with such and such a person, she was rarely satisfied with my saying, "I believe he meant this or that" or "I have a feeling that..." If the conversation was important enough, she demanded "Tell me exactly what was said " Only then, after a conversation was repeated to the best of my ability, would she be interested in my opinion or my feelings. "But what did he say..." I knew she was going to persist, and I scribbled shorthand notes to myself constantly, taking care to repeat accurately whatever seemed to be the cogent points. Ted was even worse than she was, expecting me to reel off long involved conversations with every 't' crossed and 'i' dotted. "It's all there, every word, in your computer somewhere," he would insist, "just punch the right button and voila!" It was usually Miss Buck who took the pressure off me by lightly chiding Ted with "Voila! She's not a machine."

The dust jacket on Volume I of the Biography tells how her need for accuracy was handled:

Pearl S. Buck personally chose Theodore F. Harris to write her biography, and has advised and aided him throughout. She made all her papers available to him, dictated onto tape for him her recollections of what was not in the records, and spent many hours over several years answering his questions in personal conversation. He has drawn from her things she thought she had forgotten, things she had not written about even in her own autobiographical works. The result is a life of this

Birthplace of Pearl S. Buck, Hillsboro, West Virginia.

Family portrait with Pearl, her mother and father, brother and baby
Grace.

Family picture showing Pearl and Grace with their parents and Amah.

Reprint of photo showing Pearl S. Buck receiving the Nobel Prize for literature from the King of Sweden.

remarkable woman, from her birth to the present, with a degree of completeness, of detail, of intimacy, that has not previously been available....

It frustrated, hurt, and angered Miss Buck when some detractors and critics dismissed Ted Harris as the author and accused her of writing the whole thing just as a money-making project, an ego-trip, or other unkind, untrue reasons. I was standing in the country store one day and overheard this exchange between a well-dressed elderly female customer and her well-dressed elderly male companion as they leafed through a copy of the Biography: She (haughtily) "Why didn't Pearl Buck just call this her autobiography; she must've written it herself. He (sarcastically) "It says 'In Consultation with Pearl Buck' - more like Harris was in cahoots with Pearl Buck. The real story is he probably paid her to write it." Miss Buck ghost-writing for Ted or anybody else is so preposterous that quick anger gave way to laughter, first in me and then in Miss Buck when I repeated the little dialogue to her. Ted? He shrugged and mumbled something about wishing he had the money she allegedly had given him: he could have used it to keep the Danby Project going.

The fact that the flow of funds coming into the Danby Project was not yet sufficient to keep up with what had to go out was revealed to me in the most personal way possible. For the first few weeks of my employment, my pay check (which was to have been $125 per week) was cut to $100 per week. Adding me to an already strained payroll meant some temporary sacrificing and considerable "robbing Peter to pay Paul"- until some way was found to bring in more money.

It was Miss Buck who explained to me that in order to make ends meet "Mr. Harris and Jimmy received no salary at all - existing on minimum living expenses; and Wendy and Alan were, for the time being, doing without their paychecks which amounted to $75 each per week." What they were living on she did not know, but our sacrifices were needed in order to keep paying the storekeepers and the building and decorating crew.

"We made a bargain with your husband," she said, "that you would be paid $125 per week, and so you shall be, except for this necessary temporary set-back. Can you explain this to him to his satisfaction?" She was, she said, more than willing to meet with him face to face to explain the financial situation. I said that for the time being I would try to do the explaining myself. So in answer to her question I replied, "Yes, and no." Yes I can explain it; but no, he will not be satisfied with my explanation, and he definitely will not be happy. He'd probably like me to quit." The truth is I would have been proud to have told Miss Buck I'd work for nothing until finances eased up and everybody could be paid a decent wage. There was no way I could do that, however, for I was already facing a disgruntled husband who reminded me daily that, as he put it "your little adventure in Danby is costing me money: you'll never catch up no matter what they pay you." I had already spent my first two weeks' salary on some very basic additions to my farm wardrobe, but the big bone of contention was the $2850 Volkswagen Bug which had been bought (angrily and reluctantly on his part) as a second car and needed transportation for me. The money had come out of our joint savings account. "You've got it all now - your own car, your own job, your own way. What more do you need from me?" I needed all of the things that had sent me fleeing from home to a job in the first place. I had thought I would be helping him, but as usual, as far as he was concerned, it was turning out all wrong. Nothing had changed, except that now I had a job but all the unresolved problems at home were the same or worse - the ups and downs cycled and I cycled with them.

Justifying the reasons for my lower paycheck became a little easier with the approach of the holiday season when an exciting money-making scheme for Danby was put into motion with dizzying speed. From what Miss Buck termed "Mr. Harris' brilliant idea, though I don't see how he is to get it going," was born The Pearl S. Buck Book Club, offering personally autographed Pearl S. Buck books by mail to members.

The air at Danby House and the office became electrified. The idea was to get the whole thing going and underway to capitalize on the Christmas gift season, giving an instant boost to the Danby coffers. If the idea of setting up a nice little book club sounds easy - a simple exchange of money for books - in actual fact we accomplished an incredible feat. Ted was supercharged with energy, Wendy was in tears ("I've seen him before when he gets an idea like this," she said to me, "and there's no stopping him"), and I became caught up with a colossal enthusiasm for the whole gigantic undertaking. If we had had a lot of money, a lot of people, and a lot of time, it might have been easy. As it was, there was no money and the burdens of the overwhelming workload fell to Ted, Wendy, and me with a few other "go-fers" here and there when things got really frantic. And Christmas was but a few weeks away! The workload quickly generated by the Book Club, by the way, was on top of the workload we were already saddled with.

The Book Club had Miss Buck's blessing. Her part would be in the realm of moral support and encouragement and the signing of her books to be offered to club members (there was no fee or dues involved). I felt as though I'd been shot out of a cannon; my days in Danby were exhilarating and invigorating beyond anything I had ever known. I loved the challenge of juggling all of my duties and responsibilities. When I fell short, I vowed to organize my time even better; when I was successful, the elixir of a job well done was sweet and potent.

The excitement of my day at work overflowed into my night at home and I had great difficulty soft-peddling my enthusiasm so that it would not become overbearing to husband and sons. They were usually tolerant, sometimes amused as I shared stories and anecdotes with them, but there was a point beyond which I could not share "my day." I had become, to my husband, "a part-time wife and mother, a liberated woman."

I risked hostile stares and insulting remarks if I overstepped the bounds of my balancing act between home and work, so without even knowing it I developed a sort of dual personality, finding myself much more of a positive, assertive, confident women at work than I was at home. I relished Miss Buck's poem called Dichotomy, which she recited during an apt moment for me:

Pilloried 'twixt heaven and hell,

My heart its secrets cannot tell,

Hung high upon a cross of praise,

My heart soul's saintliness betrays

O Soul!

If rise you must, up from the dead,

Leave Heart behind in that cold bed.

I was crying inside with my own Dichotomy, and hard work was a wonderful way of maintaining my equilibrium. And my dual personality which had evolved took on added meaning when, in the course of setting up the Book Club, I was officially given an alter ego named Naomi Bixby, Researcher and Librarian. Miss Buck thought it would be a wonderful idea for me to have this pseudonym, this behind the scenes personality, allowing me the additional "privilege" of handling crank phone calls or difficult letters or any sensitive situation where she felt it would be inappropriate for me to handle it as her personal secretary. I loved going "undercover" as Naomi Bixby, and Miss Buck never failed to be amused as she dictated some difficult response to some difficult person. Mrs. Bixby always got the touchiest assignments, and as time went on Mrs. Bixby was often allowed to handle situations on her own. "I trust Mrs. Bixby's judgement," Miss Buck would chuckle with that delicious wicked look in her eyes, "Let her handle this problem and keep Mrs. Drake out of it." Mrs. Bixby even developed her own very definite personality, and we had a whole glossary of information about her background and life-style: she was a widow struggling to put three sons through college, and after hours she, surprisingly, liked to ride around on the back roads with her boyfriend, who was a trucker, and he tolerated her fondness for sherry, though he was a jolly beer drinker....

That was Mrs. Bixby's personal side. At work she was all business, and one of her most enjoyable duties was as a very active officer in the Pearl S. Buck Book Club. The initial list of prospective Book Club members was taken right from the current fan letter files, and it was decided that the Book Club should have a roster of officers. It could not be known, of course, that Ted and Wendy and Bev were carrying the whole business on their shoulders. So along with Researcher and Librarian Mrs. Naomi Bixby there arrived on the scene the rest of the Book Club personnel: Mr. Carter McNeil, Managing Director; Mr. Robert S. Edwardsen, Coordinating Director; and Mr. Steven P. Michaels, Assistant Director. Fortunately, these new people required no paychecks, for they were invisible, but the result of their hard work was not. Mrs. Bixby and Mr. McNeil proved to be the most active and resourceful - somehow the others got lost in the shuffle; and sometimes Ted and Wendy and Bev became positively slap-happy as they tried to sort out whether Mr. Michaels should have sent out a letter which was actually signed by Mr. McNeil; and hadn't Mrs. Bixby written to such and such a person telling her that Mr. Edwardsen would be writing to her soon with an explanation about such and such a book being delayed from the publisher. Once again, the saving grace of laughter and good humor came to our rescue. Better to laugh than cry, we kept reminding each other, and it's a wonder we all didn't crack under the constant strain of trying to do so much with so little. It was exciting when the very first edition of Book Club News, printed laboriously on a huge rented printing machine monster which took over half the third-floor office (and which both Mrs. Bixby and Mrs. Drake refused to touch), was dedicated with much hip-hip-hooraying to Mrs. Naomi Bixby, and signed thusly:

Theodore F. Harris

and Robert S. Edwardsen

and Carter McNeil

and Steven P. Michaels....

Above this was a short quote by Elbert Hubbard, chosen jointly by Miss Buck and Ted: "If men could only know each other, they would neither idolize nor hate."

The following cover letter was one of several that went out to the first list of prospective members over the signature of the Managing Director:

Welcome to the growing number of people who wish to become informed through the works of the most widely translated author in the history of American literature, Pearl S. Buck. We of the Pearl S. Buck Book Club know that you will thoroughly enjoy your enlightenment, for reading her books is indeed a pleasurable experience.

One of the most important aspects of her work is that she writes out of her life, and all of the incidents that take place in her most important novels are actually historical events. She has yet to be found in error.

Enclosed is a brochure which describes some of Miss Buck's books, together with an order blank for your convenience.

Thank you...and welcome to the Pearl S. Buck Book Club. (A P. S. added that "members of the Book Club purchase books only when they choose to do so.")

The carefully prepared Book Club brochure, written by Ted and approved by Miss Buck, is filled with vital information which received an immediate and appreciative response from new club members. The fine response served as personal gratification to Miss Buck who was pleased to know that new and old readers were still interested in her books. The brochure is called "Discovering the World with Pearl S. Buck" and is too worthwhile to gloss over briefly. Packed with facts it is, in effect, an introduction to her writing for new and old admirers. The pseudonym John Sedges, by the way, was utilized for several novels by Miss Buck upon the urging of her second husband, also her publisher, who felt that her reading audience would not accept the fact that one woman, Pearl Buck, could turn out so many top-notch novels. In other words, nobody could write that much and be that good. Interesting to note that the publisher suggested a man's pen name. Miss Buck dismissed all this as "unnecessary nonsense," and it wasn't long before the Sedges secret was out in the open and she resumed writing under her own name. Mrs. Bixby had considerable correspondence with some difficult readers who refused to believe that John Sedges was actually Pearl Buck.

Here is the enticing introduction to the Book Club brochure:

Six Americans have won literature's most coveted award...The Nobel Prize. They were one woman and five men. Of the six only one remains alive and is writing today...the lady recently referred to by *The Saturday Evening Post* as "The Empress of American Literature"...Pearl S. Buck. In 1938 her citation for the Nobel Prize read "For rich and genuine epic portrayals of Chinese Peasant Life and for masterpieces of Biography." She has become the most widely translated author in the history of American literature. Only Mark

Twain comes near her in translations and she has doubled him. Over three-fourths of her reading audience is abroad reading her work in languages other than her own. There has to be a reason for this overwhelming acceptance of her work and, of course, there is a simple explanation. Her books are of major importance universally...and more so today than when they were written, as one can see with a little understanding of how and why she has written what she has written. First let us take a look at the women...and then her books. It is important to see her as she sees herself, as nearly as possible, with regard to her work. She has won over two hundred humanitarian awards; she is a teacher; she is a philosopher.... She is a great artist...but what does she consider herself? She considers herself first and foremost and completely a novelist...and nothing more. Her life work has been to write novels and all else has been incidental to that chosen pursuit. She herself has expressed her belief that the first and only duty of a novelist is to entertain and she has obviously succeeded in this area for more than forty years...as one can clearly see when one remembers that in 1931 THE GOOD EARTH sold 1,811,000 copies and in 1971 she had three major Book Club selections with two novels, THE THREE DAUGHTERS OF MADAME LIANG was the Reader's Digest Condensed Book and Book of the Month Club selection, and MANDALA, a novel of India, was the Literary Guild selection.

Her novels, however, attain a greater then literary importance when one considers how she writes. She does not, as some novelists do, sit down and make up stories through imaginary events that take place with make-believe people. Instead she writes out of her own life about events that have taken place during her lifetime to people she has known. Now consider what that statement has proclaimed. First, the events that have taken place during her lifetime. Perhaps the most important single occurrence in relation to world history is the decline and eventual fall of the Imperial Government of China, creating the void into which Communism firmly entrenched itself. She has gone from travel in a sedan chair to men walking on the moon. She has seen American involvement in Asia from its beginnings with businessmen and missionaries to our present tragic involvement with troops.

She lived forty years in China where she was definitely a part of life in a Chinese community and where Chinese became her native tongue, for she spoke Chinese before she spoke English. And what an important forty-years they were. From 1892, when she was taken to China as a three-month-old infant, until 1911 she lived under the last Empress of China, the true facts of whose life she wrote into her novel, IMPERIAL WOMAN.She lived through the ten-year void, when there was no central government, until when, in 1921, the Communist party was officially recognized. In 1927 she almost lost her life at the hands of the Communists in the Nanking Incident, after which she fled to Japan for a year, returning to China in 1928. She lived there under the Nationalist Government of Chiang Kai-shek until 1933 when she saw that there definitely would be a Communist rule, under which she could not live, and then she returned to the United States. When she arrived she accepted speaking engagements and wrote at length about what she had seen and learned, in order that Americans would be aware of potential danger. All of her books on Chinese subjects, though most are classed as fiction, and indeed are novels, are an historically accurate account of events that took place during those strategically important years. A good example of non-fiction on the subject of China is the book CHINA   AS I SEE IT, which is a collection of speeches end essays from 1933 through 1970, and allows the reader to see in how many ways she has been prophetic and in how many more ways she is likely to be. There is no better teacher than experience, and she has looked into her own unique past to predict the future....

(The rest of the information in the brochure appears in a special section in the back of this book).

Chapter 19

Love Is Not Enough

The Book Club intensified the already deep involvement Miss Buck had with what I called her "paper people." Many of the initial members, whose names had been taken directly from the fan letter files, had written to Miss Buck not once but several times. Along with the purchase orders for books came more and more letters of a touching personal nature, as if these people knew they were writing to a friend - or even a family member. "I wonder why this person is writing to *me?*" she would often ask out loud, perplexed at this universal chord she somehow struck in people of different nations in different parts of the world.

Many more "paper people" of still a different kind existed in her books and stories - hundreds of characters she herself had created over decades of writing. She often spoke of these characters as though they were real people. In a sense, they *were* real, these creations who reached out and touched her correspondents who in turn reached out and touched her as creator, until the circle was completed and then repeated over and over. Friendly ties, familial ties with a constant sharing of joys and sorrows. And at the center of this universal clan sat Miss Buck as matriarch.

Because so much of my time with her was devoted to keeping up with the members of this paper dynasty, I marveled at how she kept her book people in the proper books or stories, rarely confusing names or mixing up relationships. "With so many different people running around in your head," I commented, "don't you sometimes get them mixed up in your thoughts or in actual writing?" And her amused answer was, "Not any more than I get my own friends and relatives mixed up, or remembering what daughter-in-law belongs to which son, and so on."

It was to be several months before I met any of Miss Buck's "real" family - her flesh and blood younger sister Grace, her retarded daughter Carol, and the adopted children (now all adults). She often reminisced and pondered about her own relationships with her own family, and she reflected on the cleavage she herself had insisted upon between her business life and her family life - her public self and her private self. Closest to her in spirit was her sister Grace (living in Maryland with her husband) and they talked frequently by phone. But even Grace was kept at some distance for Pearl had always been and would always be the protective "big sister." "I must not bother Grace too much," she declared. "She has her own problems." They shared many things, including memories of dramatic years in China, but a noticeable distance was maintained between them because of Miss Buck's unwillingness to alter their big sister-little sister status.

Way back in 1940 an entry in the Treasure Book notes that "A letter from Grace says she wishes I would not write for the popular magazines. Aside from money necessary for these many children who so enrich and enlarge my life, the fact remains that I should not be satisfied if I did not have stories published in the magazines which the mass of people read. The finest and most beautiful do not come from these people, but still they are the root and stock of life. A person so secluded as a writer must not lose touch with them. I value their letters, often so foolish. I *feel* them. Their minds reach mine, and I try to make my mind reach theirs.

"The real objection to magazines is their editorial cutting which reduces every author to a dead level of style. This does distress me, since I tend to write at length. I am going to try to keep my stories within limits, so that such cutting at least need not be so severe.

"I must work hard today. But I am going to take an hour first to go sledding with the children."

That entry, written so many years ago, hints at the "We wish you wouldn't do that" or "Why do you insist on working so hard" objections that first Grace and later her adult adopted children directed pointedly towards Miss Buck. Well-meaning and loving as these suggestions might have been, they frustrated and irritated Miss Buck with their lack of understanding of who she was and what her life's work was all about. This lack of understanding and the schisms which developed because of it had followed her throughout her long career. The schisms were still there as she approached her eightieth birthday, and led to this reflective entry:

"It would be an interesting study, if I had time, to consider the moods of the aged. It is a period of intense solitude and melancholy which must be resolutely faced and accepted. I think it is a sense of separation, not from life, but from human beings. People relegate the aged, even very kind people. I feel it very much with my own children. Jean is wonderful and considerate, for example, unique among my children, and yet I realize that our lives are separate. It must be so, in the very nature of life itself. The other children seldom, if ever, pay any heed to me. I suppose, in a way, I have succeeded too well in making my children independent and whole, in themselves, able to function. Richard called once this year to know if I would help financially in their cellar flooding problem! Henriette called to know when the living trust would begin!....

I must not be sad, for any reason *whatsoever.*

The sadness which had been born with her only birth child Carol who was irreversibly retarded from Phenylketonuria - PKU, (the inability of the enzyme system to convert one amino acid to another) never left her. Nor did the sadness of her first marriage ever completely leave her, wrapped up as it was with her retarded child.

"There is a right time biologically for marriage," she told me many times, "and although I married a good man, he was not an intellectual - not my equal intellectually. I married against my parents' wishes, for they knew I should have married an intellectual." (Miss Buck's definition of an intellectual was, I believe, someone who possessed not only the capacity for contemplation and speculation on the universal life forces which affect all human beings, but the talents to engage in creative endeavors which go beyond mere human existence.) While she looked with compassion and tolerance on the individual whose life was devoted simply to "making a living," she grew impatient when she was drawn into this atmosphere of limited boundaries, when she considered that the confines of the mind - her own mind - could be limitless. Drawn for too long a time into the non-intellectual world with its emphasis on what she termed petty problems, she felt her own creativity stifled - her purpose in life thwarted.

As the incompatability of her life with John Lossing Buck

became painfully obvious, Miss Buck explained to me how she turned inward, going more and more to her writing, while her husband turned in frustration to something - anything - to keep her with him. "The doctors finally told me that he feigned blindness," she revealed, "and although I at first rejected this possibility, as a last resort I realized that he was trying to bind me to him out of pity." Such a relationship could not last, of course, and although the break came and the false pity disappeared, the sadness as well as her concern for this man, the father of her only child, remained. Her attitude is expressed in this letter, quoted in full, to John Lossing Buck who, during the holiday season of 1971, was living with his wife Lomay in Poughkeepsie, New York:

Dear Lossing:

Thank you and Lomay very much for the pretty Christmas card. I am glad you are comfortably and conveniently settled in your permanent home. I am sure it was a wise decision, although the farmhouse was so beautiful, as I remember.

I am sorry to hear you fractured your hip. It is hard to think we are all getting older and our lives filled with such mishaps. I stay as well as ever - I say this apologetically and keep to my usual schedules of work and life.

Most of my time is spent in my home in Danby, Vermont, where I am having much enjoyment in setting up a business with my partners in antiques. It is my first experience living in a small American village, and I am enjoying it very much.

I have kept my home in Pennsylvania, but my daughter, Jean, and her rather large family, including some

Amerasian children, live there. I keep my own rooms there and stay with them when I go to the Foundation offices to fulfill obligations. It is pleasant to know the children are near.

I feel so happy that you have your two children, and perhaps you have grandchildren as well. I have fourteen grandchildren now. All my children are married except Janice. Janice lives near me in Pennsylvania and is an extremely successful occupational therapist. She heads up the Department of Occupational Therapy in the County Home for the Elderly and Disabled, and everybody likes her.

Carol is in her usual place at the Training School in New Jersey. I took Jean and Janice with me to see her recently so that in case of my disability - when and if that time comes - and come it must - there will be two members of the family to look after her. She is now fifty, as you know. Her life has been a useful one because I have been able to make it so. Through her, much of the work in diagnosis and prevention of PKU has been made possible. Because of her, I have been able to help parents of retarded children, not only in this country, but also in Japan, Korea, and in parts of Europe. You may not know it, but Madame de Gaulle has a retarded child, and she wrote to me about her. Carol is in good health, and has become so adjusted to her life that she creates no problems.

The Training School has taken wonderful care of Carol. I have always been on the Board of Trustees; I was chairman for some years until I felt someone else must take my place, but I am still on the Board.

Forgive me for telling you all of this, but as we grow old

we remember friends, I am sure. It has been a great satisfaction that you have a good wife in Lomay and that she has been able to give you your children.

With best wishes, I am

As ever

Pearl S. Buck

* * *

Many of Miss Buck's correspondents thought that her name Buck was her maiden name, not realizing that her first published novels were published under her married name. (Quite a number of her admirers mistakenly thought she was the wife of Frank Buck, the bring 'em back alive big game hunter, and Mrs. Bixby had great fun setting straight this misconception). Only reluctantly and for a brief period of time had she acquiesced to the use of the John Sedges pen name. Publicly she was to remain Pearl Buck. Her personal choice for signing her name was Pearl S. Buck, the S standing for her maiden name of Sydenstricker. At a later date she was, as they say in legal documents, Also Known As (AKA) Pearl S. Walsh. Richard Walsh, the man who became her second husband, was first her publisher and quite her equal intellectually. Nevertheless, Miss Buck described to me her reluctance to commit herself to a second binding relationship. Still married to Lossing Buck and still wearing his gold band, she described the scene to me when she finally gave in to what she terms, not unkindly, "the relentless pursuit of me by Richard Walsh!"

"We were standing on the deck of a boat on a river in China," she recalled, "and I remember staring into the swiftly moving muddy water, listening to Richard Walsh tell me all the reasons why I should marry him. Suddenly, impulsively, I pulled off my gold wedding ring and threw it away into those muddy waters..." The end of one chapter, the beginning of another. She never gave that symbolic little story to one of her autobiographical book characters. It remained utterly private until she shared it with me just that once, and then it was never again mentioned.

Richard Walsh had children of his own and Richard Jr. eventually took over the organization called The John Day Co. which had been publishing Pearl Buck books for many years. Pearl Buck and her new husband shared a love of children, and together they started a second family. After the birth of her own daughter Carol, she was unable to have any more babies. She had already adopted Janice and after her marriage to Richard Walsh their adoptive family continued to grow to include Jean, Richard, John, Edgar, Henriette, Chieko, and two wards, Teresa and Johanna.

"I guess there is a limit to what one person can do," Miss Buck lamented, "and when my own household was not enough, I started my own adoption agency." She started to read to me a reprint of a letter she had written (before I arrived on the scene) to the editor of one of the weekly news magazines. The reprint was sent to her by an anonymous correspondent (no name - just an address) seeking her autograph - "one or two, if you have time" said the request.

Here she paused to address the subject of what she should or should not do about requests for autographs. We were alone, in one of those long morning sessions which inevitably prompted Ted's needling "And what did you talk about for so long today?" Shyly, almost conspiratorially, she asked me what I thought she should do about the endless requests for her autographs. "Mr. Harris," she said formally, "thinks I should autograph only copies of my own books and that I should no longer feel obligated to autograph all the indiscriminate pieces of paper and other personal things," as she called the array of unsolicited items pressed upon her.

"What is *your* opinion, Mrs. Drake," she prompted. I hesitated, and she smiled and I could see the merriment dancing in her eyes. I put one index finger to my nose and smiled back at her. "You obviously already know what I'm thinking; my thought must be as plain as the nose on my face. If I tell you what I think, it will sound like I'm telling you what to do, and I would never do that. It is not my place."

"Your place is to help me," she chuckled, "and you can help me now by giving me your opinion, which I value. I have always signed everything anybody asked me to sign. I would not wish in any way to offend my readers. For I need them to keep buying my books..." she trailed off, still waiting for me to say something.

"I know a very famous lady," I began slowly, "who has spent a lifetime doing a lot of things for a lot of people because she cares. She told me once, and this is a direct quote, that 'I guess there is a limit to what one person can do.' Do you recognize the quote?" I teased.

"Go on," she prodded, giving no quarter.

"Well," I continued, "your reader audience and the number of autograph seekers continues to grow because you insist on doing more and more and making yourself known to more and more people. I figure, roughly, that if you finish all the manuscripts you are now working on and complete all the articles you want to write, and still continue to keep up with your hundreds, no thousands, of correspondents (your autograph is on every letter you send out, by the way), it will

Pearl S. Buck, 1972
photo by Bruce Curtis

take you at least until the year two thousand to complete your creative work. Mr. Harris is absolutely correct in suggesting that you should cut down somewhere. It may seem a small matter, but it is my opinion that autographing only your own books from now on is a time-saving, energy-conserving good idea."

I finished with the flourish of a speech-maker warming to his subject and we both ended up giggling. Mr. Harris, I have no doubt, heard about this little morning episode. The new policy was enforced. There were no more autographs except in her own books, and Mrs. Bixby was given the task of returning the unsolicited pieces of paper, and so on. Occasionally a reader, taking it as a personal affront, became huffy. And one persistent correspondent sent a carton full of early and probably quite valuable Pearl Buck volumes, requesting her autograph in each one. This was an extreme case, but Miss Buck not only autographed each book, she directed me to ship back the carton immediately at her own expense, since no return postage had been included.

"Yes, I guess maybe there is a limit to what one person can do," Miss Buck agreed and then she read me this reprint which the magazine editor headlined "Love is Enough."

Your issue of Sept. 13 was, as always, very interesting but especially to me because of the picture on the cover of a white couple who had adopted a black baby and also because of the interesting article on interracial adoptions.

The reason for my special interest is that I faced this problem some 25 years ego when I found that agencies in the United States were not willing to make interracial adoptions. I had been given a little boy who was half East Indian and half American and almost at the same time a baby whose mother was American and whose father was Chinese. Since my own family situation made it impossible for me to adopt these children personally at that time, I tried to place them through an adoption agency. None would accept the children.

Therefore, with the help of friends, Mr. and Mrs. Oscar Hammerstein and Mr. and Mrs. Kermit Fischer, I formed my own adoption agency especially for making interracial adoptions. In spite of the fact that we had graduate social workers and took great care with the adoptions legally, we received much criticism from other adoptive agencies.

We persisted, however, and the agency, Welcome House, has continued with outstanding success all through the years and so continues this very moment. Its headquarters are in Doylestown, Pa., and its president now is Mrs. David Burpee; I am chairman of the board. With the Second World War and the engagement of American servicemen in seven countries of Asia - please note not only in Vietnam - we have placed for adoption many half-American children from Asia as well as in the United States.

I might just add as a personal note that two of my own adopted children are black. I adopted them years ago when they were small; they are now married and leading pleasantly successful lives.

The purpose of this letter is simply to reassure white parents who adopt black babies that these adoptions have worked and do work. A child's color has nothing to do with the love which parents give him. The problems are not insurmountable as he grows into the knowledge of his own background.

Love is enough.

But love is not enough, it appeared, to bridge the separation between Miss Buck's real life family and her real life work, which even now, nearing eighty, she felt compelled to continue at her frenetic pace. Every poignant conversation I ever had with her left no doubt that she was fiercely determined to keep these two worlds separate and apart from one another. Knowing that all of her adopted children were adults and had had the benefit of her influence during their formative growing years, I puzzled over her uncompromising and unyielding position. Not yet understanding, I finally asked her bluntly, "Why?"

Her answer, surprising to me, came readily: "Because the pain that results from keeping these two worlds separate is easier to bear than the pain that would result from trying to bring them together. Not one of all of my children, with the possible exception of Jean, is at all suited to helping me in my work, and Jean is busy with her own large family. Not one of my children is - an intellectual." She said this slowly and carefully, drawing out the word "intellectual" as an admission of a truth which hurt her deeply. I was instantly sorry I had forced the issue. On the other hand, I already knew her well enough to know that if she had not wanted to answer me, she would have dismissed my question, and with no further explanation forthcoming. "So they cannot possibly understand me," she continued, "though they think otherwise, and I must find my own ways of letting them know I love them - all of them. It was easier when they were all children. Do you know what I mean, Mrs. Drake?"

Now she had bluntly asked me a question and I answered as best I could, "I think I do understand. We are responsible for our children when they are children - we do our best for them - but we cannot be responsible for them as adults. We might wish them different, but they are who they are. I would hope that my own two boys, when they become adults, could at least understand me and I them, so that we can appreciate each other's worlds, different though they may be. I shall always love them very dearly and deeply, but love is not always complete understanding - though maybe it should be."

Miss Buck's separation of family and business, then, was her way of coping with the lesser of two pains, but I would be doing her a grave injustice if I gave the slightest impression that she wallowed in self pity over the situation she herself had instigated and now perpetuated. Self pity, she said, was a time waster, and she had no time to waste. Her thoughtful musings on the "why" of things were basic to her complex personality. Her awareness of a more intense feeling of melancholy and wistful solitude was part of the "moods of the aged" which she took time to ponder only briefly. She rebelled at any frailty of her mind or body, and if at this time she had any premonition of impending disaster in the form of illness which would take all her strength to fight, the only indication to those few of us around her was an ever-increasing desire to hurry up and do more and more and more.

She wanted a holiday party to include all of the people associated with the Danby project - from the antiques dealers and their spouses, to the dark-haired young mother who quietly cleaned her rooms each morning, to the interesting assortment of local young employees who were carpenters and plumbers and general workers.

It fell to Ted and Jimmy and Wendy to bring together this mix of people at Danby House, where a huge glittering

Christmas tree was installed and a sumptuous evening buffet was prepared, including some of Mr. Choi's Korean specialties. Miss Buck presided over the affair, seated regally in her gold velvet chair, singling out first one and then another of her guests for a personal chat.

To my husband she talked of world affairs and military issues, "picking his brains," she later told me, "in an effort to get to know him better." In my presence, she made a special point of thanking him for letting her borrow my "excellent secretarial services" and being understanding about the financial difficulties which necessitated lowering my salary temporarily. She was charmingly feminine and persuasive and I could see that Bill had very reluctantly fallen under her spell. He was charmed by her but he was far from charmed by my "leaving home" and I knew I would get some far from charming comments later.

Before we left Danby House that night each guest was given a smell red lacquered bowl inscribed in gold with Miss Buck's initials in Chinese characters (Bill and I were given an additional two bowls, one each for Tom and Jim) mementos of the evening and the season.

Shortly after this holiday affair, Bill and I were invited alone to Danby House to dine with Ted and Miss Buck. Served was a lovely candlelight dinner, complete with exquisite china and crystal which Miss Buck insisted upon using every night.

The morning after Bill and I, (he at his charming best and I on pins and needles at this meeting - this intimate meeting of my two worlds) Miss Buck and Ted together caught me unaware with a very direct question: "What would you think of our asking your husband to come and work for us as a part of the Danby Project?" His brain power, they said, could be put to excellent use as a sort of assistant manager to Ted.

I needed no long drawn-out thinking to answer stiffly and unsmilingly, "You may choose either him or me - but not both of us, for I cannot work for you if he is here too. I thought I had explained to you how I had literally run away from an impossible personal situation, and now you're asking me to run right back into it for twenty-four hours a day with no respite whatsoever."

I toned down my caustic objection by adding, though still stiffly, that "Yes, my husband is brilliant - difficult but brilliant, though maybe he would not be as difficult for you as he is for me. But if he can be of more service to you than I, then I will gladly bow out and return to the farm full time, with regrets, of course. I love what I am doing here, I love the whole idea of what *you're* doing here, and I thought you were genuinely pleased with my work." I was sounding petulant and pouty, and I was sorry I was sounding like that.

There followed such a shower of words on the part of both Miss Buck and Ted to soothe my obviously ruffled feathers - of course, they said, they never meant that they should do anything to lose me. However valuable Bill might be to them, it seemed they thought I was infinitely more valuable. I wasn't fishing for compliments, though I got them now in abundance. My stiffness disappeared and my sense of humor quickly returned. And, as so often happened among the three of us, a very trying, serious situation was put into proper perspective by interjecting a light touch.

"It is unconscionable," said Miss Buck with a merry glint in her eyes, "that I should risk losing Mrs. Drake *and* Mrs. Bixby."

"I must admit," I said, "you both had me on the proverbial sticky wicket; no," I amended, searching for a stronger expression, "you really had me where the hair is curly." Horrified, I gasped at my unladylike, uncharacteristic gaffe. To my added discomfort, Miss Buck and Ted both broke into gales of laughter.

"Mrs. Drake - or is it Mrs. Bixby - I do believe you're blushing scarlet," Ted observed.

"I am - that is, we are," I agreed, laughing along with them.

And quickly the matter was dropped, and we returned to the ever waiting work at hand, each one of us comfortably aware that there was an ever-strengthening bond of trust and friendship among us - an indefinable something that went far beyond everyday words and paychecks and nine to five boundaries. My destiny seemed somehow linked to this lady who was in such a hurry to finish so many things, and to this unusual man upon whom she relied to carry out her every wish.

Chapter 20

Going to China

There was an increasing wistfulness, a growing "Wouldn't it be nice if..." attitude when Miss Buck talked about China, brought about by the opening up of China to visitors and the renewed interest in Chinese fashions, Chinese food, Chinese everything. "My earliest memories are of the people of China," she was to write as the very first words in her book in progress called CHINA PAST AND PRESENT (published during the first six months of 1972). Her curiosity about what was going on in modern-day China was endless. She wasn't satisfied with the tantalizing tid-bits of information reaching her in the form of letters and postcards from travelers and business associates. She longed for on-the-spot reports, and she announced to me one morning that Ross Terrill, recently returned from China and someone who was working on a book about China, would be coming to Danby to talk with her. Although it would be an informal meeting, I was asked to sit in on the conversation and take detailed notes in case she wanted to refer to any of the information for the book she was writing.

When I found out that she had allotted a whole day and maybe a bit more for her talks with Ross Terrill, I had visions of my scribbling in shorthand hour after hour after hour. I doubted the advisability of this marathon note taking, and suggested to Ted that we use a tape recorder placed unobtrusively. Even before I finished asking him about this, he shook his head and said Miss Buck detested "those machines" and had had more than enough of them during the time he had been writing Volume I of the Biography. No machines, therefore I had no choice but to place myself unobtrusively upstairs in Miss Buck's pink sitting room, where the meeting took place.

Armed with not one but several steno books and a fist full of pens, I was a silent and ultimately weary scribbling machine, even carrying pen and book downstairs and writing on my lap while we ate lunch and Miss Buck and Mr. Terrill continued talking, a day and a half, all told. In truth, I do not even remember what Ross Terrill looked like, so intent was I on listening. Naturally, it was impossible to capture everything that was said, so I concentrated on picking out the meat of the sentences and discarding the frills. This worked fine as I started transcribing my notes right away, until more urgent business necessitated my setting them aside for some days. My concentration cooled, of course, and when I went back to my notes some of the pages made no more sense to me than Chinese shorthand. This, coupled with the horrifying discovery that someone had inadvertently ripped out some of the pages for scrap paper, telephone notes, or whatever, made me fume to Ted that "I told you we should have used the tape recorder." "Do your best." he soothed, and ultimately Miss Buck was satisfied with what I called my chewed-up notes, using them merely to jog her own excellent memory. She had her own tape recorder in her head. The shorthand notes were redundant, but she seemed to very much appreciate my, as she put it, "uncomplaining, lady-like presence." I sat in on many such visits with many different visitors, but thank goodness I was never again asked to run a notetaking marathon.

Not long after Ross Terrill's visit, when the newspaper and television news was full of the exciting announcements of President Richard Nixon's visit to mainland China, Miss Buck had her own exciting announcement.

"Are you ready for this? You better sit down," Ted said, excitement in his own voice. I was already sitting down, but I was totally unprepared when Miss Buck looked at me intently with those bright blue eyes and declared. "I'll be going to China, and you and Mr. Harris will be going with me."

Me? Going to China? How could I leave my husband, my sons. It was impossible. Me going to China when I wasn't even supposed to travel anywhere at all with Miss Buck. "Me? Going to China?" I whispered incredulously back to Miss Buck and Ted, question marks all over my face.

And in the way that she had, she said with bright finality, "Of course, it's all settled, and we must begin planning right away. The first thing I want you to do, Mrs. Drake, is call The White House..."

Chapter 21

Supremely Natural

Call the White House — We're going to China!

Had Lady Peasbee struck again with her velvet sledgehammer?

As I faced Miss Buck and Ted incredulously and tried to digest this latest dizzying development which I knew was a *fait accompli* even with all its implications and complications, I was struck by something else, something which I once before had chosen to call Destiny. We may all be victims of destiny as we thread our way through life, but we are not always so consciously and immediately aware of the active presence of Destiny. The first time I had met Miss Buck, Destiny was surely at work, yet I was not aware of it until later in retrospect. This time I was very definitely aware of that same invisible casting director forcefully and forcibly moving us around in a new dramatic episode from which there was no escaping center stage. It was a strong force that could make the invisible seem visible, the intangible seem tangible. It was a strong force that left us apparently no choice but to be swept along in this continuing drama.

Talking about an invisible casting director-an unfathomable force so strong it becomes an almost seeable, hearable presence - is touchy material.

Yet, since my mission is to give you the essence of the

private lady Pearl Buck, I must continue to attempt that balance of not too much, not too little, even when articulating the touchy material.

After years of careful contemplation, and reviewing my feelings in this and other similar incidents, I believe that both Ted Harris and I were with Pearl Buck, sharing her deepest and most intimate thoughts, because she early divined in both of us a capacity to instinctively understand those deepest and most intimate thoughts. To function successfully, as a person and as a writer, she demanded this understanding. This is not to say that others could not have performed our tasks or that we two were clairvoyant super-human beings. Not at all. We happened to be two who were around her during times of urgent need. She was in a command position to make use of all of us. And use us she did. When Ted came into her life, her goal was not only to continue her writing under her specific conditions, but to actively set up an organization to help the half-American children whose plight she felt was being ignored by governments and existing relief groups. That was in 1963 and she voiced the concern then that she needed about ten more years. She hoped ten years would be enough to accomplish all that she felt she must accomplish. When I came into her life, she was approaching that ten-year self-imposed deadline, and her speeded up pace early in 1972 gave credence to her hinted at fears that she was running out of time.

As we were running faster and faster along with her, it certainly seemed no mere coincidence that Ted and I were, in a manner of speaking, tuned into her on the same wave length and therefore she didn't have time to waste on lengthy explanation. At least most of the time, we knew *how* she was feeling and *what* she was feeling.

"I hate explanations," she grumbled through one of her characters in MANDALA, a novel set in modern-day India. "Either one knows the meaning or one doesn't. Either one understands or there is no possibility of understanding."

Of such things as invisible casting directors and other unfathomables which confound quick and reasonable explanations, she said, "There is no such thing as the supernatural, only the supremely natural." Indeed, of science and religion - both of which are called upon to explain away unfathomables - she felt that they are one and the same. Man *en masse* had not yet reached the point where they are recognized as one and the same; but she was convinced that the two are drawing closer together and human understanding would eventually reconcile them to be inseparable. If they *are* drawing closer together, then by what or by whom? Invisible casting directors? She used the term "supremely natural," and used it often.

I grew accustomed to her term "supremely natural," and I personally took it to mean Miss Buck's own all-encompassing euphemistic description of religion and science intertwined; that is, *all* religion, *all* science known to Man. But did Pearl Buck believe in God?, comes the inevitable simplistic question. If we take God to be a simplistic euphemism for some omniscient force beyond the comprehension of Man, yet still the object of human faith and hope, most definitely Pearl Buck believed in God. But her God was not *de*finable or *con*finable in terms of any one religion, any one church doctrine. Her God did not assume a benevolent human likeness in flowing white robes presiding over a Heaven and Hell. I choose my words carefully as I say that. In my opinion, Pearl Buck's God was a supremely natural synthesizing of not only God and his powers in the Christian-Judeo tradition, but included everything from Confucius and the God-leaders of all religions straight back to the Sun, worshipped by our primitive ancestors. All are one and one is all in a supremely natural intertwining.

Pearl Buck's unconventional opinions or comments on conventional spiritual or religious topics frequently left her open to puzzled, even shocked criticism, such as the time she was asked to speak, early in her career, before a group of prominent religious leaders. Expecting no doubt to hear some comforting unabrasive comments by the well-known author whose own parents had been dedicated missionaries, her audience was stunned when she used the occasion to issue an impassioned plea for what she termed "more highly educated missionaries," even angrily chastising those uneducated and misinformed missionaries as being perhaps the primary cause of most of the world's human suffering. She was not, of course, chastising all missionaries and her plea for greater understanding and sensitivity was directed at those who were sent to foreign lands totally uninformed - or even worse, misinformed - about regional traditions, customs and beliefs. Confusion and misery, she said, have too often been the results of well-intentioned though mis-guided Christian love and dedication. Though her stance was defensible and explainable, it was unexpected uncoventional remarks like this one that were often misinterpreted and misrepresented. This outspokenness branded Pearl Buck early in her public life and dogged her throughout the decades.

"I will *not* be quiet," was still a favorite expression of hers as she approached her eightieth birthday. It is still easy to visualize the intensely curious little Pearl Comfort she once was whose constant chatter and probing questions often forced her exasperated mother to tell her small daughter to sit in a chair for five minutes without uttering a word.

It is interesting to note that large numbers of her "paper people" - those many admirers who wrote to her - related to the often subtle spiritual-mystical side of her writing, and shared with her off-beat experiences of their own which apparently they had never been able to share with anyone else. I pick an example quickly at random from the hundreds and hundreds of letters which came to Miss Buck. This one comes from Spokane, Washington in the winter of 1973:

Dear Pearl Buck:

A strange thing happened to me which I cannot explain. Two days ago in my mail was a copy of MODERN MATURITY, to which I subscribe, but while addressed to me, it was the October-November issue of 1971 containing your article Essay on Life. Where this copy has been for the last year and a half I don't know. But I couldn't have received it at a more opportune time. I have buried all my family - father, mother, brother, husband and my two sons. My last son died either Christmas Eve or Christmas Day in New York, the hospital didn't tell me exactly when.

Why I am writing this is to thank you for the splendid article. It is very helpful and comforting to me. It gave me courage to think that somewhere my two beloved sons are going on.

Thanking you again for such a comforting philosophy.

I have long been an admirer of you and your work. May it long continue.

I am 85 1/2 years old but am still giving piano lessons, which I have done for over 70 years.

A least at the end of her life, during the months I was with her, she had all but given up the tedious and time consuming task of justifying what some considered controversial, even unacceptable actions. It is not surprising that the rapport she developed with sympathetic and understanding correspondents was both a relief and a release.

The same book that produced the "I hate explanations" statement also contains a cameo episode concerning one human being meeting another human being, one of whom is a small child. Strangers to each other from different parts of the world, there is instant recognition - a deja vu intimacy. No explanation is necessary. This is, of course, a poignant and simple example of a large and difficult subject called reincarnation. Such an incident occurred personally to Pearl Buck and was, in her words, one of those supremely natural happenings. It was, I believe, probably the singular most important reason for writing MANDALA. The *New York Times* generalized blandly that this book was "an enjoyable and profitable experience." In a short piece about MANDALA written in 1972 for a *Library Guild Bulletin,* Miss Buck quotes from the preface of the Chinese novel ALL MEN ARE BROTHERS, which she translated from Chinese to English: "Alas, I was born to die! How can I know what those who come after me and read my book will think of it? I cannot know if I, myself, afterwards, can read this book. Why, therefore, should I care?"

Other spiritual-mystical unfathomables are woven into Pearl Buck stories, sometimes overlooked or overshadowed by colorful characters, plots, and sub-plots. During her lifetime there were some critics who carped that she should write more "scholarly," more "in depth." She dismissed those detractors by adhering steadfastly to her own style of writing. "I cannot write the way some others would have me write," she noted aloud on occasions when suggestions came to her that she should write thus and so about such and such. "I write from my life experiences and all my stories are historically accurate, based on sound research." This became a familiar litany as I typed manuscript after manuscript penned in her bold black handwriting. The warm and gratifying letters that kept coming from her readers convinced her that she should keep writing the way she wrote and without apology. Again I pick quickly at random, this time a letter from Midland, Texas, dated November 10, 1972:

Dear Miss Buck:

I hesitate to come again and take any of your strength, even for reading, so I shall wait until some distant eternity where, last of all, I may come into your rest. (I say "last of all" for I am sure there will be others before me, and "eternity" for they will take so long!) But then there will be strength enough for both of us - and time.

May I ask now if, in some fresh, faultless morning, some dew-cooled early autumn morn, I may walk with you in that eternal Eden?

I have just completed a beautiful landscape. From the left of the canvas the sunlight is breaking in brilliance through a forest and striking in full strength across a trail that rises from the forefront of the scene. The rest of the rock-strewn trail is in deep shadow. Were I painting autobiographically I would have included two figures: you standing in the white light on the trail extending an arm to a small figure in the shadows - drawing her out of darkness into light and life.

Thank you for your gentle touch upon my shadowed

solitude these heavy years, and for your rich wholeness which kept me whole. The ideals first struck to life by your flame still live - and lead me. That is enough. Lovingly....

Psychic phenomena fascinated Pearl Buck and often a chance letter from a reader sparked a train of thought which eventually found its way into her writing. Tracing such sparks from start to finish was apparent only to those who were steeped in her daily work. For example, a lengthy letter arrived one day from a reader who had taken some snapshots of Miss Buck at some Foundation function. Each small photo, in color, revealed a hazy but unmistakeable "halo" effect around her upper body. A flaw in the film or camera? Odd atmospheric conditions? A hoax? Could be or could not be. The photographer was convinced that it was her personal "aura," her energy field emitting impulses of her personal life forces. This aura theory found its way into one of the manuscripts I was typing for her, the never published GENIUS BOOK.

The GENIUS BOOK, by the way, was sparked by so many personal experiences, beginning with the mystical first paragraph:

He lay sleeping in still waters. This was not to say that his world was always motionless. There were times when he was aware of motion, even violent motion, in his universe. The warm fluid which enfolded him could rock him to and fro, could even toss him about, so that instinctively he spread his arms wide, his hands flailing, his legs spreading in the sprinting fashion of a frog. Not that he knew anything about frogs - it was too soon for that. It was too soon for him to know. Instinct was as yet his only tool. He was quiescent most of the time, active only when responding to unexpected movements in the other universe..."

Pearl Buck herself was born early on a dew-cooled June morning in Hillsboro, West Virginia. Of this, her own birth, she insisted "I remember when I was born. I am sure I remember..."

Farther on in the GENIUS BOOK, the central character, still an inquisitive small boy, is obsessed with knowing about the beginning of life. He marvels thusly: "Everything in the world, all that lived, began with a seed! 'In the beginning,' the Minister intoned one Sunday morning in the church, 'in the Beginning was the Word and the Word was God.'

"Is God the same as the seed?" he asked his father on the way home.

"No," his father replied, "and don't ask me what God is, because I don't know. I doubt anyone knows, but everyone with any intelligence wonders, each in his own way. It seems as though there ought to be, or even must be, a beginning, but then again perhaps there wasn't. Perhaps we live in eternity."

"How you talk!" his mother said. "The boy can't understand."

"He understands," his father said.

The boy looked from one to the other of these, his parents, and he loved his father the better.

"I do understand," he said....

Had Pearl Buck completed the GENIUS BOOK, I believe it would have been a final wrap-up of her considered opinions over a long life-time on being a genius and living in America, all based, of course, on her own personal experiences. She found a quote of Samuel Butler to be appropriate to her current era, although Butler died at the beginning of this century: "I do not think America is a good place in which to be a genius. A genius can never expect to have a good time anywhere, but America is about the last place in which life will be endurable at all for an inspired writer."

If she did not consider herself to be an inspired writer (although I believe she did), she considered herself to be a writer compelled to write. And while she wrote, she probed and pushed to the limits not only her own inquisitive mind, but those minds closest to her, frequently insisting on ideas, if not definite answers, to disarming direct questions such as "Do you believe in an after-life?" or "Do you have ESP?" or "Have you ever known anyone with a gift of prophecy?" The perplexing unfathomables which seemed so much a viable component of her own existence and which she pondered constantly became topics of on-going lively discussions.

She always laughed when I tried to side-step an answer to a difficult question by gracefully phrasing some non-committal platitude. I tried but never got away with something like this: "I believe that there are those of us who seem to have the capability of understanding things which others don't seem to understand." Here she would always smile at me, not content with such platitudes, even when I protested that I believed what I said to be true.

Ever searching for answers of her own and having reached no definite conclusions about the mysteries of the universe, even as she approached the end of her life, Pearl Buck insisted on pulling ideas, if not definite answers, from me when we talked. This became a habit, a sort of counterbalancing to the day's more mundane affairs. For her, at least, I believe it was an enjoyable form of mental relaxation and stimulation. For me it was more stimulating than relaxing when we pursued, for example, one such on-going discussion concerning the make-up of the human brain. For I, who had never even had the advantage of high school physics or chemistry, much less advanced philosophy or theology, found myself being stretched into exploring with her the possibilities that if the brain is made up of matter and matter exists forever, then it merely changes from one form to another; and if this be so, then does the brain continue to function and exist after death in some invisible (to the human eye) state, and so on, and so on.

These mental journeys into unfathomables were never-ending, and even as I applied myself to the hectic mechanics of traveling to China with Pearl Buck, the presence of Destiny hovered no longer in the background but tantalizingly in the foreground.

CHAPTER 22

A Frustrating Wait

Once Miss Buck had announced her plans to return to China, she pursued with her usual impatient determination and tenacity. It never occurred to her that she would *not* go, only that she *would* go and the sooner the better. My first call to the White House became the first of many calls to the White House, seeking (and for the most part getting) helpful information from the personal staff of the first U.S. President in modern history to visit China. President Nixon's upcoming visit to mainland China was being loudly heralded as an historic opening up of official East-West relations. It was further thought that Communist China, so long shut off and remote to most Western visitors, would actually be opening up to tourists, with Nixon and his entourage again leading the way.

With no precedents to follow, no one at this time was positive as to the proper channels to follow in order to be allowed entry into China, but we were told that written visas, medical documents, carefully approved travel itineraries, and other papers were essential. Members of President and Mrs. Nixon's personal staff, as well as assistant secretaries of state and security officers who offered what specifics they could, assured Miss Buck that the one prerequisite for traveling to China was approval from the authorities in Peking. Without fail, my introductory announcement to each person with whom I made telephone contact, that I was calling on behalf of Pearl Buck, the noted Nobel Prize-winning author, etc., became an introduction to a cordial conversation. Indeed, on many occasions, the officials slipped out of their official roles to inform me that they were fans of Miss Buck's and particularly enjoyed one or another of her books.

As travel negotiations got rapidly under way, I thought at first that it was well within the realm of possibility that Miss Buck was going to ask or be asked to travel with the official Nixon group. Being a part of this politically delicate situation, however, was not to be, and it became apparent that any travel by Pearl Buck would be unofficial and definitely not politically motivated or even suspected. Even as an unofficial visitor, she was aware that she was not exactly an ordinary tourist. Her intimate knowledge of Chinese history, her outspoken condemnation of the Communist take-over, the fact that she had been driven out of China by Communists, barely escaping with her own life - and then continuing to write about China - all these things prevented her from ever being just an ordinary tourist. Nevertheless, in the sunset of her years, so to speak, motivated not by politics but by a deep personal desire to see the China of her childhood once more, she pushed her plans forward with confidence.

In addition to gathering information and working through official government channels, Miss Buck concurrently began writing to old acquaintances, associates and friends of long-standing who had maintained direct contact with mainland China, as she had not. Many such individuals were dubbed "old China hands" by the press, and she sought their expertise.

Correspondence with Benjamin Tan, then President of the E. Philip Corporation in New York in the summer of 1971, serves as a sort of prelude to subsequent events. Mr. Tan, whose neatly typed letters in English were interspersed with small precise Chinese characters (Miss Buck still read and spoke Chinese as I was soon to find out) wrote that he had been granted permission to visit China, would be leaving in a few weeks, and offered to visit and take pictures of the gravesites of Miss Buck's mother and father. Mr. Tan's salutation to her is "to an outstanding genuine Pearl who is more like Her Kind Grand Aunt than just a true friend of China."

He continues, "enclosed herewith please find an article which appeared in today's edition of the *Wall Street Journal* titled 'Calm in Peking, China Regains Stability, Economy Rises, but Woes Remain' written by Robert Keatley - an article written by a capitalist newspaper whose view may be objective; I still prefer first hand and direct communication.

"My contemplated trip is not only to see my sick sister, but also to find out for myself so that I will have a better understanding in presenting a more accurate perspective for the program in Chinese culture at Dag Hammarskjold College..."

To which Miss Buck responded "Of course, I am deeply touched that you want to visit my ancestral graves. Please do not do so if it makes you any trouble at all. I would not have anything disturb your visit or put you in any danger.

"My father's grave is in the foreign cemetery on a hill in Kuling in Changsi Province. It has a headstone which I have not seen but which gives his name, Absalom Sydenstricker.

"My mother's grave is in the foreign cemetery near Chinkiang. This cemetery was an old one with a wooden gate. It is situated not too far from Golden Island and yet not very near. There are many westerners buried there. My mother's grave has a headstone and the name Caroline Sydenstricker. In the same cemetery to the left of the gate as one enters there is the grave of my brother and sisters. Their names are Clyde, Edith and Maud. It may be that only the name of Clyde appears on the headstone for I am not sure that my parents were able to move the graves of the sisters from Shanghai."

A "P.S." urges, "Please be sure to let me know when you return. I shall be interested to know how China appears to you now."

I puzzle over an unfiled letter from that same summer of 1971 (before I was with Miss Buck). It appears to be from a Dutch television executive and concerns events which, to my knowledge, were not even under contemplation until many months later. It even occurred to me that a typographical error dated the letter 1971 instead of 1972, but the later date would be just as puzzling. Either way, Miss Buck never mentioned it to me, but I offer it here in interesting speculation.

Amsterdam - July 2, 1971

Yesterday, the Chinese (Peking) legation in the Hague informed us definitely, that no news had come from their Government, as to our official request to travel to China in order to film a reportage of your return visit to the land of your youth. Permission was granted to film the Canton trade fair and several other projects, but nothing was said further on inviting you to come to China. I have also been in constant touch with ambassador Djawato in Peking (even had him on the phone) but for the moment, we have the impression, that they are not prepared to receive you or invite you.

The legation added that as soon as they had information, they would contact me, but knowing Asia, as I do, that might be any time between now and the year 2,000.

I still hope, of course, that sooner or later, we have good news for you. I certainly will contact you at once if we do. Our request and project remains on top of our file of course. The more so, since I have one more card to play. A Dutchman does not give up so easily!"

There seems to be no connection between that letter and all the correspondence which emanated from Danby House, starting with a letter to Prime Minister Chou En-Lai dated February 26, 1972:

"My dear Mr. Prime Minister:

Upon my desk at this moment is a letter from you, written long ago from Chungking. This letter kindly offers to give me information on the "background and conditions" of your people at that time, because you had heard I was planning to write a novel dealing with the areas in northern China defended by your army. I replied immediately, date November 15, 1943, saying that I was not planning such a novel then, but that I might wish to write such a novel at a later time.

"That later time has now come, and during these intervening years I have endeavored to keep alive the basic friendly feelings which my people have always had toward your people. Indeed, I myself do not distinguish between our two peoples. I spent the first forty years of my life in China. My parents, my two brothers and two sisters, are buried there. I look on China as my other country. During the years I have followed closely all available sources of news about the Chinese people.

Now I wish to learn directly of the new China and its tremendous achievements. I should like to present them to my own people as they are today. I do not wish to hear of China only through American or even Western sources. I should like to learn through direct Chinese sources, now that communication between our peoples is possible.

May I call upon you today for the help you offered me so generously in the past?

Yours respectfully,

(signed) Pearl S. Buck

She swiftly followed this letter with another dated March 2nd, again to Chou En-Lai:

Pursuant to my letter to you of February 26, 1972, I would like to say further that if I am given permission to visit your great country, as I hope, I shall be accompanied by my personal secretary, Mrs. William Drake, also by my biographer, Mr. Theodore Harris, and my photographer, Mr. James Pauls. My personal physician, Dr. Albert Bender, is preparing pertinent information regarding my health for one of your Chinese physicians, which my biographer will bring with him. I am glad to say that my health is excellent, and that I expect no problems.

Further, it is my earnest hope that we may leave the United States on or about April 15, 1972. We must return by May the fifteenth at the latest, if we are allowed to stay so long, since my fellow citizens in the United States are making preparations for the widespread celebration of my eightieth birthday upon my return and I do not wish to disappoint them.

All Americans have been looking eagerly and with greatest interest at the pictures of the Chinese people and the beautiful scenery shown on our television. We are impressed that the Chinese people look healthy and happy and that all the children are in school now. I am eager indeed to see with my own eyes the great differences between the past and the present. Please do not consider me in any way political or official. I really wish to come as a long-standing friend of the Chinese people.

In conclusion, I would like to report that copies of my first letter to you, dated February 26, 1972, were sent to The Embassy of the People's Republic of China in Ottawa, Canada, and also to your Embassies in London and Paris, in order to facilitate matters, if possible. Copies of this letter will be sent to the same Embassies. My age compels me to think in immediate terms.

With every good wish, I am..."

On March 1st she dispatched what was termed an "Urgent Telegram" to President Nixon at The White House:

"My dear Mr. President:

I have followed your China visit every step of the way and I congratulate you and Mrs. Nixon. I am very proud of you both. I had planned a trip to China recently but preferred to wait until you had made your historic visit. Now, due to my age, I would like to leave as soon as possible for China, approximately April 15th if arrangements can be made with the Chinese to this end. I have resumed a former correspondence with Premier Chou En-Lai and am in touch with the Chinese Ambassador Huang-Hua. My visit would be for about a month and four people will accompany me. I have no political interests in going to China, but merely wish to observe the changes in the life of the people for my own information and interests. As you may know, I spent the first 40 years of my life in China and my Chinese friends have urged me to make a visit now. I would appreciate anything that you can do to facilitate my departure for China by April 15, 1972. I have asked my biographer to send you copies of his recent volumes on me, and though with deep respect for the value of your time, I take the liberty of asking you to note my letter to Eleanor Roosevelt of March 22nd, 1943 and appearing on page 320 of Volume Two. Again my congratulations and appreciation, with best wishes to you and Mrs. Nixon, I am yours most sincerely....

Ted's letter to The White House went out the same day:

Dear Mr. President and Mrs. Nixon:

Miss Pearl S. Buck has requested that I send to you copies of my two volumes of her biography, which have been sent to you under separate cover. These editions are the only ones that I have at hand. I have called my publishers and requested that they prepare for you special leather-bound presentation copies, which you should receive within three weeks. I am sending the interim copies only because Miss Buck would like you to read her letter of March 22, 1943, beginning on page 320 of the second volume.

May I take this opportunity to express my deep sense of pride and gratitude as an American for the magnificent accomplishments of you and Mrs. Nixon on your visit to the People's Republic of China. We considered your visit perfect in every way.

Respectfully yours,
Theodore F. Harris,
Biographer of Pearl S. Buck

A letter dated March 14, 1972, from United States Senator from Vermont, Robert T. Stafford:

Dear Miss Buck:

Since talking with you by telephone, I have discussed the situation with the gentleman in charge of the Asian Affairs Desk at the State Department, Mr. Richard Kilpatrick.

He tells me that the Chinese Embassy in Canada is flooded with applications for visas to visit China. He says he is sure that the personnel at the Embassy would be well aware of the fact that you are no ordinary person making a request to visit China.

However, he suggested that you have your secretary call the Chinese Embassy and volunteer to come up to Ottawa to discuss the visa request made in your behalf and members of your party.

He suggested that if letters urging you to come to China are from officials of the Chinese government, that the Embassy may be made aware of this, but that if the letters are from unofficial sources, it would be best they not be mentioned.

His final suggestion was to the effect that if you are on friendly terms with Madam Sun Yat Sen that you might wish to write to her in connection with your proposed visit to the Chinese People's Republic.

Hoping that these suggestions will be of assistance, I am

Sincerely yours,

Robert T. Stafford, U. S. Senator

Another letter to Chou En-Lai dated March 20th, this time started with Dear Sir instead of My dear Mr. Prime Minister:

You will by now have received my letters, and I have been in touch with the Embassy of The People's Republic of China in Ottawa, Canada. They have been most kind and courteous.

This letter is to say simply that I am now including in my party my eldest daughter, who lived the first nine years of her life in China with me. As I told you before, my party includes four other persons. They are my secretary, my biographer, my photographer, and my publisher. To these I would like now to add my daughter, Janice Walsh. My daughter is a very successful occupational therapist, especially interested and expert in the education of the handicapped, both old and young, using crafts as therapy.

I hope very much that we can come to China about the middle of April, when the weather is most suitable for me. I look forward with keenest pleasure to seeing the tremendous improvements in the lives of the people of China, especially of the peasants, whom I used to know so well, and about whom I have written always with love and sympathy. Now I will see their happier life, their children in school, and so many benefits.

Yours cordially,

Pearl S. Buck

A letter from the White House dated April 1, 1972, signed by Henry Kissinger, then Secretary of State:

Dear Mrs. Buck:

The President has asked me to reply to your telegram of March 1, in which you indicate that you hope to travel to The People's Republic of China this spring with a party of four to observe changes in the life of the Chinese people. He wants me to thank you for your kind words concerning our efforts to normalize relations between the United States and China.

Knowing the prominent role you have played in portraying life in China to the American people through major literary achievements, we hope that your efforts to return to this country where you spent so many years will prove to be successful. On the basis of our own brief experience in China during the past year, I know there is an interesting story to be told about changes in this ancient society.

I understand that my staff has been in contact with you concerning the matter of obtaining a visa to travel in China. I trust they have been of some assistance to you. I wish there were some way in which we could insure that you and your party obtained visas, but as you know such judgments are made only by the authorities of the People's Republic. You can be sure, however, that your communications with Premier Chou En-lai and Ambassador Huang Hua are getting through to the right people.

The only additional suggestion we might make is that you contact the Embassy of the People's Republic of China in Paris. This Embassy has now been established as a contact point for exchanges between China and the U.S.

We wish you good fortune in your efforts.

Best regards,

Henry A. Kissinger

Again a letter to Premier Chou En-lai dated April 21st:

Dear Mr. Premier:

My letters to you of February 27th, March 2nd, and March 20th have remained unanswered. I quite understand that you are very busy indeed and that the Canton Fair has meant that there has been a crowd of visitors to China, putting a strain on accommodations.

I am approaching you again, however, first because I must arrange for other plans during the next few months, and also because I do not like very hot weather.

I called upon Madame Huang Hua last week. She was very encouraging and very kind. Since I was on the Voice of America that same day and I knew I would be asked whether I would visit China, I asked her what to say. She told me that I could say I would be visiting China but that the time was still indefinite. I am asking now for a definite appointment, since your Embassy in Ottawa cannot send us applications until Peking approves.

Meanwhile I continue anxious to see the new China with my own eyes. It would be easy for me to write from the reports of others. Dr. Ross Terrill, for example, spent some days with me and gave a full report. I do not like to write, nevertheless, without seeing for myself in order that I may give a true and fair picture of the many improvements that have taken place in the new China.

Thanking you again, I am

Yours sincerely,

Pearl S. Buck

A copy of this latest letter was sent to Embassies in Ottawa, Paris and London, all of whom we were in contact with by telephone. And all of whom did not speak fluent English. When halting English proved too frustrating, especially on a trans-Atlantic conversation, Miss Buck occasionally took over in high-pitched careful Chinese.

Her personal visit to Madame Huang Hua in New York needs a comment. Accompanied by Ted and dressed in one of her stunning Chinese robes (which were now being made for her by Sandra Stone, a young local seamstress I had recommended). Miss Buck had no illusions that the visit would produce immediate results in the form of visas or travel approval. As much as anything, she was curious about Madame Huang Hua herself and the atmosphere of the Embassy. I gathered that little substantive conversation took place, although they were received cordially enough, Miss Buck reported when she and Ted drove back from the city. She had the impression that the small Embassy staff was ill at ease and quite unprepared to entertain visitors. Lapsing into a hilarious monologue (with no disrespect intended), Miss Buck regaled me with intimate details of the scene as she and Ted were awkwardly served tea (which no one touched). Her exact words were "I was seated so that I faced the bathroom. The door was open and I was forced to stare at a most unattractive toilet with the seat up." The scene was a comic gem; and while no disrespect was meant, these observations might not have been appreciated by official Chinese sources. "I fear they have much to learn" she ended this episode and returned to the serious side of the whole China affair.

Confident of eventually making the right connections and getting an affirmative reply to her travel request, Miss Buck kept up a barrage of letters to officials. Ted and I were also directed to dispatch messages, sending helpful information wherever she thought it might prove helpful.

Over my signature as Miss Buck's secretary, a letter dated April 24th went to Madame Huang Hua in New York, the wife of the Ambassador:

Dear Madame Huang Hua:

Your answer to my call last week was very much appreciated by Miss Buck. She wishes me to thank you.

Knowing of your interest in having the new China presented fully and fairly, it occurs to me that you might like to see the enclosed advertisement which is appearing now in one of the most important magazines. It is true that Miss Buck has devoted herself to keeping alive the friendship between her two countries, China and the United States. That this friendliness has been made evident here in the United States is largely the result of her books, which are so widely read.

I know that she is very anxious to continue to present a fair and friendly picture of China to the American public who read everything she writes. Her chief desire now is to portray the new China and help the American People to understand and appreciate the new Chinese as they create the new China.

The enclosure to this letter was a full-page ad headed "to millions of readers around the world America's most translated author, the Nobel Laureate Pearl S. Buck is China." There followed a list of her China in fiction and China in nonfiction books.

Next a letter signed by Theodore B. Dolmatch, the President of Intext Publishers Groups. Intext was the conglomerate of which the old Pearl Buck Publishing Company, John Day, was now a part. Miss Buck greatly admired Mr. Dolmatch, as she always called him, and often spoke of his business acumen. He could be both fiery and feisty, and he and Ted Harris often engaged in shouting matches over the telephone until one bested the other over some business procedure or problem. Miss Buck approved of the following letter and hoped it might somehow help in gaining ultimate approval to visit China.

May 5, 1972

To the Honorable Huang Hua, Ambassador
"My dear Mr. Ambassador:

You may recall that Miss Pearl S. Buck has asked to be allowed to visit the People's Republic of China. She has also requested that I, as her publisher, be permitted to accompany her.

I am writing now to request an appointment to see you or your representative. I should like personally to indicate how much Miss Buck wishes to visit your country. She has, over a long and honored career, been the preeminent interpreter of the Chinese people to the American people. Her love of the land and those living on it is apparent in her works, from THE GOOD EARTH of 40 years ago until today. Indeed, her Nobel Prize citation reads "for rich and genuine epic portrayals of Chinese peasant life..."

As she approaches her eightieth birthday, she has said to me that she wishes no gift or honor other than to be allowed to see "her first homeland" again.

Because of her age, the many demands on her time, and because - most of all - she can be and wishes to be one link between the Chinese and the American people, may I ask that you use your good offices to help her return to China very soon.

I look forward to hearing from you....

Many weeks had gone by now and all of Miss Buck's avenues of request had received frustrating maybes or vague answers or worst, no answers. While her confidence may not have been at an all-time high, there was no doubt that her patience was at an all-time low. As usual, her staff was left to deal with the added pressures as best we could. At the end of a file folder full of formal letters and telegrams to President Nixon, ambassadors, embassies and travel bureaus, I came upon an unexpected tension-breaker, a mood-lightener. No, not exactly unexpected, for laughter never failed to lighten the load. "To Go to China" I penned with a smile and it helped to doodle away some of the increasing tensions:

Dear Chairman Mao,

Will you tell me how

To go to China?

Dear Chou En-lai,

Are my plans awry

To go to China?

Dear Ambassador Huang

For me it's wrong

To go to China?

Dear Mr. Harris

Should I go to Paris

To go to China?

Dear Miss P. S. Buck

It rests with Lady Luck

To go to China!

This bit of frivolity is followed by my serious letter to Mr. Yao at the Ottawa Embassy:

"At the suggestion of a Chinese friend, I called the Department of International Travel Bureau in Peking concerning Miss Buck's visit. They suggested we send an itinerary of the places we wish to go.

Miss Buck hopes to stay at least two weeks, with a possibility of three, if her time permits. She would like to visit Peking, Nanking and Chinkiang, the capital of Kiangsu Province where Miss Buck spent her youth. She would also appreciate seeing any villages that are possible, since she has always been interested in the life of the peasants. She is delighted to know that their life is so much better now than it was in the old days. That is the main reason she wants to visit China. If it is not possible for these places to be included, then we would leave her itinerary entirely to the decision of The People's Republic of China.

Thank you for your assistance, Sincerely..."

That phone call to Peking was left entirely in my hands at Miss Buck's insistence. Not only had she grown impatient with the waiting and wondering, she was weary of dealing with all the details. She ignored my concern that Peking might not speak English, and her firm "You handle it, my dear" left no doubt as to what I had to do. Calling at that time was no quick dial-it-yourself undertaking. At the end of the day I still had not reached anyone in the Department of International Travel Bureau and I was instructed to continue my efforts from my farm kitchen phone, assigning the charges to the Danby phone. That was taking my job home with me, something I was still trying unrealistically and unsucccesfully not to do.

Chapter 23

Impatience Grows

Not really knowing how to drop the announcement to my family that I was going to China with Miss Buck, I decided that the only way to do it was to drop it quickly, like a bomb. While my initial announcement produced some traumatic repercussions for me to deal with, taking the positive tack that "anyone in his right mind would jump at the chance to travel to China with Pearl Buck," made the repercussions easier. Miss Buck's personal intervention and explanations helped enormously in easing the situation. Bill's unabashed admiration for her usually superseded his queasiness about the role I was playing and how it could cause (and was causing) an upheaval in our family life. He limped through all the emotional lows as well as the highs, and I really tried, to the extent that it was possible, to include my family in the excitement of the adventure that had been made available to me. We all practiced eating with chopsticks, an art that my left-handedness refused to master, and I promised to write daily accounts of everything I was seeing and hearing.

While all the travel arrangements were taking place, it wasn't only my immediate family being affected. Travel plans included Ted and Jimmy, but not Wendy (so long a part of the inner sanctum) or her husband Alan. Wendy was piqued - and I don't blame her - when she learned that I was going and she was staying home to tend shop.

But much to her credit, and I'm not at all so sure that I could have done it as graciously, Wendy swallowed all her envy and threw herself into the enormous task of preparing to keep the Danby businesses running while the boss was away. Interestingly, Miss Buck elicited a promise from Bill Drake that he would "keep an eye on things" while she was away, giving him status and a direct personal link to her.

So the chosen little band of people around Miss Buck continued in their individual and concerted efforts to support her desire to see China once more. Our travel plans had grown to include not only Ted and Jimmy and me, but Ted Dolmatch and daughter Janice as well. Typically, travel plans had also grown to include not just a quick junket to China and back directly, but an almost around the world last fling for Miss Buck, it would be fair to say. My notes dated March sixth, for example, state that I talked to a travel agency in Manchester, Vermont, getting prices for a route that had us flying from Philadelphia to Seattle to Honolulu to Hong Kong; then train from Hong Kong to Peking and staying in China approximately April 17th to May 15th. Open tickets from Peking to Rome to Paris to London, renting a car in each place and staying approximately seven days in each location. By boat from Southampton back to the U.S. Rough cost per person round trip fare was $1430, $300 extra when returning by ship. Accommodations European plan per night would be about $20 per person.

For Miss Buck's perusal, time was spent in compiling a detailed list of major city highlights. Three pages of things to see and places to go included items like the Empirical Society of Teachers of Dance and the British Museum in London (read *Queen*, *Vogue*, or *What's On In London*, I noted). A list of famous restaurants in Paris, the Borghese Gallery with its Titians, Tintorettos and Grecos, and the Cappricioso for superb pizza at a moderate price in Rome, the Royal Coach Museum and Botanical Gardens in Lisbon, the rose-colored Prado Palace in Madrid, and so on through a fascinating array of ideas.

If it all sounds like we were going on some glorious fun-filled holiday, I knew that I, at least, and Ted, would be coping with timetables, appointments - gruelling schedules every day and that somehow we would have to fit in voluminous note-taking - not only for Miss Buck, but for ourselves as well. We had thought that in addition to whatever work Miss Buck thrust our way, and we knew there would be plenty, we would attempt to collaborate on a book of our own, given our unique traveling circumstances.

So much for the more personal side of the travel negotiations. The daily affairs of the antique shops in Danby, the Country Store, Miss Buck's appointments, her occasional travels to the Foundation and back with Wendy continued uninterrupted. As did her own writing routine and the spate of letters she sent to those "old China hands" she thought might be of some help to her somehow. Letters went back and forth to the widow of author Edgar Snow, to John Service at the Center for Chinese Studies in California, and to another friend living in Shanghai, who wrote informally:

What a relief to know that you have actually applied to come and see! I'm counting the weeks already.

Of course at first you will see the Capital and Premier Chow (her spelling). If you have not already listed them on your application, be sure to ask to see the scenes of your early years here, a commune or two, acupuncture in action, the work of the China Welfare Institute, the big State stores, book stores, and to be sure, enjoy some real Chinese chow....

Give my regards to your right-hand lady, Mrs. Drake, who wrote me such a nice letter. I want her to know I have not touched a typewriter for donkey's years and so apologize for this tacky attempt. She'll be coming along if all works out as you have planned, say, come mid-April, so keep plugging away at that visa!

We all kept officially plugging away, and to Lois Snow Miss Buck wrote:

Your card came this morning and I am delighted, for it is the first sign that mail gets through to Peking. Two months ago I wrote to the Premier, expressing my wish to come to China as soon as possible, hopefully this spring, since I cannot take a hot summer at my age. I am in perfect health and travel without the slightest problems, except that I do mind heat.

At the same time we went through the prescribed formalities of applying at the Embassy of The People's Republic of China in Ottawa, Canada. We have heard nothing except to "wait patiently." We have also had a meeting with Mrs. Huang Hua at the Chinese Mission in New York. She, too, was very courteous but simply said that we must "wait patiently."

Pearl Buck wrote a correspondent:

I wrote a second time to the Premier but have received no reply. Then a week ago we called Peking by telephone and talked with the Information Officer of the Ministry of Foreign Affairs. He spoke excellent English and said that he would bring the matter to the attention of the Premier and the Minister of Foreign Affairs. Since then we have heard nothing and my anxiety continues to come to China - not for a long time, for the most time I could expect to spend there would be about three weeks - but just to see two or three places where I lived for many years and also to see, particularly, the improvement in the life of the peasants.

In a curious way I spoke for the Chinese peasants against the young Chinese intellectuals who were the elite of my youth and my friends, since my father was a scholar and their fathers were his friends. In those days I begged the young intellectuals to pay heed to the peasants who constituted such a majority in China, then as now. They were interested in writing books imitative of Western writers, especially the Germans. When I suggested that they write about their own peasants, they said no one would be interested, whereupon I said I would do it, and I wrote THE GOOD EARTH and a succession of books thereafter. I knew the peasants because we lived in Chinkiang, the provincial capital of Kiangsu province. When we lived in the northern areas we lived outside the city among the farm people. I knew them very well and I knew their hardships. Now I want to see as many villages as I can because I hear and read of great improvements....

Now I am asking a favor of you, which is to speak on my behalf to the powers in Peking and ask if I may be allowed to come for a short period of time.... Since summer is so near it would mean a *great* deal to me to receive immediate words, 'yes or no,' although I hope and pray for 'yes.' I feel sure I could do much in the present difficult times here in the United States to help the American people and even officials in Washington to understand the present situation in China and deepen the friendship between our two people.

Early in May, feeling the backlash of Miss Buck's impatience and frustration, Ted wrote to one of these correspondents himself:

Your correspondence with Pearl S. Buck has come to my attention as her business manager. I am writing to you out of pure confusion, with the hope that you may be able to help me at this point.

We have, in the past two months, not only knocked on the door, we have begged, pleaded, cajoled, sent flowers, and everything else we could think of to get some kind of answer from The People's Republic of China concerning a visit by Pearl S. Buck. While they have been kind, considerate, pleasant and generous with their time, everyone has been totally noncommittal. We do not understand this, frankly. When Pearl S. Buck writes a letter to anyone, it is at least acknowledged, even if evasively, and so far, her letters to China have remained unacknowledged. She will, of course, write a book about the new China, which she can do based upon reports from persons who have returned. It was my idea, however, that she should visit China in order that she could write such a book based upon first-hand information. This book is the next one on Miss Buck's schedule, whether she visits or not. But I still feel that my alternative is the correct one. I know from your correspondence that you agree with me. And so, this letter.

Has common courtesy disappeared from the scene there? Is it not strange that for two months her letters have remained unacknowledged? Is there anything we can do besides 'wait patiently,' which, of course, we cannot do?

There must be someone out there in the great beyond to whom we can appeal for help. In short, is there anything that we can do in order that we can proceed with some sort of intelligent plan in Miss Buck's eightieth year?

A last letter to the friend in Shanghai from Miss Buck, dated May 15th:

Until now we have had nothing but a polite 'please wait patiently' from Ottawa and Mrs. Huang Hua in New York. I am inclined to agree with you that I should now wait until the autumn. I want to attend the P.E.N. international meeting in Japan on November eighteenth, and I would like to make my visit to China before then so let us hope for September or October. It is very interesting to see the difference between the China of yesterday and the Chinese who are here in the United States now - I mean, of course, the ones in missions, etc.

I always speak extemporaneously and I do not, therefore, have a copy of my speeches, but I am sending you one of my books which covers a lot of ground. As you will see, it contains my thoughts about China over the years and my efforts to help our people to understand China better. Now, of course, I feel I must understand the new China, insofar as it is new, for at the end of every dynasty there has been a strange similarity with the incoming groups.

The daily routine at Danby House continued undiminished in intensity. Still hopeful of firming up our travel plans any day, we made a detailed inventory of Miss Buck's valuable personal and household possessions. It was decided that many of these priceless treasures should be temporarily stored in a safe location while Danby House was unoccupied. We met with the Curator-Director of the Bennington Museum in Bennington, Vermont. After a lengthy meeting with Miss Buck, he agreed to transport and store select items while we were away. Miss Buck often wove a story about her possessions. The following colorful pot pourri of things surrounding her weaves its own story about the author. One can almost see her moving about from room to room:

> 3 pieces Steuben ivory glass, candlesticks & centerpiece - c. 1900-1920
>
> 3-piece girandole Sandwich - c. 1840-1860
>
> 10 5-piece place settings Baccarat crystal - c. 1860-1880
>
> 10 second-grind Pamona finger bowls - c. 1886-1890
>
> 1 Thomas Webb cameo vase
>
> Amberina vase
>
> Art glass vase lamps - sandwich glass, sauce dishes and compote
>
> Satin glass rose bowl
>
> Opalescent rose bowl
>
> 10 Tiffany service plates
>
> 10 Tiffany dessert plates
>
> Picard demi-tasse
>
> Nippon dresser set

Occupied Japan figurines

Rose medallion vase

Ginger jar and ginger jar lamp

Nippon tea set

Caldwell Company clock

Pennsylvania Grandfather clock

Jade urn given to Pearl S. Buck by Lin Yu-tang

Jade or Jadite lamp

Peking cloisonne lamp

Inlaid jade and ivory panel

Small jade medallion

Jade water buffalo

Ivory chess set

Netsuke ivory

Ivory snuff bottle

Inside painted snuff bottle

Italian monk's table

4 Chinese tables

English walnut burl shaving mirror

English inlaid dressing table

English tavern table

Round Victorian table

English round hall stand

Kwan-yin (goddess)

Chinese shelves

Charles II screen

English sea chest

Pearl S. Buck at Danby House
by Bruce Curtis

Small Chippendale batchelor's chest

Decorative boxes

Esmeralda lamp

Victorian chair and table

Captain's chair

Silver box from Madame Pandit

Jewelry - good and junque!

Each one of these treasures has its own story to tell - observed together, like observing invited guests at a house party, they draw a vivid outline portrait of the hostess. While it is not fair to say that Pearl Buck was possessed by her possessions, it *is* fair to say that it was very important to her to be constantly surrounded by her beautiful objects.

The "good and junque" description applied to her collection of jewelry applied also to our methods of coping with her growing impatience at hearing nothing definite from Peking, from Ottawa, from Paris - from anywhere. January, February, March, April slipped away and blossomed into mid-May and still no word. We would have snapped under the tension had it not been for the light bantering humor we tossed to each other. Slipped in among the growing file of letters, telegrams and log of telephone calls, I find this scribbled mood-lightener. I started out doodling with the titles of two of Miss Buck's recent books on China, CHINA AS I SEE IT, and CHINA PAST AND PRESENT and doodled on with a junque rhyme for a smile and a laugh for all of us:

China as I see it
Past, present and albeit.

Is full of no's, not now's
From Chou's and Mao's and Yao's.

If they only would say yes
To a lady in distress.

Then nothing could be fina
Than to be in Peking, China.

Chapter 24

A Perfect
Traveling Companion

Towards the end of May Miss Buck prepared to travel to New Jersey to fulfill a speaking engagement at the Vineland Institution where her daughter Carol had been a resident for so many years. This trip, and even the elaborate birthday celebration at the Foundation in June, was completely over-shadowed by a cloud of doubt and silence surrounding the China trip. Wendy, of course, had been scheduled to accompany Miss Buck to New Jersey and Pennsylvania. Then abruptly, due to some urgent business matter in Danby which made it imposslble for Wendy to get away for the Vineland appointments, Miss Buck announced that I would accompany her, as a sort of test run to see what kind of traveling companion I would be. She was still confident that the China trip would somehow someday take place.

The way was smoothed for me - with Miss Buck doing most of the smoothing - and we were driven to and from New Jersey in a chauffeured Cadillac from Vineland. The teenage daughter of the Director was a passenger with us on the first leg of the journey. It caused quite a stir and a lot of surprised looks as we stopped at rest stops along the Taconic Parkway and crowded roadside restaurants. It's no wonder we drew curious stares - Miss Buck in vivid make-up and striking Chinese robe, a uniformed driver complete with peaked cap, a casually dressed teenager and an ultra-conservative looking woman scribbling notes from time to time and paying all the bills along the way. (Miss Buck never carried money with her, always delegating the responsibility of purchasing and paying to one of her staff).

Miss Buck was given a private suite at the home of the Vineland director, while I was assigned fine quarters in a nearby guest house. We dined both nights with the Director's family, and the second night was an outdoor barbeque with a large number of faculty and friends invited to meet Miss Buck. Julie Nixon Eisenhower was a scheduled speaker along with Miss Buck, and we met her before the formal gathering at an informal reception, where she was friendly and charming, although constantly surrounded by hovering Secret Service agents. Miss Buck made time for a visit with daughter Carol. I was surprised at her insistent invitation that I accompany her to the cottage which she had had built for Carol many years before. It was an emotional meeting to face the tall, robust woman with the piercing blue eyes who looked first at me and then at her mother and murmured one word only, "Mama." Somehow there is a tendency to think and speak of retarded or mentally handicapped persons always as "children." Carol was older than I - built like her mother, a picture of her mother in many ways. But behind these piercing blue eyes was THE CHILD WHO NEVER GREW - and I could see how it tore at Miss Buck to view this woman who looked like a woman but was really a child, her child, her only birth child.

The trip back to Vermont proved to be long, hot and tiring. The car air conditioner acted up and finally quit altogether, as did the engine, and we found ourselves stranded in the middle of a super highway at a spot called the Hawthorne Circle. With the hood raised and the temperature inside the car soaring to uncomfortable heights, we waited for help which did not come in a reasonable length of time. I could see that Miss Buck was becoming more and more impatient and agitated. She had little confidence in machines any time and here she was again at the mercy of a big one. Finally we had no choice but to abandon the car and go for help - help being in view in the form of a gas station off the highway, across the median, and on the other side of the dual-lane traffic traveling the other way. The three of us set out - Miss Buck striding along as best she could in her high heels and robe, the driver with his peaked cap, and I trying to look as matter of fact as I could, as if this were just some every day occurrence.

I called Danby to tell them of our dilemma and how impatient Miss Buck was getting (I could hear Ted's knowing laughter in the background). While the car was being worked over and made road-worthy again, I sat grimly facing Miss Buck in the tiny cubicle which served as the station office. The floor was grimy, the windows were grimy, the bathroom was grimy, and the only reading material was a dog-eared map of New England, which some other stranded traveler had no doubt left there. Miss Buck was in no mood to chat pleasantly about any subject - we were both feeling grimy ourselves - I was concerned that she was noticeably weary. I don't remember what we talked about, but it was enough to while away a couple of sticky hours. When at last we arrived at dusk in Danby, I was more than relieved when Miss Buck, before heading upstairs to rest, announced to Ted that I had been a perfect traveling companion. I had passed the test run for China.

Chapter 25

The Letter

While the waiting continued for some word from China, Miss Buck busied herself with completing the CHINA PAST AND PRESENT book, for a publication deadline had to be met, whether or not she could incorporate first-hand observations. It is, in fact, in Chapter Nine of CHINA PAST AND PRESENT that she describes her thoughts as she is waiting and the trauma that occurs when the waiting is finally over. I sat across from her day after day as the drama unfolded. Many mornings, seated perhaps downstairs in the Danby House living room, or more often upstairs where her pink sitting room was flooded with bright Spring light and she could enjoy the show of red and yellow tulips on the hillside below her window, she reminisced at length and let thoughts flow out freely, thoughts I later found myself typing into the manuscript. Sometimes the thoughts were word for word, as if she had had her own tape recorder going during our conversations. Actually, she did most of the talking, and I the listening. Always, always, each reminiscence was preceded and punctuated by some comment about "the letter, the expected letter from China."

She began by saying "All these days I have been waiting - waiting for the letter. While I waited I have been remembering the China I knew better than I knew my own country, the people I knew better than my own..." She remembered the love and sacrifice and dedication of her own parents. And the three Murdock sisters, missionaries who had renounced all comfort to live among the Chinese, taking as their special cause the abandoned girl babies left outside the city walls. These sisters saved what babies they could and raised them as their own. Miss Buck murmured so low I could hardly hear her. "The Murdock sisters loved them all the way."

"...Oh, the memories that flash into my mind because of this letter, lying open here on my desk..."

And oh the memories that flash into *my* mind now, years later because of this same letter - the original one - now lying open on my desk in another time, another place, but still that same letter. It was I, and Wendy and Ted, who first saw this letter as we opened the pile of mail at the office, as was the custom. I saw that letter before it was carried to Miss Buck at Danby House. That same letter lies in front of me this instant and I feel the same disbelief, hurt, anger, confusion - all the things I felt then. Silently, not knowing what to say, we had presented the letter to Miss Buck.

"The letter came this morning. I had waited weeks..."

And she talked about the good men and women she knew, all the good missionaries who protested when even some of our own people were unjust to the Chinese. And she lamented for the Chinese poor and oppressed and murdered.

"...and the letter," she said, "the letter is here on my desk..."

And she told me again of how her father and mother often stayed up all night with one or another grieving or needy neighbor. I see her father as she describes him to me walking with his arm around a Chinese opium addict who was near death from an overdose.

She did not sob with tears, but her very words are sobs.

"Oh my beloved father, I shall never see even your grave - never, never. The letter is here, and it commands me never to return..."

And the memories of her mother helping, healing, helping wherever she was needed, and her terrible tragedy of burying four children, her babies born in a foreign land far from comforts and loved ones.

I can feel all her hurt and anger even now as I steal a look at the letter and I can hear her saying:

"This letter lies here. It is a menacing fist. What does it mean? The letter is written to me, but I am only one person. What does it mean to the whole world that a Chinese man, even a mere second-class official, can show such narrowness of understanding, such ignorant vindictiveness?"

I feel her anger and suspicion as she looks at the letter, as I look at it now.

"The letter - the letter. It lies there like a living snake on my desk - a poisonous snake..."

She quickly returns to the good memories of how her parents taught her to respect and even revere the Chinese because of their great and glorious ancient civilization. Though she was driven out of China by the Communists, she knew and understood and even forgave them for what was happening for it had happened all before - different names, different places but the same pattern repeating itself over and over, in the endless bid for power. "But China is old and wise," Miss Buck declared, leaving no doubt that the current revolutionary furor would eventually wear itself out until intellectual sanity would once again prevail and China could resume its courteous, venerable place on the new world scene.

She found an analogy in what was happening now in China in a little gift, a memento of the President's trip to China, which had recently been presented to her by Julie Nixon Eisenhower. The gift was a set of nested lacquer boxes, each one nesting within the other and growing smaller and smaller until the last one is so minute that it could contain nothing. She drew a parallel by saying that in China now - temporarily - there was control, control and more control until there is - nothing.

She called the rude letter an attack. "It is violent, it is uninformed, it is untruthful," she condemned it severely.

She knew from this violent attack that the writer, whoever he was, had never read one of her books, although they had been widely translated and read in the China of earlier times. A Chinese writer once said of THE GOOD EARTH that his only criticism was that it should have been written by a Chinese.

Her reminiscing, first aloud and then in writing, had a profound effect of causing her hurt and anger to subside and in its place there remained nothing but pity - pity for the new people of China who had, at least for the present, lost track of their own illustrious history. It is a pity when anyone, for whatever purpose, causes his own inheritance to be destroyed.

There remained, briefly, some pity for herself, for now she would never again see China. She would have to write her next novel, THE RED EARTH from what she read and from what others told her. These others, she lamented, would now have to visit her in secret, fearful for their very lives if they were in the company of one who had been banished by the current powerful and ignorant rulers.

But to live too long in self pity would be a waste of time, and Pearl Buck never had time to waste, not even minutes. And so the letter lay on her desk and as she talked, the letter ceased to wound her further and she looked with pleasure at the bright tulips and the rushing waterfall.

"Somehow," she wrote, "while I have been writing these pages," referring to that last chapter of CHINA PAST AND PRESENT" the sting has gone out of the letter. I do not care any more. The wound is healed, the discourtesy ignored. Therefore, I am able now to quote the letter as it is, as it has been, laying before me on my desk, these several days..."

And as I type these words above, her words, I reflect that it is the second time I have written them and this second time the menacing letter has been laying open on my desk. I can look at it now with pity. It is but a limp bit of paper, its message no longer able to harm or hurt. Here is the letter:

**The Embassy of the People's Republic of China
In Canada**

May 17, 1972
"Dear Pearl Buck:

Your letters have been duly received.

In view of the fact that for a long time you have in your works taken an attitude of distortion, smear and vilification towards the people of new China and their leaders, I am authorized to inform you that we can not accept your request for a visit to China.

Sincerely Yours,
(signed) H.L. Yoan

The Embassy of the People's Republic of China in Canada

May 17, 1972.

Dear Miss Pearl Buck,

Your letters have been duly received.

In view of the fact that for a long time you have in your works taken an attitude of distortion, smear and vilification towards the people of new China and their leaders, I am authorized to inform you that we can not accept your request for a visit to China.

Sincerely yours

(H. L. Yuan)
Second Secretary

She called or wrote to many of the people who had been helpful to her in her initial quest to travel to China. Typical of the response was a letter from John S. Service at the Center for Chinese Studies in Berkeley, California:

May 23, 1972

Dear Pearl Buck:

The news you gave me this morning was a surprise and a shock, and perhaps I don't think very well that early in the morning.

As I keep turning it over in my mind, one thing seems more and more obvious. It is not the kind of decision nor the type of letter (to a Nobel Laureate) to be the decision or phraseology of a minor bureaucrat such as a second secretary in the Chinese Embassy. It is possible (as I suggested) that it could reflect a new "get tough with Americans" policy based on Chinese resentment of Nixon's escalation of the Vietnam war. But I think, if this is the case, that there would have been some mention of the war. My impression, over the telephone, was that there was no such mention in the letter.

My present conclusion is that your hope of making a return visit to the land of our birth has run head-on into another famous author - Mao Tse-tung. Mao is, by all reports, an omnivorous reader - but only in Chinese. One must wonder, then, how fair an idea he has of your views and attitude. *The Good Earth,* certainly, but what else? Speculation is probably a waste of time. But if my hunch is correct - that you have received an unfavorable "review" from a thin-skinned, dogmatic, old Mao - then there is very little chance of obtaining any reversal. Perhaps when John Fairbank returns from China, he may be able to shed some light - but I understand that that will not be until some time in August.

I am sincerely sorry to hear your bad news..."

Her reply to him dated May 31, 1972:

Dear Mr. Service:

Thank you very much for your letter of May 23rd. None of us has any idea as to who or what is behind the really vicious letter of refusal from a small official in the Ottawa Embassy. We have not quite decided how to use it but must accept it as it stands for the present.

Thank you for your help and if you hear anything from John Fairbank, I shall be pleased to know of it..."

Next to this correspondence I have a single-page draft of a proposed letter to Premier Chou En-lai. Carbon copies were to have gone to President Nixon, Henry Kissinger, Marshall Green, Assistant Secretary of State, Ambassedor Huang Hua and Mrs. Huang Hua, John Service, Embassies of the People's Republic of China in Canada, Paris, and London, Theodore B. Dolmatch, and 32 foreign publishers. To my knowledge this letter was never sent, but I include it here as an interesting aside to the chain of events which had been taking place.

May 23, 1972

My dear Mr. Premier:

The most incredible letter from the Embassy of The People's Republic of China in Canada has arrived in my mail today. It seems to me impossible that the leaders of the new China could be as misinformed as to say that I have "taken an attitude of distortion, smear, and vilification towards the people of new China and their leaders."

In view of the fact that my Nobel Prize citation reads "for rich and epic portrayals of Chinese peasant life," it must occur to the Chinese people, new or not, that for millions of readers around the world I am the leading authority on life in China. If, in fact, the "new" China is, in fact, so good, then why not show it to me and let me tell my millions of readers around the world how good it is. As things now stand, I fear that perhaps things in the new China are not so good as they may seem on the surface, and I fear that under the circumstances I shall have to say so.

I wish hereby formally to withdraw any request I may have made to visit China and to inform you that I now consider it impossible that I shall ever desire to visit China again.

This letter brings my every sincere wish for your good health, for after your death I fear the Chinese people will have a very difficult time indeed..."

One final emotional letter, in the form of an open letter to the people of China deserves to be quoted in its entirety. Miss

Buck called it 'L'Envoi.' Is it the end of the CHINA PAST AND PRESENT book and it is the end, in a sense, of the trip to China which never took place.

L-Enovi

"O my dear people of China! Dear because of all my childhood in China, all my Chinese friends through all my youth and young womanhood, even until half my life was spent, I speak as your lifelong friend.

You have much to endure before your future is clear and peaceful. When this Emperor dies, this Mao Tse-tung, there will be wars among you as there have always been when an Emperor dies and there is no heir to take his place. There will be a struggle in all your members, a regional struggle, until the new Emperor appears. And the struggle for his emergence will be, as it has always been among the young generals. They are waiting in every province in your country, their armies trained and poised, each army loyal to its own general, and only to him. The victor in this struggle will be your new Emperor, whether you call him that or not. His will be "the mandate of Heaven," because what you, the people of China, want is always the mandate of Heaven. By whatever name you call yourselves, you are still the people of the Middle Kingdom, the Center of the World.

I shall never see you again, nor will you see me. It has been forbidden us. You will smile, perhaps, when I tell you that although I have been many times invited to visit Taiwan, I have never accepted, lest your rulers take it as a political act and forbid me a visit to you on the mainland. But this does not matter now. Already the son of President Chiang is negotiating the return of Taiwan to

China. This is, of course, inevitable, whether the people of Taiwan wish it or not.

No, I shall never see you again, my beloved people of China. My feet will never again tread the hills, the villages, the cities I know so well. Yet, though this is true, it, too, no longer matters to me. I am a part of you forever, as you are of me. You formed me, you fed me, you shaped me as I am forever.

A part of me remains eternally with you. My parents lie in your earth. They spent their lives with you and for you. In death they are with you still. With them are also my two brothers and two sisters who died in childhood of diseases endemic in your country. They never saw America, their ancestral land. They are forever a part of China, as I am also, save that I still live and am safely in my native land, for here I, the only one of seven children, was born.

Here, too, in freedom, I have done my work. I have steadfastly helped my American people to understand, respect, and even love you, my Chinese people. I have had my part in our President's visit to Peking, for our people wished him to go. They do not feel you are strangers, whatever the difference in our governments. I am proud to know that through my writings I have helped to create and sustain this feeling. I shall continue to do so.

All that China gave me, the friendships, the beauty, the excitement, the dangers - yes, there were dangers to my very life and the lives of my family and we were saved by our Chinese friends - all my experiences for so many years, I have poured into my books. My books have taken me, and you with me, far and wide upon our Earth.

I am glad for your sake that I am the most widely translated author my country has ever had, for that means
that you, too, are also widely known. To the best of my
ability, I have tried to speak for you. I was proud that
the Nobel Prize for Literature was awarded to me for
"rich and genuine epic portrayals of Chinese peasant
life."

I was humbly happy that my parents were also mentioned in the added phrase, "and for masterpieces of
biography." For in their time my father and mother
obeyed the mandate of Heaven as it was given to them:
"Go ye into all the world!"

In my own way, in my own time, I too have obeyed the
mandate of Heaven. For me it is expressed through the
words of eternal truth spoken by Confucius, who yet
lives though he was born five hundred years before the
Christian era.

"Under Heaven," he said, "All are One."

Danby House

Danby, Vermont

May 30, 1972

Pearl S. Buck's 80th birthday celebration at Green Hills
June 1972 - by Lorston Studios

Chapter 26

Miss Buck Calls for Help

L'Envoi, the epilogue to the China book, also ended the real life China episode we had been involved with for so many months. There was too much work to be done to dwell on what might have been or should have been. The manuscript was delivered to the publisher in New York, the China trip was relegated to the past, and Miss Buck, with renewed writing vigor and determination, handed me page after page of the GENIUS BOOK and the short stories she enjoyed writing from time to time.

When she and Wendy went away for the big eightieth birthday celebration in Pennsylvania, Ted and Jimmy were also gone on antique business. For a brief few days, the third floor offices were quiet except for my whirring typewriter. At the top of my ever-changing priorities of work to be completed were the Nobel Peace Prize letters. This was an ambitious project instigated by Ted as a birthday surprise for Miss Buck. Writing to prominent people all over the world - people familiar with the humanitarian and literary accomplishments of Pearl Buck, Ted was requesting their assistance in having her nominated for the Nobel Peace Prize. From the response which was pouring into Danby many others shared Ted's belief that she was more than a worthy candidate. Copies of their letters, addressed to the Nobel Peace Prize Committee in Oslo, Norway, attest to

their feelings. The letter writers included university profes-
sors and presidents, premiers, governors and senators, as
well as distinguished writers. I paused to reflect then, as I
pause to reflect now, on the outpouring of feelings:

From Richard Curry, History Professor at the University
of Connecticut:

When Pearl S. Buck was awarded the Nobel Prize for
Literature in 1938, it could hardly be predicted that she
was destined to become equally distinguished in still
other areas of endeavor.

Through her writing, by the establishment of The Pearl
S. Buck Foundation, by her personal example in adopt-
ing nine children of all races, and by her courage in fighting racism and the ugly spectre of McCarthyism in the
United States during the 1950's, Miss Buck has
profoundly affected the lives of countless thousands all
over the world.

Hers has been a lonely, yet unrelenting struggle to
demonstrate to all mankind the potential of the human
race for achieving unity and dignity - and this despite
the omnipresence of countervailing forces that threaten
to engulf and destroy the human race.

I can think of no one who deserves the Nobel Peace Prize
more than Miss Buck....

From Governor of Vermont Dean C. Davis:

There is, living in a beautiful rural town in the State of
Vermont, a lady who is soon to be eighty years old, Pearl

S. Buck. It is a pleasure and an honor to nominate her for the Nobel Prize for Peace.

In this world of complexity, impersonalizations, change and strife, the greatest way to peace is through compassion, commitment and understanding. Through her writings, her work with children of the world, and her role as ambassador among people of every race, nationality and creed, Miss Buck has built a bridge of communication between the peoples of the East and West that has fostered the realization that all of us, the people of the world, are of one great family and that peace must be our way.

I know of no other citizen of this Good Earth who is more deserving of the Nobel Prize for Peace than Miss Pearl S. Buck....

From Tad Danielewski of the Directors' Guild of America:

John F. Kennedy put into simple words a very profound concept: "The men who create power make an indispensable contribution to the nation's greatness. But those who question power make a contribution just as indispensable, especially when that questioning is disinterested. For they determine whether we use power or power uses us."

Pearl S. Buck in her lifetime of work as artist and humanitarian has helped many men of power to adjust their actions to reality until many of them are closer to her perception of it and thus a step closer to achieving lasting peace for all of us on this planet..."

And from Carlos P. Romulo, Secretary of Foreign Affairs of the Phillippines:

Some years ago, I had the pleasure of collaborating with Pearl S. Buck, then already a writer of renown and a recipient of the Nobel Prize for Literature, on a book, FRIEND TO FRIEND. She struck me as unique in many ways. She wrote books not so much to make money as to express a deeply humanitarian concern for societies in a state of development and frustration, and for people. Such was THE GOOD EARTH, for instance, and the score of other books which she wrote that the West may have a glimpse of the soul of the East.

It is this humanitarian urge which, in my opinion, has moved Pearl Buck to fresh labors. She is eighty, but if age has meant anything to her, it is that she is bequeathing all of herself to humanity so that thousands of children without identity, with no place in society to begin with, with a future darkened by an ambiguous past, may live as persons if not as links between East and West. I refer, of course, to the Pearl S. Buck Foundation, which is setting up those Opportunity Centers in suitable capitals in Southeast Asia, including Manila. The war has spawned among other things an army of orphans, whom we vaguely call Amerasians, and who can't all be adopted. Mrs. Buck's intention in setting up those Opportunity Centers is to educate, rehabilitate, and develop these youngsters in their own milieu before they become social problems.

What is unique is that Mrs. Buck has given virtually all her earnings as an author to the Foundation - more than a million dollars to start with - to support a great humanitarian project which is bound to have a tremendous impact on Asia's attitude towards the West. On top of that, Mrs. Buck herself has been working ceaselessly to hasten the setting up of this network. This is not merely a gesture - it is commitment at its fullest. We cannot even begin to think of peace as a universal desideratum unless the human being is offered an opportunity to realize himself within a civilized framework. Mrs. Buck has given her all to make this possible....

The list goes on, and I use that brief interlude of quiet between the China episode and what happens next to indulge in some random observations - more personal. In the relatively short period of time since I had entered that closed circle of Pearl Buck associates, I had amassed an incredible array of feelings and facts about my lady boss and her complex life, as well as Ted, Wendy and Jimmy - those three personalities I had once called The Three Bears.

Miss Buck herself commented to me often that her daily life at Danby took on many aspects of a colorful and fast-moving soap opera. She relished this aspect, as she relished all aspects of daily life. Sometimes she was responsible for setting in motion the entangled interaction of the participants, like the chaos she caused when she decided that her "Dream for Danby" was not moving rapidly enough. Indeed, from the outside Danby House itself was still an eyesore on the scene - half-painted, half-remodeled, unlandscaped. When she discovered that the brook behind Danby House was polluted and that the tumble-down old house (she called it a shack) next door had no proper plumbing facilities and was responsible for much of the nearby brook pollution, she set out to "clean up the sludge in the brook," as she called it, and "buy up the shack next door," thereby hurrying along - on *her* terms - the beautification of Danby. All of this was a noble, but unrealistic approach. She knew it but pursued it anyway. Her letters and phone calls to first one Vermont governor and then his successor would not let either ignore the sludge in the brook problem. "And what are you going to do about it?" she persisted relentlessly. And I, as both Mrs. Drake and Mrs. Bixby, was dispatched to write, telephone, and visit in person the local family living in "that shack next door," with offers to buy their homestead which they and their ancestors had occupied for several generations. Humble as their home might be, the residents of that shack were not about to move. It was the only home they had known and they were not about to give it up, not even to the world-famous lady next door waving money at them.

There were some testy exchanges, but no real animosity involved. Miss Buck understood them and their attitudes. "Peasant attitudes" she called them, combined with Yankee stubborness and lack of education. She stated her opinions, but she never looked down disparagingly on any of her neighbors. Many times I watched her absorb with pleasure the wonderfully naive and unworldly manners of a farmer friend who told her all the problems he was having with his "bull-nozer," as he insisted on calling his earth-moving machine.

For as long as I was with Miss Buck, the sludge and the shack remained. Had there been enough time, I have no doubt that the sludge and the shack would have been beautified, if not removed from the scene altogether. Her methods might be controversial, but her motives were not.

Everywhere she traveled away from Danby, Miss Buck was driven, occasionally in the old but still serviceable Chrysler New Yorker, vintage of another era. Most often she was driven by Ted or Wendy in a small but comfortable Volvo sedan. Occasionally even I had been pressed into service with my little red bug to escort her to a doctor's appointment when no one else was available or no one's car was running and mine was. When I asked Miss Buck one day if she herself had ever driven, I was surprised when she replied, "Of course, I drove one of the first early model automobiles in Japan." I was surprised again when she told me that at one time she was quite fond of smoking little cigars. Like her driving, her smoking had ceased years ago. She intensely disliked anyone smoking in her presence for any length of time, and she was always scolding Ted for smoking too much, even when he wasn't in her presence, which he usually was for she demanded it.

My reflections went back to Ted, Wendy and Jimmy, and I tried always to see them as *she* saw them. Ted, even with his known faults and frailties, was always set apart as special and cherished by her - not above reproach but loved and needed by her. She appreciated and leaned on his strengths; she forgave and tolerated his weaknesses. Friends, lovers, business associates, I have never waivered in my feelings that Pearl Buck and Ted Harris enjoyed an extraordinary and unusual relationship based on complete trust and confidence.

Trying to figure out the twisted ties around Ted and Wendy and Jimmy and Wendy's husband Alan was as futile as trying to sort out the who's and what's of a television soap opera which had been grinding on for years. "Just accept it; don't try to understand it or change it," Miss Buck admonished me on more than one occasion when I seemed perplexed at the questionable actions of one or more of these friends who were so inseparable most of the time. It was from Miss Buck herself, as a matter of fact, (though I learned it in bits and pieces from others as time went on) that I discovered that Wendy, married now to Alan (a former milkman who had once been a dance instructor with Ted) used to be married to Jimmy and that Ted and Jimmy, though mostly Ted, had transformed a chubby little teenager named Minnie from Texas into the chic Wendy who cheerily (for the most part) cha-cha-cha-ed through her chores with the lightness and grace of the dance partner she used to be to Ted.

The rambling way I wrote that, on purpose, is pretty much the way Miss Buck described those four to me. The ties that bound these four puzzled her, as they puzzled me, but she accepted this diverse group for what they were, relying on what she termed Ted's great abilities to keep them all mobilized in her best interests under his direct supervision. "My Several Worlds," noted Miss Buck concluding one of our many conversations about Danby people and problems, "include Danby, for that's where I am now."

And it was in Danby that I found myself once again alone in the third floor office on the first Saturday afternoon in July. Even with the China trip behind us, at least one big manuscript completed, and the Book Club running along smoothly, I was somehow always behind on Miss Buck's voluminous personal correspondence. Determined not to begin another Monday morning with unfinished work, I was concentrating on the mountain of fan mail beside me when the phone rang. It was Miss Buck and she was surprised when I answered for I had never before worked in the office on a Saturday. Concerned, she said something about not staying too late because Colonel Drake would not like it. "Do you know where Mr. Harris is?" she asked. I replied that I thought he was in the corner antique shop. She hesitated and so I asked if she would like me to have him call her. "No, no, he's busy and I don't want to bother him..." She hesitated again, so I asked if there was something I could do for her. "It's probably nothing," she said then, "but I have a slight pain in my side; I've been writing and perhaps I should rest a while." She repeated, "It's probably nothing." I debated whether I should go and find Ted and tell him of the phone call I had just received, for he had instructed me always to keep him informed of any little thing out of the ordinary or unusual in Miss Buck's normal routine. I was debating this within minutes of that first phone call, when a second call from Miss Buck left no doubt as to what I had to do.

"Mrs. Drake," she began formally, "I'm afraid the pain is quite bad now and seems to be getting worse..." I was aware instantly of the strain in her voice. All my antennas told me that something was wrong. Don't panic I told myself; you'll panic her and you'll panic Ted. Slowly, with a calm I didn't feel, I said, "I'll tell Mr. Harris right away - we're on our way right now to Danby House."

I flew down the stairs, taking them two or three at a time and ran as fast as I could up the street to the corner shop where I could see Ted inside talking with a group of customers. I forced myself to stop and take a deep breath. Then I stepped through the open door and put my hand gently on Ted's shoulder and said, as quietly as I could, "Don't panic, Ted, but drop whatever you're doing and come with me right away to Danby House..."

Chapter 27

The Goddess Abides

It was neither personal panic nor false alarm that drove Miss Buck, Ted and me to the Emergency Room of Rutland Hospital on the afternoon of July 1, 1972. A quick telephone consultation with the doctor before we even left Danby set us on our rapid course of action that would see the three of us involved in a medical and personal drama with side effects more complicated than any story Pearl Buck had yet written. That redoubtable presence of Destiny was with us once again as Ted and I nervously watched Miss Buck being wheeled into the examining room for preliminary tests and x-rays. "Such a bother, such a waste of time," she complained. "Probably just too much birthday celebration," she diagnosed her own discomfort. Ted and I had already voiced concern to each other that she had seemed unusually fatigued upon her return from Pennsylvania. And we could only guess the toll on both mind and body that the vicious China letter had taken.

"I am in perfect health for a woman my age," she announced in her most imperious way to the doctors in charge. The doctors firmly reminded her, nevertheless, that she was eighty years old and advised that she would have to be checked into the hospital for further observation and examination. Quick diagnosis, they said, was not only unwise; it was impossible. If they suspected what was wrong, they cautiously said nothing.

Following her instructions, I took care of the paperwork to admit her as "Jane Doe." This insured, at least for a short time, her protection from the press and unwanted prying eyes. Since the receipt of the China letter, Miss Buck had become more and more insistent that everything be done to insure her privacy. She was adamant about having every detail of each day exactly as she dictated. We weren't at Danby House; we were at a large busy hospital, but she made it more than clear that she wanted no fuss, no publicity, and to the extent it was possible, she demanded *her* routine. We knew that she could not remain anonymous Jane Doe for long, but as we checked her in, she herself was already anticipating checking out. We were thinking short term, not long term.

Wendy was summoned to bring a suitcase of personal articles, including Miss Buck's choice of reading and writing materials. Jimmy was asked to bring the Winnebago travel trailer which usually was parked unused near Danby House, pressed into service only occasionally for transporting antiques. They could use the trailer during these current crisis hours.

I already knew that Ted was pretty much at Miss Buck's beck and call, but this emergency pointed up that pretty much translated to all the time. "When do you have any time for yourself?" I asked. His instant answer, "I don't. For over nine years I have given all my time to Lady Peasbee. She's a full time job and make no mistake about it." I was beginning to realize that she was a full time job for me, too.

Family members had to be notified immediately and Ted took care of calling daughters Jean, Janice and Henriette. Sister Grace was out of town and could not be reached right away. Despite any coolness or disapproval that some family members might have felt towards Ted Harris (I had been told by Miss Buck that there was plenty of both), I found it to his credit that he outwardly ignored their feelings and did what he felt he had to do for her and what she would consider his proper conduct. Usually he acted on her direct instructions, but I was reminded that some weeks ago he had telephoned on his own, to several of the adopted sons and daughters to gently suggest that (if they had not already thought to do so) a special message for Mother's Day would be warmly received. Miss Buck had mentioned that she hoped to hear from at least some of the children but doubted that she would. Jean seemed to be the one exception who always responded with kindness and fondness. Miss Buck had enjoyed the lovely pink azalea in her bedroom which had arrived from Jean and her family on Mother's Day. Sadly, she had mentioned often to me that Henriette had not called or spoken to her since her request to her mother for money, a request which Miss Buck had refused, though she said that many times in the past she had given money freely. As Ted began calling first one and then another family member, I realized that I still had not met any of these people. I had talked two or three times with Jean when she called asking for her mother at Danby House. These few conversations had always been brief and fairly formal.

My own family had been expecting me home for an early supper on that Saturday night. My telephone call of explanation of where I was and what I was doing ended with the statement, "I'll be home as soon as possible, but I don't know when that will be." My "please understand and don't worry" became a fervent plea which I was to repeat again and again as circumstances dictated that I spend more and more time with Miss Buck and less and less time with my family.

It was dusk when I finally was able to leave the hospital, satisfied that I could do no more that night to insure Miss Buck's comfort and calmness. I was asked to return early the next morning, Sunday. She was in good medical hands, and Ted had made arrangements to park the Winnebago in the visitor parking lot where he and Jimmy would be on constant call all night and would be allowed access to Miss Buck any time should she wish it. This, of course, violated usual hospital regulations, but was the first of many concessions to be made by the cooperative medical and administrative staff.

I was actually grateful for my half-hour drive home through the soft summer twilight, for it gave my racing thoughts time to slow down. We still had no idea what was wrong with Miss Buck, except that she was experiencing pain "under the rib cage," as she described it, and she seemed unduly agitated most of the time. "Wired," one of the nurses described her. While I did not want to exaggerate the seriousness of the situation, neither could I minimize it too much, for I had to justify to my family why I had to return to the hospital on a Sunday morning. I was therefore grateful and relieved when I found concern and sympathy waiting for me at the farm. There was no doubt that my job had long ago turned into more than just a job and, rightly or wrongly, I couldn't back away from it now. I knew I was needed.

For all his displeasure at me for becoming a part-time wife, and in spite of all the unresolved friction between us, Colonel Drake had become an ardent admirer of Pearl Buck and when he said, "She's a special lady," I knew he meant it. I remembered to tell him that she had asked me to thank him for allowing me to be with her so much. And she had also mentioned again how pleased she was to have the rose-colored needlepoint footstool to use in her sitting room at Danby House. Bill had completed this as a surprise birthday gift for her which I had started but never found time to finish.

It is more than understandable that any reader who has read this far in the story may start to doubt my credibility and raise a skeptical eyebrow at how my tiger of a husband - the same man I first describe as distraught and distressed and so difficult to live with that I ran away in desperation - could suddenly turn into a pussycat meekly sitting at home doing needlepoint for the very same woman he himself once condemned for taking away his wife and threatening his lifestyle. While I could not pause then to philosophize on all the whys and wherefores of what was happening and how there seemed to be a sort of moratorium on the up and down cycles that had torn at our marriage for so long, I was once more aware of the extraordinary influence Pearl Buck had on Bill Drake. It was obvious to me that she brought out the best in him, just as I observed that she brought out the best in Ted Harris. These two men, though touched by Pearl Buck under dissimilar circumstances, were bonded to her by her uncanny ability to recognize what she called their raw materials,the potential they possessed. But more than that, she had the power to elicit and sustain a high caliber performance from each of them by putting their intellect to work - *always for her own purposes.*

What I have to say next is based on my reflective judgment after years of sifting through the circumstances I lived through - all the observing, acting, reacting, and absorbing of endless private conversations with Miss Buck. This, in the final analysis, amounted to an intimate portrait of the complete woman: wife, mother, friend, lover, business associate, author, humanitarian. "Thank you for your infinite variety," said her second husband Richard Walsh to her as he lay dying. And plague your infinite variety, I am sure more than one man has said to this same woman who could not walk but could only run through life. I know she was not after power or fortune or glory, though those might come to her. She was after the ways and means to accomplish what she perceived as her essential role on the world scene. She was compelled, perhaps for reasons beyond her conscious control, to try to right what she considered to be some of the world's wrongs. An idealistic view, laudable and shared by many, but rarely brought into realistic and workable proportions. Utilizing her own considerable powers, she mobilized the resources of those she chose to aid her. Her own Foundation for the half-American children stood as the prime example of what her powers could do. But she wasn't through with her dreams yet, and she continued to elicit the best from the individuals who could help her the most.

I have digressed a bit in order to get back to how she influenced Ted Harris and how she was affecting Bill Drake. I saw her extracting the kind of devotion from these two men that a lover reserves for his beloved. And indeed, this is the point I wanted to make in the first place. Ted Harris and Bill Drake were enamored with Pearl Buck, for the goddess abided within her - and men always fall in love with a true goddess. I believe that every man who crossed her path and whom she ensnared as someone able to help her in her life's pursuits - every one of these men had been obsessed with her at one time and would probably remain so, even when she no longer had any use for them. *Do not misunderstand what I am saying.* Do not sully the purity and refinement of the love a Muse-poet has for his goddess. Do not try to tell me that Ted Harris and Bill Drake were lured into the arms of a dirty old woman for perverted mischief. I beg you to try to soar into another dimension of love on an altogether different and higher intellectual plane. Such a love accounts for a seemingly changed Bill Drake, a tiger turned pussycat for his goddess, and Ted Harris, a diamond in the rough whose diamond side always shone brilliantly in the presence of his goddess. I was going to say here merely THE GODDESS ABIDES, but I think it appropriate to repeat the entire quote Miss Buck used to introduce her own book on this very theme. If you did not comprehend it the first time I used it in this story - and I do not say this to be demeaning or derogatory, for goddesses are beyond understanding for many human beings - I hope it will touch you this time. In Pearl Buck, THE GODDESS ABIDES. To understand the woman, you must accept the goddess.

A Muse-poet falls in love, absolutely, and his true love is for him the embodiment of the Muse. In many cases the power of absolutely falling in love soon vanishes; if only because the woman takes no trouble to preserve whatever glory she gets from the knowledge of her beauty and the power she exercises over her poet-lover. She grows embarassed by this glory, repudiates it, and ends up either as a housewife or a tramp; he, in disillusion, turns to Apollo who, at any rate, can provide him with a livelihood and intelligent entertainment - and goes out of circulation before his middle-twenties. But the real, perpetually obsessed Muse-poet makes a distinction between the Goddess as revealed in the supreme power, glory, wisdom and love of woman, and the individual woman in whom the Goddess may take up residence for a month, a year, seven years, or even longer. The Goddess Abides.

How, you may still be asking, does this fit into the whole story? Does Bill Drake remain a pussycat forever? Will Mrs. Drake give up being Mrs. Bixby and return to the farm? Will the powers of the goddess diminish with illness or age? Will Ted Harris carry on alone the work of the goddess, or will he return to a rougher Fred Hair?

Wait. Be patient. It is too soon to answer these questions, for there is more to the story. But I thought it important to interject here that Miss Buck was completely responsible for what gentling changes seemed to be taking place in Bill Drake. I had nothing to do with this and take no credit for it. In nearly two decades of trying, I had failed. It took a goddess to succeed.

At the hospital, there was an agonizing waiting period of two or three days before we had a diagnosis. We talked small talk and continued to hope that it was just too much birthday. Cutting through this optimism more times than I could count came Miss Buck's knife-sharp question: "Mrs. Drake, I want you to tell me the truth. Have the doctors told you something they are not telling me? I want you to promise me that you will tell me exactly what you hear, even if Mr. Harris tries to hide the worst from me." I promised. I even told Ted what she said. "That lady is too much." He shook his head and knifed through his own shaky feelings.

"What are we going to do, how are we going to cope if it's, if it's (he didn't even want to say the word serious)." What do *you* think, Bev? Come on, gut feeling, woman's intuition. What do *you* think is wrong? Ted's first two questions could only be answered by I don't know; we just do the best we can, whatever that is.

What do I think is wrong with Miss Buck? I repeated, stalling for time. I shrugged. At best it's too much birthday, at worst it's some sort of heart problem. I neither believed nor disbelieved what I said, but I had to say something.

When at last the diagnosis was handed down, the explanation was lengthy and the terms unfamiliar. We had hoped for the best, prepared for the worst, but never expected to be devastated.

Chapter 28

Rutland Hospital

It's an aneurysm, came the pronouncement from the two Rutland doctors caring for Miss Buck, plus two more specialists called in for consultation from the Medical Center in Burlington.

In dictatorial tones, Miss Buck had informed the doctors that Mr. Harris was in charge of all her affairs, that he was, in fact, closer to her than her family. " My family has nothing whatsoever to do with my affairs, business or private. You must deal directly with Mr. Harris *and* Mrs. Drake," she added. "They are with me and know me. I am comfortable with them and they are quite capable of handling everything. They will, of course, keep my sister and the others informed and do whatever has to be done..." No mistaking what Lady Jane Doe wanted.

So it was that the doctors accepted Miss Buck's specific directives and Ted and I became the individuals they would have to consult with and advise. And so it was that Ted and I were to be responsible for the awesome task of coping with the patient's care and well-being. "Coping" does not begin to describe the specialized needs and problems of caring for an impatient patient with an aneurysm. "I think a heart problem might have been easier," I murmured to Ted as we sat tensely and listened in a state of shock and worry. First the definition of an aneurysm: It is a ballooning out of the wall of an artery which has somehow been weakened. It can suddenly rupture, causing sometimes fatal loss of blood.

Next we heard what had to be done for an eighty-year-old aneurysm patient: There would be a "wait and see" period when the aneurysm was monitored to determine whether or not it was increasing, decreasing, moving around or? Or? An aneurysm can burst if it keeps growing and gets too thin and stretched. Like a balloon that is blown up and blown up and blown up until it finally reaches its breaking point and pops. An aneurysm is operable only under certain circumstances. An aneurysm is a risk with a capital R. What specifically was to be done with Miss Buck and *her* aneurysm? Ted and I were told that in her case the aneurysm (and they were not absolutely positively sure that it *was* an aneurysm, though all the doctors agreed that at this time it was the best diagnosis that could be offered) - in her case, the aneurysm was in a difficult spot in the chest cavity; very difficult to positively identify on the x-rays which had been taken so far. It would be essential, during an extended period of observation and monitoring, to keep the patient utterly serene and calm, avoid all stress and strain, avoid all conflict, avoid even the smallest annoyance, avoid anything at all that might upset the patient.

How long was the "extended period of observation" to be? At this point they could not project. Days, maybe weeks. In the hospital? Probably. What was to happen at the end of this period? Again too soon to tell. But the possibility seemed to exist that the aneurysm might remain unchanged, static. And? And if an operation was ruled out, there remained nothing to do but to continue - preferably at home - to insulate, isolate, insure the patient's continuing calm atmosphere. The danger of an aneurysm popping? Always there. It would be like living with a ticking time bomb but never knowing when the bomb would explode or *if* it would explode.

"Oh my God," Ted and I both gasped. "You don't know Miss Buck. We can't possibly keep her life utterly calm and serene."

The doctors listened patiently and sympathetically while we exploded emotionally about the recent trauma of the aborted China trip, the important writing she was in the midst of, and what were we to do about her family? The doctors listened to our outpouring. When we protested that they were asking us to do the impossible, they even agreed but said, "You have no choice." For their part, they told us that they would do everything medically possible and would keep us informed of everything, good and bad. Then they said that if we needed their assistance in dealing with the family (and they thought we would because the mere appearance of disagreements and difficulties *must* be kept from the patient), we were to use our own best judgment. They told us to tell everyone that we were under strict orders from the doctors.

Impossible, it's impossible.... Ted and I almost shouted it at each other in our frustration with the inevitable. We realized we were in an untenable position. And if we can't carry out this totally calm environment, we wanted to know....

You risk the patient's life, was the numbing reply. You risk the possibility that the balloon will pop. You want to do what's right for her? She's counting on you two, obviously....

Well of course we want to do what's right for her - It was insulting to both of us to think otherwise.

Then you have no choice. The doctors once again underscored their impossible dictum. There were more questions and answers but, to my ears, the answers were cautiously worded maybe, possibly and wait and see. No cure-all pill or serum, no fool-proof corrective surgery was possible now, maybe never. Careful medication perhaps to relieve physical discomfort or aid in the emotional serenity of the patient. And then? And then more wait and see. Did Miss Buck at least have a fighting chance for productive years ahead with this monstrous "thing" inside of her? She had much unfinished work....

But the doctors refused to project more than hours or days ahead, weeks at the most. Ted and I were seeking definite answers where there were no definite answers. We wanted to know that the medical men facing us were miracle men. They would do everything they knew how to do, and if we did everything we knew how to do, would the aneurysm go away? Would a miracle occur?

In spite of everything we *all* do, the end result may be out of our hands, came the final sober answer.

Out of our hands...out of our hands.... As the dread pronouncements swirled around us, I knew that we would have to step over, push aside, out-run, and try to overcome the overbearing presence of that damnable, damnable, damnable director called Destiny.

There was now no time to waste on pondering the unfathomables, if indeed they existed at all. There was work to be done and no time to waste in speculation. Years later, as I stare at my original notes of those terrible hours, I remember exactly how I felt. The sounds and smells of the hospital return and alien images crowd my mind now, as then. I felt like we had been deputized forcibly into functioning in this unfamiliar world. I had already gone through, I thought, a crash course in Pearl Buck and her several worlds. Now here I was - here we were - in yet another of her several worlds. My own knowledge of hospitals was limited to two brief and untraumatic periods in military quarters when Tom and Jim were born.

A word of apology here if my explanations of aneurysms in general and Miss Buck's in particular are medically unsound. I relate only how it was for me - what I heard, how I reacted and how the story continued to unfold. I remember it all, exactly how I felt when I stared at Ted and wondered just how we were going to do what was expected of us.

Reading my thoughts, Ted said aloud "Anybody can do easy things - we have to do the impossible."

To me he said one word - "Go!" He didn't have to say more. I knew this meant Go! Do what you have to do, Mrs. Drake, Mrs. Bixby. Set everything in motion to cope with everything. Move the office to the hospital. Coordinate with Danby. Coordinate with everybody necessary.

"Go!" he said. And I went. Just as the doctors left on their appointed rounds, so I left on *my* appointed rounds and indulged in no self-pity. There was a lady upstairs alone in a hospital bed who was counting on me - on us. On her behalf, I quickly enlisted the assistance of everybody who could help us with our particular and peculiar needs. If the hospital staff resented our sudden intrusion and special requests, it rarely showed. I had the feeling that they were actually grateful for the help Ted and I were providing them in the care of their rather special patient. We tried never to be a bother or a hindrance and I like to think that most of the time we succeeded.

First I borrowed an unused typwriter and telephone, and it wasn't long before we were offered a whole unused office, which became our busy headquarters for as long as Miss Buck was at Rutland Hospital. Not surprisingly, the day of the diagnosis from the doctors was the day the Jane Doe cover was blown and Pearl Buck was discovered by the media. With full cooperation from the hospital public relations people, we kept the official news of Miss Buck's hospitalization as low-keyed as possible, though media people tend not to keep news of famous personalities low-keyed. Nevertheless, we tried, and the news release dated the Fourth of July is typical of the kind of information which was released regularly.

"Miss Pearl Buck remains in the Intensive Care Unit of the Rutland Hospital. She was examined this morning by Dr. David Cross, attending physician in consultation with Dr. John Davis, Professor of Surgery, University of Vermont and Dr. Lawrence Coffin, Chief of Thoracic Surgery, University of Vermont. Every indication is that her pleurisy condition is improving under the present program of treatment."

"Pleurisy condition" may have stretched accuracy a bit, but it was deemed medically acceptable and more low-keyed than describing the day-by-day progress of a probable aneurysm patient.

In my notes for July sixth, I find that I talked by telephone to Miss Buck's agents in New York who handled her complex book affairs with her many foreign publishers. Cablegrams were to be sent stating "Please inform all news media. Miss Pearl Buck resting comfortably and responding beautifully to present treatment. No danger."

Again on July sixth, the hospital released to the media: "Miss Pearl S. Buck remains in very satisfactory condition in the Rutland Hospital. Late last evening she received a personal telegram and she has given permission for its release:

> It saddened me to learn that you are in the hospital and I hope you are now resting comfortably and regaining strength. As a long time admirer of your indomitable spirit and unfailing courage, I am confident that you will soon be fully recovered and able to continue with your work. With my prayers and best wishes, (signed) Richard Nixon"

It wasn't long before flowers and cards and letters from everywhere began arriving at the front desk. First a trickle - a pretty card or two which Ted and I opened and showed Miss Buck. Then a stream of get well messages and gifts which overflowed baskets and boxes - the likes of which the hospital staff had never seen, and the likes of which Ted and I had never seen and didn't know what to do with. We gave this problem to Mrs. Bixby who began sending out notes that Miss Buck was "resting comfortably but would not be personally answering her mail for some time..." Mrs. Bixby tried but found it utterly beyond reason to respond personally to every message. And for the first time ever, every message was not shown to Miss Buck. The sheer numbers were overwhelming. Being overwhelmed was not keeping her calm and serene, and it became our practice to select however many pieces of correspondence we thought her frame of mind and spirit would want to cope with. The doctors approved of our selective methods. We were not hiding anything from her, as we were later accused of doing by misinformed persons, but we *were* protecting her.

There is no easy way to describe how Miss Buck accepted the diagnosis and that first hospitalization in Rutland, which lasted three weeks. That is, it is not possible to use catch-all words like "fine or resigned" to give a quick analysis of how she did or did not accept what was happening. She was facing an unknown she had never before encountered, and she was too perceptive to totally ignore the spectre of death somewhere out there too. Her own mortality was at stake, and I know her brain was turning this over and over.

I have already related that she seemed both fatigued and agitated - the conditions that were evident when she returned from her birthday celebration the end of June. These conditions continued in the hospital, sometimes simultaneously and they cycled in erratic patterns. Creating a stable atmosphere for any length of time was a constant struggle, for the doctors and for Ted and me. The doctors monitored her closely, sometimes prescribing medication supposedly to keep her calm, but which all too often affected her in unexpected ways and actually caused greater fatigue and increased agitation. "Her mind fights the medication," one of the nurses observed. Being fatigued to the point of exhaustion yet agitated to the point of flying apart, so to speak, and mind over medication - this all seems contradictory and ambiguous, if not erroneous. In my own unmedical way, however, this is the way I observed it and the way we lived through it.

The fatigue and the agitation, entwined as they were, seriously hampered Miss Buck's ability to calmly accept the fact that she was living, and might be living for some time to come, with an aneurysm. There were so many variables involved. I cannot say that either the fatigue *or* the agitation was caused by the aneurysm. I do not know. I only know that both were present in varying degrees and did much to sap the physical strength and the mental fortitude of the patient.

With the doctors' blessing (and they came to rely more and more on our presence as "medicine" to keep the patient calm) either Ted or I was in constant attendance all day. Sometimes we were together but more often we were with her one at a time. At first Ted assumed the greater share of the burden sitting with Miss Buck, talking quietly of things she wanted to talk about, or sitting quietly nearby when she did not feel like talking. I came to appreciate just how dependent she was on Ted for companionship and emotional comfort. It was lovely to see the delight she received from his daily gifts - flowers, a bottle of cologne, a small piece of jewelry - and lovely too to observe her unmistakable pleasure his presence gave her. She always had a smile, no matter how small, for him.

Only one gift, prescribed by the doctors, actually displeased her and threatened a stubborn rebelliousness. I was there with her when Ted gingerly presented her with a pair of thick-soled substantial-looking white nurses shoes. "Ugly boats" she called them. "I won't wear them." "Yes you will," Ted insisted gently. He held up a pair of her spike heel pointed pumps and told her the doctors wouldn't allow her to wear them, at least not for a while. She noted disdainfully that the nurses wore the ugly rubber boats so "they can sneak up on patients." I saw the hint of that wicked humor in her eyes as she looked to me for assistance. She got none this time. "They *are* ugly," I agreed, "but better on slippery floors than your high fashion shoes. Besides, now you can sneak up on the nurses." She finally relented, but only after Ted exchanged the tie variety for a slip-on style and we had trimmed the sides to make them more low-cut and comfortable. "Ugly" she always mumbled as she steered her big white boats around the room or down the hall. The nurses smiled understandingly and she usually smiled back.

The extraordinary rapport shared by Miss Buck and Ted was not only obvious to me; every staff member who saw them together mentioned it time and time again. In a very real sense, there is no doubt that Ted provided the best medicine available. He was steadfast and gallant in carrying out his duties; but being on call night and day, trying to keep a complicated business running smoothly, and trying not to worry about the future was a super-human burden. After the first few days, we knew that he could not do it all, and we carefully rearranged the twenty-four-hour regimen to provide relief for Ted while assuring Miss Buck's maximum comfort and safety. I purposely use the word "safety" here - a strong word which would seem to have no place in caring for a patient in a large modern hospital. A highly trained medical staff was on duty twenty-four hours a day, as were security personnel trained to deal with any problem that might endanger any patient, including Pearl Buck. What then, did safety have to do with our care of Miss Buck? It involved the fact that she herself felt safe, calm, serene only when one of the immediate staff was with her or right near by. Some of this, we thought, was the fear of the Chinese officials responsible for the cruel letter. "You mustn't let any Orientals anywhere near me," she implored. This was an unreasonable, paranoid fear which never left her. An entry from her Treasure Book on June ninth provides some background to her thinking:

This morning, after several days of rain, the mountains seem to be clearing. Yesterday I did not feel well - curious aches, pains, depression, of which I did not speak. In the morning a sad piece of news on television. An old couple, each 81 years old, the woman ill, the man no longer able to care for her, and the children, married and with their own families, unable financially to put them in a rest home, unwilling to take care of them, and the old man said, "I guess Mom and I have lived too long." He went into the bedroom, shot his old wife and then himself.... There *are* such things in this country! I am fortunate. I want to leave TFH and Jimmy safe for their old age. But can any old person be *safe?* I will try."

Because her fears were so real to her, one of us had to be with her night and day, in spite of the medical and security staff which were also available as well. In the interest of that calm and serene atmosphere we were charged with maintaining - or trying valiantly to maintain - we carefully rearranged our night and day routine. Keeping Miss Buck at ease was delicate and tricky. Ted and I were literally on duty all day and therefore could not be on duty all night as well. Wendy and Jimmy floated back and forth between Danby and hospital, coping with paperwork, personnel and problems too numerous to mention. Their days were full and long and they could not be expected to pull night duty. Mr. Choi was not available (and I don't think Miss Buck would have tolerated him anyway) because he had recently drifted out of the scene entirely, after an upsetting episode some weeks before in Danby when he had confronted Miss Buck and demanded that she give him $10,000 so that he could bring his family to the United States from Korea. His officious request was graciously refused by Miss Buck, who explained that she did not have that kind of money to give anyone. Mr. Choi accepted her refusal ungraciously and left shortly thereafter, a disgruntled ex-employee.

First one and then another of the few persons available to be with Miss Buck at night were either unavailable or unacceptable. Relating our dilemma wearily late one night when I arrived at the farm, Bill Drake quietly volunteered that, if Miss Buck would have him, he would sit with her at the hospital at night - in her room, outside her room - whatever had to be done to insure her comfort. It was a surprise move that was instantly acceptable to Miss Buck. Bill pulled night duty for as long as Miss Buck was in Rutland Hospital, sleeping during the day when I was at the hospital, and spending his nights like Ted and I spent our days - talking with Miss Buck when she wanted to talk, sitting quietly nearby when she wanted to be quiet. Her sleep was erratic and she told me they spent many hours talking of the problems of war, conflicts between nations and families, economic disasters, historical lessons which we never learned, and so on. Bill was a voracious reader, as she was, and he fell into a habit of bringing her books, many of which she read and they talked about together. It was an unusual and moving interlude that Bill Drake and Pearl Buck shared during the long quiet night hours, and it cemented an unusual and moving bond between them, different from the bond that existed between Miss Buck and me or Miss Buck and Ted, but a very real bond nonetheless.

The nights, like our days, were not always easy and filled with pleasant talk of books and world affairs. There were periods of agitation and aggressive insistence on Miss Buck's part that she could move about the room on her own and wanted no one to help her with anything. On more than one occasion she slipped and fell, and Bill found himself picking her up off the floor - no apparent damage done, but a frightening experience. He didn't talk much about it, but I think his night duty gave him a deep insight into my day duty. We came and went on our shifts, hardly seeing one another for days at a time.

Ted's burden remained enormous, but steadily, little by little, we discovered that Miss Buck accepted my presence more and more in Ted's absence, relieving him to work in our borrowed office downstairs and occasionally slipping off to Danby to cope with pressing matters there. We worked as a team, taking over where the other left off - drifting in and out of Miss Buck's room with intuitive understanding as to what had transpired, how the patient was feeling at that particular moment, and the mood that was required of us to adapt to her mood.

It was a highly unusual partnership between Ted Harris and me - two of us working in unison, disciplining our own personalities for the benefit of a third.

Ours was a relationship based on the same kind of trust and confidence that I had always observed between Ted and Miss Buck. It was also unusual in that Miss Buck so readily accepted me, another woman working in close harmony with Ted. I knew, for she had discussed it many times, that she could be jealous, even vindictive, concerning Ted's most casual encounters with other women. He had no social life of his own, for she took up all his time - business *and* social. I was a business associate, even though hand-picked by her. Just how Miss Buck categorized me I cannot say for sure, except to state that she accepted me and trusted me totally, and there was never the slightest bit of jealousy or uneasy doubt on her part concerning my extraordinarily close working partnership with Ted. It was as if she had dubbed us in tandem to do her bidding.

I myself find it difficult to categorize my relationship with Ted, so closely were we allied. But we were allied for her, not each other. There was an altruistic nature about our togetherness which transcended any man-woman friendship or association. Working for Miss Buck as we did was working in another dimension. For want of a better analogy, we were electrified directly to her, and the strong currents which flowed between Ted and me were directed right back to her and used by her.

If what existed between Ted and Miss Buck was unique, it is fair to say that what existed between Ted and me was also unique. We shared the tears, frustration, exhaustion, and even the occasional laughter of an extraordinary set of circumstances. The burden we shared deeply affected me as a person, as a human being searching for answers, the why of existence. Little wonder that I had great difficulty explaining to even my own family the intricacies of each day.

A little levity now and then - even bittersweet levity - was a blessing, and I am reminded of my forty-first birthday, spent in the hospital. July seventh was a day that saw Miss Buck starting out early in the morning in a high state of anxiety. The early morning nursing and cleaning chores had been dispensed with, the doctors had not yet made their rounds, and when I arrived on the scene, she greeted me briskly with "We're going home, Mrs. Drake; I shall not spend another hour in this abominable place." She then attempted to get shakily out of bed, changed her mind, and directed me instead to start packing - everything and just as she demanded. I knew that arguing with her would be futile and would agitate her more, so I proceeded to play along, meticulously packing and arranging things, once dropping the suitcase on purpose so I had to repack everything slowly, deliberately. Several times she attempted to get up, fussing and fuming all the while, and I finally settled her in a chair by the window, where she continued to direct the folding of lingerie and the exact placement of cosmetics and other articles. I knew that it couldn't be too long before someone - nurse, doctor, Ted, someone - would be along to check routinely, so I continued to talk lightly about going home, going back to Danby, what might be going on when we arrived, how Ted would probably have masses of fresh flowers waiting for her.... On and on I went, packing and talking, all the while keeping one troubled eye on her as she slowly, slowly wound down from the high state of agitation and slumped into a child-like bundle of dejection and fatigue. Finally, after what seemed like hours but was probably a matter of minutes, a nurse and doctor both appeared, to be followed by Ted. I knew the room looked like a disaster area and I babbled inanely "we've been getting ready to go home." After order had been restored and Miss Buck was safely back in bed with all thoughts of going home totally forgotten, and I had been assured by nurse and doctor that I had ad libbed beautifully through a potentially dangerous situation, the humor - bittersweet though it may have been - of this little episode made us all laugh till we cried.

There was a birthday cake waiting for me when I got home that night very late and very tired, and I had with me a bottle of sherry that Ted had presented to me with a promise that forever and ever on each birthday Mrs. Bixby-Mrs. Drake would be presented with a special birthday bottle. We both knew it was a pledge which would never be kept, but it was a nice gesture. I had cake and sherry sitting at the kitchen table with Tom and Jim and, in the soft dark of that summer evening, they proudly escorted me into the sitting room-bedroom-bathroom suite which they had helped their father finish as a long-awaited surprise for me. This project had been started some years before, never finished, and had been a continuing source of frustration and disappointment.

It was a very strange birthday, with both laughter and tears and I was grateful to my family for walking the extra mile with me. I knew I had Miss Buck's strong influence to thank for drawing Bill to her; and in so doing there was a blessed, if only temporary, hiatus in the personal problems between Bill and me. It was *her* command presence at work, even from a hospital bed. The relief that I was allowed at this time helped me in no small way to deal with the members of Miss Buck's own large family, now entering the scene.

Chapter 29

"No Visitors"

Prior to July 1, 1972, when Miss Buck was hospitalized at the Rutland Hospital, I had not met any of her adopted children. (I quote directly from my original notes). I had talked two or three times over the telephone with Jean when she called asking for her mother. She had called the office number and I had answered, calling Miss Buck on her private line at Danby House and telling her that Jean was on the other line waiting for her. On July 1st, when Miss Buck was hospitalized, Mr. Harris called Jean, Janice and Henriette to inform them of their mother's illness. They all asked "was it serious" and "should we come to Rutland." We tried many times to reach Mrs. Yaukey, who was near Ithaca at a Quaker meeting. She finally called us several days later, upset, and offering to come if necessary, or she would keep in close touch with us and Jean. Henriette came one time to the hospital to see her mother when she was sound asleep, and left without seeing her, saying that she would return again soon. She came back several days later, saw her mother briefly and left. Jean and Joe (her husband) arrived for a day or two some time during the first two weeks, arriving early in the morning when Bill was at the hospital with Miss Buck. Janice and Joan (friend) arrived briefly, stayed overnight, were entertained at dinner at Danby House by

Mr. Harris and Jimmy, and said they could not stay because they were on vacation and just happened to be in New England. Theresa (not a daughter but a ward of Miss Buck's) arrived at the hospital with her boyfriend. My notes summarized that Theresa spent some time with Miss Buck.

Outline comments like these fleshed out from time to time my impersonal running log of phone calls and visits with which we kept Miss Buck informed. The doctors advised that I should handle all incoming calls for Miss Buck until or unless she could resume doing so herself. The phone in her hospital room was restricted to minimal personal use. It was at my discretion or Ted's, fully backed up by the doctors, that Miss Buck received or made phone calls or was allowed visitors.

A "No Visitors" sign was posted on her door and the first violator, who startled and upset Miss Buck to the point of fearing for her very life, was a mild-mannered, self-described "do-gooder, a man of God." He was, in fact, an area preacher who took it upon himself, he said, to regularly visit patients at random and dispense Bible-inspired comfort. His efforts, he whined, were usually well received.

Not here, I snapped. Your discourteous random do-goodery is unwelcome here. Don't return. He didn't, though Miss Buck warned each and every nurse to beware of "Bible-toting evangelists."

My frequent phone contact with daughter Jean and Sister Grace during this trial period of stabilizing a touch-and-go illness was friendly, understanding, and helpful. It set a pattern which was to continue in the weeks and months ahead. I was more than grateful for their support, for other family members proved not so supportive and many times sabotaged, or attempted to sabotage, the kid-glove way Ted and I tried to maintain the fragile balance around her. Charged with keeping all persons, including the family, at arm's length if they threatened to upset this tenuous balance, I frequently found myself a hostile target.

Jean and Grace together assumed the roles of family peace-keepers. They were caring, gentle women, but they were outnumbered, or at least over-ruled when dissension occurred. Where there might have been unifying family attitudes of let's all pull together, let's all forgive past misunderstandings, let's swallow our misplaced pride that Mr. Harris and Mrs. Drake are performing protective duties that perhaps should have been ours in this crisis, etc...instead there was a snide sniping away at everything we were trying to do, a lack of understanding of the strengths, and now the weaknesses of Pearl Buck, adoptive mother to not only her own nine orphans, but adoptive mother to the thousands of orphans whose American eyes and freckled cheeks she could not ignore in the slums of Asia. How dare you shake your fist at Mr. Harris whom your mother chose, when all others refused, to bend the rules until her relentless cries for help succeeded. It was your mother who silently watched day after day at a U.S. military camp in Korea - watched the long lines of women and children standing patiently by the G.I. garbage cans outside the mess halls. She watched with growing dismay the women and children waiting to steal the leftovers that were carelessly tossed out after each meal. If we could afford to throw away food, your mother reasoned, we could afford to give away at least a portion of it. Do I need to say more? It was your mother, with Mr. Harris at her side doing much of the rule bending and arm twisting, who saw to it that G.I. eggs, bacon, milk and bread were freely shared with the starving scavengers at the garbage cans.

How dare you shake your fist now at this same Mr. Harris, or me, both of us here now because *she* wants us here. And we are not acting on our own against anybody's wishes. We are following doctors' orders - orders from respected men and women who devote their lives to helping others in times of pain and suffering. Can't you see that we are here for one purpose and one purpose only - to help your mother? We didn't ask to be here. We don't call her mother. We call her Miss Buck. Yes, we think she's special, just as millions of her readers and admirers do. How dare you insinuate that Mr. Harris and I are getting handsomely paid for performing, or that we are forcing her to pay us against her wishes. Listen, and listen well, for I want you to know that what we're getting from your mother are cries for help. Are we paid off for what we can give in return? Not on *your* terms and probably not in terms you can understand. She gives us token pennies of this world and glimpses of supremely natural things of another world. We're very rich, but not rich in ways you think *we* covet. You don't understand? Maybe that's why we are here, and you are not. We don't understand everything about your mother, but we understand what she needs of us. You've made her angry sometimes in the past. You'll make her angry now if you don't let us help her. You're making me angry for her and I haven't time to waste in anger. I pity you, and I haven't time to waste in pity. If you really don't know how to help, and if you really care about your mother, start by reading one of her books - any one. She's there, talking to you. If you won't listen to me, try listening to her. And oh yes, read the book she sent you which Mr. Harris wrote about her, but please don't refer to him ever as "what's his name" - it hurts her and it offends her. She may not tell you, but it makes her very angry. Don't make her use her strength in anger - or pity. Please help her....

This passionate tirade ran through my mind at the hospital, whose origins go back to Edgar's first phone call to the hospital. At first I tried to dismiss my uneasy feelings about Edgar. Something in his attitude, his approach to his mother's illness didn't seem right and I tried to justify it by saying that it was natural that he was miffed, upset, hurt, even angry that he, the son, could not talk to her, the mother. I could understand that he did not want to deal with me, the secretary. I could also understand that his unsympathetic manner had much to do with the fact that I, although a relative newcomer, was part of "those people" who had surrounded his mother and isolated her from her family. Miss Buck had warned me from the start that Edgar especially held to these totally false views. I could expect a certain amount of coolness when I became the instrument that made direct contact between son and mother impossible. But impossible is not the right word - although from Edgar's point of view I was making it impossible. Following doctors' orders, direct contact at times between patient and *any* person was not advisable and not acceptable, based on sound medical reasons. On the other hand, direct contact with family, friends, and associates became not only possible, but beneficial when the patient's condition warranted it - again doctors' orders and their trust in my judgement and Ted's.

Edgar called quite often and usually had to talk to me, which he did not like at all. When I told Miss Buck he had called several times and was waiting anxiously to talk directly to her, she pierced me with her blue eyes, "I do not want to talk to him just yet; I do not want to be upset by anything he says. You have my permission to tell him, though I doubt he will understand - tell him I appreciate his concern and I will call him when I am ready and not a minute before." Even as she said this, I could sense the agitation rising within her and I knew that I would bear the brunt of Edgar's dissatisfaction and his discourteous attacks.

After that first phone call from Edgar, when I did my very best to make him understand what his mother needed (she needs your love and understanding, I pleaded) and I heard rebuffs and cloaked threats, I thought thoughts I didn't want to think and hope I would never have to speak. I don't like your attitude, Edgar Walsh - your attitude is not the one of a loving son, not even a concerned son. Where have you been all these years when your mother - and yes, Mr. Harris, could have used your support and assistance. I have worked for your mother many months now. Not once have I ever taken a phone call from you to her. Not once have I seen a letter addressed to her from you. This is not the attitude of a son who cares. Why are you insisting that you talk to her now, why do you want to know the name of every medication being prescribed, and why, how could you bluntly ask me on your very first phone call "Is she dying?" Maybe that's your blunt way, Mr. Walsh and maybe you mean well, but I'm thinking that I don't like you. I don't like you at all.

My most passionate inner thoughts, some in the form of a prayer to something, some invisible, supremely natural something, were fervent pleas for help and strength. Actual words like these were never spoken by me to Edgar or to any member of the family at any time. It was not my place to chastise or criticize. I tried only to enlist their understanding and help. We needed them, all of them, as friends, not enemies.

My silent tirades let off inner steam when the going got especially rough and I found a fist near my face. Inwardly, briefly, I got fighting mad. These thoughts took far less time to think than to type, but were no less meaningful or pertinent.

In reality, a precocious little stranger put into perspective my doubts and fears regarding the bad vibes I had received from meeting Edgar by phone. It was one of those chance encounters which Miss Buck so relished and so often wove into her stories.

My encounter with the little stranger after that first strange phone call with Edgar went like this:

At the doctors' suggestion, arrangements had been made for me to be paged over the hospital intercom so that no matter where I was I could answer in-coming calls for Miss Buck. A surprising number came in for her, not just from family but from fans, those paper people of hers who poured out love and concern and wanted direct contact with her. All of these calls were referred to me to handle. I remember I had just picked up the over-flowing box of letters and cards which Ted and I had not yet looked at that day. Ted was upstairs with Miss Buck and I sat down in the main lobby next to a bright-eyed little boy of about five or six who immediately started chattering to me.

Hi, my name is Eric. My Grandmother is here in the hospital. She's very sick. She may die. I'm here a lot. I see you here a lot with a man with red hair. Is your grandmother sick? What's her name? Does she tell you stories? I call my grandmother Mary and she tells me stories when she's not sick.

I hadn't said a word yet when I heard "Mrs. Drake, pick up on Line 2..." The loud, measured announcement broke into the background recorded music which floated through the corridors. I sighed, put aside the box of letters and walked to the front desk. It was, I remember, a long conversation, with Edgar not accepting my careful explanation of why he couldn't talk directly to his mother. I didn't ask for her secretary; I didn't want to talk to her secretary; I want to talk to my mother; what's the name of the medicine she's getting; who's giving it to her; and, that incredible question "Is she dying?" We fervently hope not, I remember saying in stunned disbelief.

When I put the phone down the unspoken tirade went round and round in my head. I had forgotten all about the chatty little boy Eric till I felt a tug at my elbow. "Guess you're Mrs. Drake," he said. "Who's Edgar?" He grinned disarmingly. "I was listening. Are you mad at me?"

I laughed and it was a good laugh, wiping away angry, unpleasant thoughts. The laugh put me back in focus. Out of the mouths of babes. I smiled at Eric and ruffled his hair. Then I answered in one run-on sentence all the questions he had thrown at me.

Well, Eric-with-the-grandmother named Mary, no, I'm not mad at you and Edgar is the son of the lady I work for and the name of the lady I work for is Miss Pearl Buck and she tells lots of stories, in fact she writes books so people all over the world can read her stories.

Miss Buck was fond of saying that "the strong take care of the weak, but who is to take care of the strong." And there is a beautiful quote which says that "It is the weak who are cruel. Gentleness can only be expected from the strong." Laughter has its place between the two. It can be a bridge between gentleness and cruelty.

Chapter 30

Dolphus Crow III

I brought none of the dissension to Miss Buck. Her welfare was my primary consideration at all times, and I redoubled my efforts to keep the smallest worry of my own from permeating her atmosphere. Ted did the same, but she was more perceptive than ever to our slightest sign of fatigue or worry. If she detected either, she would pounce with "What's wrong? what's happened" or the question we were to dread, "Do you know something you're not telling me?" We reassured her that "all's well" and the only thing we wanted her to worry about was getting better. She herself provided us with the very best example to do what we had to do, for we continually marveled at her determination to overcome her bouts of exhaustion and discomfort. She fought even the medication, as she would fight through battles to win a war. And as her beautiful outward manifestation of the fight she personally was waging, she kept herself - her own person - made-up and decorated in her usual bright way, hair brushed and piled high, and a stylish brooch or set of earrings in place, even if she were forced to wear a shapeless styleless hospital gown. She never allowed visitors (the nurses and I were the exceptions) including, or perhaps it's more accurate to say especially, Mr. Harris, before she was what she called "presentable." She was not always satisfied with her efforts but everybody else was always astounded. She put on a front for visitors as an actress would slip into a character role.

The doctors smiled at her spirit, her grit, but because of it, they had great difficulty reading whether or not she was in discomfort and if so, how much. They suspected that she had what they called a very high threshold of pain. Ted and I learned to read her eyes, or rather what we suspected was behind her eyes, and we tried to act accordingly.

If I had discussed my worries about any of her children at this time, she no doubt would have told me to do exactly as I did. I was courteous and honest at all times, and I worked very hard to win their sympathy.

Perhaps, if I had asked Miss Buck now about her children, she would have said what she said in response to a letter from one of her readers who wrote to her in anguish about her own children.

Dear Miss Buck:

Thank you for your article.... Sometimes I feel as if I'm living in a pack of wolves - my biggest problem is in raising my three children. While they were very young and their minds open and gullible I taught them to be kind and open. Now I find them being taken advantage of - I taught them to say what they mean and they're baffled to find their supposedly best friends lying to them. I know how they feel and how you feel too - because I move among the throngs but live a solitary life. I wonder, has it always been this way? Can people change? Do I try and toughen my children up? But how do you teach them things you don't believe in? I've taught them to curse prejudice and praise fairness but life becomes a constant battle and life is short and I sometimes I wonder if it's all worth it. Thanks for reading...."

And Miss Buck's response:

Thank you very much for your thoughtful letter. I wish
I knew how to advise you about your children. I can only
say what I have said to myself as I reared my own, that
I taught them to believe in that which I believe. It was
the best I could do and if life changed their beliefs, theirs
is the responsibility....

Miss Buck saw very few people during her three weeks in
the Rutland Hospital. Daughter Jean, sometimes with just
her husband Joe and sometimes with one or more or her
children, came several times. Their visits were always good
experiences for Miss Buck. I came to rely heavily on Jean for
her quiet loving manner with her mother and her consisten-
cy in supporting Ted and me in our roles. No wonder Miss
Buck spoke of Jean as "unique among my children."

The wife of Richard Walsh, Jr. (son of Miss Buck's second
husband) was the first visitor to the hospital, other than the
staff. She arrived even before Jean did, and although Miss
Buck initially seemed agitated at having to "put on a front"
for her, she decided that maybe she would enjoy a brief visit
after all and so we tried it. My notes at this time say that I
talked at length to Mrs. Walsh before we went upstairs to
see Miss Buck and she proved to be quiet, gracious and understanding. She only stayed a short time, brought a lovely
Chinese-style robe as a gift, and I was either in the room
during her visit or right outside discreetly - doctors' orders.

Another visitor, other than the few family members, came
from Philadelphia and arrived during a time when Miss
Buck had been quite heavily sedated after a bad anxiety at-

tack. The visitor was Frank Davis, a Foundation employee. At times when Miss Buck was most talkative and seemed most physically strong, she felt compelled to talk about Foundation affairs. When Frank Davis had called and offered to visit in person to talk about current activities, she appeared pleased and declared that Davis, a former Arthur Murray dance instructor and friend of Ted Harris, was "a good and dedicated worker." Among other things, they were to discuss what was being done to help Elizabeth Taylor and Richard Burton adopt a baby from one of the Asian countries. They had asked Miss Buck to intervene for them. "I cannot help them personally," she said to me, "but I trust that Davis will see to the problem." Davis and a friend visited and carried on a rather lengthy discussion, but Miss Buck later said she could not remember ever having seen them or talked with them. She said she could remember nothing at all and in confusion and dismay to me she announced, "Davis cannot have been here; I do not remember talking with him." That total lapse of memory deeply bothered her. Her medication, she said, was no excuse. "Are you sure Davis was here?" she asked me repeatedly. I'm sure, I always replied gently. We did our best to minimize the worrisome lapse of memory, but Miss Buck never forgot it and suggested defensively that maybe we had all been mistaken about Davis being with her. Maybe we were wrong. She, who had always prided herself on the fact that she never forgot anything, that she had total recall, grappled uneasily with even a temporary drug-induced memory loss. Many months later she would come back to that glaring incident and ask me two direct questions. "Was Davis really with me that day?" and "Did the Burtons ever get their baby?" I never had an answer for the second question, but was delighted when Miss Buck went on to describe her first meeting with the glamorous Elizabeth.

Miss Buck and the young actress had been in contact years before about a film version of Miss Buck's epic novel IMPERIAL WOMAN. "When I walked into the hotel lobby," she described the scene to me, "where I was told Elizabeth Taylor would be waiting for me, I saw no one but a slight young woman dressed in a simple cotton dress and sandals and no make-up. She was a lovely natural creature with the most extraordinary eyes...."

I find an undated draft of a letter which I believe Ted and I discussed with Miss Buck while she was in the Rutland Hospital. The proposed letter was in keeping with our optimistic attitude about the future; that is, Miss Buck was going to regain her strength, resume most of her activities, and plan new projects. The letter is addressed to Elizabeth Taylor at her last known address, which at that time was Budapest, Hungary:

Dear Mrs. Burton:

Congratulations on the recent article in "Life" magazine commemorating your birthday, in which I read that you intend to make a picture based on the life of the last Empress Dowager of China, from a novel by Pearl S. Buck. Miss Buck and I were both delighted to hear of this.

After careful consideration, I wonder if it might not be advantageous to all concerned to have Pearl S. Buck cooperate in some way in the making of this very important film. Her production company, Stratton Productions, with whom you and Mr. Todd had dealings some time ago, is no longer in existence. However, in an advisory capacity of opening doors and obtaining cooperation, it is undeniable that Miss Buck's services are invaluable. To say that the name Pearl S. Buck is synonymous with China and the Chinese people and that the Burton name is synonymous with excellence in films should put together a package altogether unbeatable.

May we have the benefit of your thoughts on this?

A devoted admirer,

Theodore F. Harris,
Business Manager and Biographer
of Pearl S. Buck

Miss Buck thought Elizabeth Taylor would be ideal now to portray the Dowager Empress of IMPERIAL WOMAN, but at the time of their first meeting she confessed to thinking that the actress was not mature enough to attempt the demanding role. The appeal now of Pearl Buck collaborating with Elizabeth Taylor was very strong, and although nothing ever came of it, we tempted our patient with the possibility as we faced the future with positive thoughts.

When it was certain that Miss Buck was going to be allowed to go home to Danby towards the end of July, we were confronted with a whole new set of problems, not the least of which was finding a satisfactory houseman to replace Mr. Choi. We knew that Miss Buck would be reluctant to have a stranger introduced into her household, someone unfamiliar with her old routine, let alone a new routine geared to her new circumstances. The new circumstances she was struggling with were the changes she would have to make in order to go forward with her life while learning to live with her aneurysm, still there, apparently unchanged, but making every minute of every day hazardous and harrowing. How, Ted and I wondered, could we possibly find a perfect someone who could step into this situation and smoothly assume the role of butler-chef-valet-driver. He would, of course, have to be totally acceptable to Miss Buck with impeccable personal habits. He would, of course, be satisfied with a pittance in salary, for there wasn't enough to go around now. Impossible, of course, but weren't we always being asked to perform the impossible? Because of the immediacy of the problem (we were given a hospital discharge date of July 20th) we by-passed the standard employment procedures of running ads in the newspapers or registering with employment agencies. Instead, we tried the most outrageous long-shot and it worked. Ted and I wrote a perfect character into the script and Miss Buck delightedly concurred.

Our perfect character was born one day as Ted and I sat sorting through a stack of correspondence.

"Here he is," Ted exclaimed, handing me a hand-written note. "What do you think?"

What I read was a simple, straight-forward letter from a young man recently returned from Vietnam, where he had been appalled at the misery and suffering he had seen, particularly among the children, so many of them abandoned and forgotten. He wrote that he was aware that Miss Buck was trying to help and he admired the work she was doing. He had not made any definite plans for himself yet. He had returned temporarily to his family home in the Deep South and was there anything - anything at all - that he could do to help Miss Buck. The young man signed his name Dolphus Crow III.

Long-shots can rarely be explained rationally or reasonably - that's why, I guess, they're called long-shots. How Dolphus Crow III came to be hired as Pearl Buck's houseman happened on a roll of the dice - one letter pulled from thousands. A shot in the dark that worked. It was only after Ted had made the phone call to Dolphus with arrangements for his flight to Rutland so Miss Buck could make the final decision that I said musingly. "With a name like Dolphus Crow III, do you suppose he could be a big black young man?" This was not meant to be derogatory or prejudicial, but I could not help wondering what would happen if a big black Southern DC 3 (as he was inevitably nicknamed) winged into Yankee territory. Would it cause more problems than it solved?

"No," Ted answered, "Dolphus won't be black." I don't know how he knew, but he was absolutely right. And Dolphus was dubbed the perfect person for the part by Miss Buck who saw much beyond the soft southern accent and shy manner of the young man just back from Vietnam. He was immediately outfitted with black trousers and tie and white shirt that Miss Buck preferred, improvised amiably through his unusual new duties, and when it was discovered that he was an accomplished hairdresser, he became indispensable and irreplaceable.

As we prepared to return to Danby, Miss Buck's strength seemed to be returning and her moods stabilized somewhat. With this returned a measure of her old velvet sledgehammer techniques. It was a good sign, we knew, but gave us more impossible tasks.

Proud of her new houseman, who would also be her chauffeur when she went for occasional rides in the country (as she was quick to point out that the doctors had prescribed these), she started needling Ted in the way we know so well. "Mr. Harris," she began, I caught Ted's fleeting look of resignation. And I was present during the first of many discussions about how the Volvo Ted usually used was very nice but quite small and not as comfortable as the old Chrysler which was in need of major repairs and wouldn't it be nice if he could get a fine big automobile so Dolphus could drive them around the lovely mountain roads. Danby House is beautiful and I am very comfortable there, but I cannot stay there all day every day and nice leisurely rides in the country would be relaxing and just what the doctors ordered - and on, and on, and on....

So it was that Mr. Harris waved his magic wand, danced a fast two-step while he juggled the hard-pressed corporate finances, and put a down payment on a Rolls Royce with what I know, but what was never ever discussed with Miss Buck or me - was a rather large hot check. Somehow, some way Ted would succeed in juggling the books some more to make the check good. In the meantime, while explanations and promises flowed back and forth to the disbelieving Rolls Royce people who didn't know about velvet sledgehammers, Lady Peasbee got her wish for a lovely big fancy automobile with Dolphus at the wheel and a stoically resigned Mr. Harris beside her. Privately I couldn't imagine how long they could keep it, or even if they could keep it, and I silently promised to visit them in jail if the Rolls Royce people came after them. Publicly, we issued this press release:

Pearl S. Buck's company, Creativity, Incorporated, specializing in all forms of creative endeavors, such as antiques, and the restoration of a group of old buildings in Danby, Vermont, today expanded into yet another phase of their corporate structure with the purchase of a vintage Rolls-Royce, a Silver Wraith touring limousine, built in 1956. The Rolls Royce was purchased as an eightieth birthday gift from a friend who prefers to remain anonymous. It was delivered to her home today in Danby, Vermont, where she is recuperating from a recent bout with pleurisy.

Lady Peasbee, true to form, had done it again.

Chapter 31

Out of the Hospital

It was a colorful and happy exit from the hospital. Miss Buck for once agreed to obey hospital rules without much fuss and traveled from room to waiting car in a wheelchair. Dressed in a bright Chinese robe festooned with jewelry and surrounded by an entourage of doctors, nurses and baggage bearers, she was at her imperious best, joking about the ugly white boats she was trying unsuccessfully to hide under the hem of her robe, and threatening good-naturedly to write a behind-the-scenes story of life in a hospital. As she stepped resolutely from the wheelchair, it was easy to imagine a royal personage exiting her be-jeweled coach.

"Definitely one of a kind - we'll never have another like her," one nurse ventured to say.

Whatever her faults, however demanding and impatient her ways could be, she had won the unabashed admiration of those in attendance. More than one hospital staff member that day marveled at her spirit, her ability to laugh, and her determination to outwit the devilish time bomb within her. Not one of us could foresee or foretell the future, and hopes were high.

While the ticking unpredictability of the aneurysm made one location as physically hazardous as another, there was an air of safety and assurance at the hospital which disappeared when we returned to Danby. Doctors, nurses, medicines and monitoring machines were no longer heartbeats away. Although the iron-willed lady in her pink and white living quarters had a phone at her finger tips, a car at her doorstep and medical personnel who made house calls, those in her immediate household were now responsible for keeping the calm and coping with any emergency which could arise night or day. The doctors had warned Ted and me that it was the kind of nerve-wracking responsibility that many family members of patients could not or would not accept.

Miss Buck insisted that when she went home to Danby, "Mr. Harris will see to everything...." She issued orders that her routine was to be as normal as possible; she would resume as many of her activities as her strength allowed, and she did not want to be hovered over or made to feel she was an invalid. Ted and Jimmy would retain their third floor quarters, Dolphus would be on duty each day as houseman, and Wendy and I would travel back and forth from the office with paperwork. All would be in the patterns Miss Buck liked.

But it wasn't long before each of us, especially Miss Buck herself, realized that July first had changed everything. Routines and patterns had been broken and turned upside down. We would have to learn to compromise and forget about putting everything back the way it was.

"You'll be moving your office to Danby House - temporarily, of course," Miss Buck announced to me a couple of days after we had returned from Rutland. "Mr. Harris and I have discussed it and he will arrange everything. Are you coming right away?" The question, I knew, was actually a command and once again I picked up typewriter, files and office supplies. I prepared to spend my days at Danby House - her private world, and now a very precarious world. The intuitive protective manner with which Ted and I had inched through each day at the hospital would somehow have to be carried on now. We wasted no time in worrying about the harrowing circumstances we were dealing with and set about establishing a new daily routine, one which Miss Buck could accept as being workable and which would insure her greatest peace of mind.

I set up shop in the already crowded kitchen, where my so-called office would be out of sight but I would be easily accessible at all times and free to quietly drift in and out of Miss Buck's rooms upstairs. She knew and appreciated the delicate way Ted and I approached each problem. We never had to reassure her that everything we did, every move we made, even every phone call and letter which was dispatched, was in her best interests. She knew that, and there is no doubt that the complete trust and confidence that flowed between us accounted for our being able to function in what could easily have become an impossible situation, especially for the patient.

The kitchen was far from ideal, but we made it work and, as so often happened with us, there was a measure of humor in it. Miss Buck pointed this out the first and only time she inspected my new headquarters. "Oh," she said, pushing open the swinging door, "here you are. I had to see for myself," I could see the old mischievous sparkle in her eyes. She looked around critically. I was jammed between the parrot's cage and a small table littered with books, recipes, and kitchen clutter shared by Dolphus, Ted and Jimmy. As Miss Buck and I grinned at each other, the parrot cackled "Oh Hell," and laughed ridiculously. The three of us also laughed. Miss Buck never returned to my kitchen office, but she frequently chuckled over what she called my "kitchen companions and all those gadgets that never seem to work correctly."

Miss Buck adopted a positive air of hope and enthusiasm for the future. She insisted that the present arrangements were only temporary set-backs in her still vivid Dream for Danby and encouraged all the employees involved to push forward her plans. That she was recovering from her bout of pleurisy and needed a great deal of rest remained the official explanation used in all correspondence and to the many visitors who came to Danby that summer and were disappointed because the colorful lady herself was secluded most of the time at Danby House.

I too was secluded most of the time at Danby House, spending hours each day in the house by the side of the road, curtained off, at least downstairs, from the outdoor sights and sounds of Summer. Danby House had become a sort of floating island, on the one hand beautiful and protected and remote, on the other hand in danger of sinking without warning and disappearing into what we could only imagine. Miss Buck bravely put forth her air of hope even when fatigue and the dread agitation interrupted her day, and she chastised me if I showed too much alarm over her welfare. Like the lovely sunny afternoon I went upstairs to see if she had completed autographing the stack of special limited edition Book Club volumes she had been working on a few at a time. The books, with her felt tip pen and glasses on top, were piled neatly beside her chaise lounge, along with an empty tea cup. The radio by her bed played softly, but her rooms were otherwise quiet and Miss Buck was nowhere in sight. I called her name. No answer. Swiftly I walked the few paces from bedroom to bath, but the doors were open and the rooms empty. I found her then, perfectly all right, and enjoying the sun on the little balcony outside her bedroom, but not before I had had a chance to wipe away my frown of worry. She saw it and rebuked me with "If you and Mr. Harris *must* worry about me, do so in private." The rebuke was mild, however, and tinged with her own worry and sadness. We talked then, or mostly she talked, about the wonderful majestic mountains in the distance which always reminded her of China. And then, "I wonder if we shall ever be able to bring Danby to its full beauty. Things seem to move so slowly these days..."

I spent many reflective hours with her as she voiced concern over how all this tension and added responsibility was affecting Ted. She demanded my daily assurances that he was all right. She seemed more than pleased when I told her that Mr. Harris was spending a great deal of time writing - not just business writing, but creative writing. He had started what he was calling a sort of Good Earth Southern Style, peasant images based on his own Carolina background. This writing became a part of Ted's days at Danby House, and he and Miss Buck encouraged one another. And she kept reminding us that she still had every intention of completing her own RED EARTH novel.

If Ted Harris was Miss Buck's primary interest and concern, I must not minimize her worry about what I was doing for her and how it was affecting my own family. She understood that my move to her private world meant my total commitment to see her present predicament through to the end, however long it might take. She had already elicited more than ordinary employee loyalty and devotion from me, she said, and far more than ordinary help and understanding from my husband and sons. My deeper involvement with her threatened an even deeper schism between work and home. Sensing all of this without my having to say anything, she came to my assistance as she had many times in the past. First, she saw to it that I was paid the long-promised but never delivered $350 which I had been authorized to spend for a carefully chosen travel-to-China wardrobe. Lack of payment had long been a big bone of contention on the homefront. How Ted ever managed to juggle the books for this, I don't know, but I *was* paid. I never had anything to do directly with Danby finances, but I was more than aware that funds were tight and getting tighter and Miss Buck's illness had created a tremendous strain on the cash flow. Along with the check came an unusual thank you letter, addressed to the entire Drake family, written by Ted in his own handwriting at Miss Buck's insistence, and with her blessing. It was a lovely, spontaneous message and did much, I think, to assuage the anxious and perplexed feelings of Mrs. Drake-Mrs. Bixby's family. It was addressed to Bev, Bill and the younger Drakes and is dated July 22, 1972:

I once thought it would be helpful to have a Drake in my office, hospital, home - corner! Now I know that Drakes, like all birds of a feather, flock together. They rally round the flag and come on as a team - they take over, work out the details and move forward in a way that lets all concerned do whatever they do best and do it well....

To Jim and Tom - my special thanks for giving up time with two wonderful people you are fortunate enough to have as your own private parents - and generous enough to share - and we know this put you out, too, and all we can say is that we are very grateful and you have helped us very much at a time when a very great lady needed for you to do so. May you always be happy with the thought that you may have helped the world to have a few more really great books.

Bill - Miss Buck has told me that Bev is lucky PSB is not a younger woman or Bev would have a problem with you and her 'cause she has not seen enough good men to let one go. As for me - I can only say that we've made it this far and we definitely, positively could not have done so without your help. Apart from saving a great lady - if my life is ever considered worthwhile - then add one. Perhaps Bev is also lucky I don't really have my 'vices versed.'

And Bev - it is indeed fortunate that I don't have to try to even begin to tell you what you have meant to me for this three weeks - it would have been difficult enough before, but now? What more can I say, my friends, other than the two least expressive words, thank you...and my love and gratitude and Miss Buck's....

One of Miss Buck's first prescribed rides along country roads was, at her suggestion, to the Drake farm in Wells. A representative from the Rolls Royce company was the driver that day, and with me sitting in the passenger seat and Ted and Miss Buck sitting in back, we pulled into the gravel driveway next to the porch where Bill and Tom and Jim and a barking golden retriever greeted us.

"I don't like dogs," Miss Buck announced, "for they always remind me of how the dogs ate the remains of the girl babies left to die outside the gates of the villages in China. But he's a very lovely dog," she amended, not wishing to hurt my feelings. While she surveyed my flower garden, weedy and neglected ("You spend all your time, in Danby, I realize," she mused), the boys and the dog inspected the shiny Rolls and all but ignored the people. We had cake and coffee in the new sitting room. It was a brief but pleasant visit. What I remember most was Miss Buck's slow, deliberate walk through each room downstairs, pausing and observing, pausing and observing. She said very little and we did not intrude on her perusal, except my apologies for the peeling paint and wallpaper in unfinished rooms. When she had completed her slow walk, the visit was over. She had seen what she had wanted to see. She didn't have to explain that she had needed to see this other world of mine that I shared with her world. Months later she would bring up details of that slow walk through the farmhouse, even mentioning a title of a book she had seen or the color of the peeling wallpaper. From such minutiae, I knew, came her stories and books. She seemed satisfied with her visit to my world and it helped somehow to bridge the gap between Wells and Danby. For my part, I recall I had a strange sense of detachment and aloneness as we waved good-bye to the farm and headed back to Danby House.

Chapter 32

Sparring With Death

Bill's direct duties to Miss Buck, so to speak, ended when his night shifts at the hospital ended, but he continued to show his care and concern for her with little gifts of flowers and fresh vegetables from the garden, and occasional visits to Danby to chat with her in person. On one such occasion he brought her some special tea and she sent this handwritten thank you note dated August 20th:

Dear Colonel Drake:

It is so delightful to be stocked with delicious Indian tea, and I thank you warmly. Much China tea is given me, but I like India tea. And I have been to Darjeeling and have seen the steep mountain sides planted to tea bushes and have watched the tea pickers, wondering as I watched how either people or tea bushes could cling to the steep earth.... So beautifully wrapped the tea boxes were, too. Thank you!

We greatly enjoyed our visit to your home—indeed, we greatly enjoy the Drakes.

Your friend, (signed) Pearl S. Buck.

Gestures like the thank you letters, the visit to the farm, the wardrobe check, and any number of small but significant connections Miss Buck initiated between Danby and Wells helped to make my own divided life smoother. Indeed, without her help and her continuing reassurances to my family that she greatly needed me, I would have been out on a limb swinging all alone with my problems. It was her perceptive help to me which allowed me to continue to help her.

Problems with her own family members were not quite so easy to resolve, for one thing because of the sheer numbers of people involved. Jean was our liaison between Danby House and the rest of the family, relieving us of the necessity of calling several people each day or repeating the same message to those calling us. When Jean was not in Danby herself (she and Joe and a daughter visited the farm in Wells once), we were in daily contact. When anything new developed, or the doctor had been in for a visit, Ted or I or both of us together called Jean, giving explicit information about the day's activities and events.

One of the first family visits to Danby House was from son Richard (her adopted son, not Richard Walsh, Jr., the publisher). He arrived on a Saturday, one of the few days when I was not in Danby, but I heard from Miss Buck soon enough on Monday morning how distressed she had been and how upsetting his visit was for her. I had not yet met Richard, but I knew the extent of Miss Buck's distress when she handed me the carbon copy of the letter she had had Wendy type up and send off to Richard. Her anger and hurt are obvious:

July 27, 1972

Dear Richard,

Today, after you and your family left, Mrs. Frank Sitterly, our manager for the dealers and an employee, reported in surprise and embarrassment, that you had asked her many personal questions about my business which of course, being only an employee, she did not know how to answer. She did not wish to be rude to you, as my son, but she did not consider it your business to ask such questions.

I told her she was quite right, that it was rude of you, and apologized for your not knowing better. After this, if you feel you want to know *my* business, ask me, or my attorney, Gale Raphael, or my business manager, who has done more to help me than anyone in the world and does still, and will as long as I live. He has managed my affairs and helped you children, thereby, for more than ten years. Moreover, his name is *not* "what's his name." It is Theodore Harris, a name highly respected by all who know him. He is my only authorized biographer, has sent the two-volume biography as a gift to *each* of you children, and not *one* of you, except Jean and Janice, has had the decent, ordinary good manners to thank him - or, I suppose, even to read it. *He* is a gentleman and it appears my sons are *not,* although you were all taught how to be.

At any rate, if you have questions to ask about *my* business affairs, which I have handled successfully since I was seventeen years old, ask *me* and not other people behind my back.

You will see I am *very* angry. I was glad to have you visit me with your family, but for me such visits had better not be made if I have to apologize for my children to my own employees.

Don't let this happen again!

Love, (signed) Mother

Not wishing to prolong the anger which had prompted the letter, I commented in general terms that perhaps the children would understand better as time went on - surely they had not meant to be rude. Not with anger then, but with fierce determination and pride, Miss Buck said to me, "We have no time to wait for their understanding. My affairs must be carried out exactly as I have planned them with Mr. Harris in complete charge. My children are not part of my plans for Danby." She made me reaffirm my promise that I would do everything possible to insure that the whole Danby Project remain in Mr. Harris' hands. "This is to be a home and a business for him as long as he lives." I could do nothing to quell the anger which crackled as she said slowly and distinctly, "Everything here in Danby goes to Mr. Harris when I am gone. If any one of my children dares to question my plans, I shall rely on you, my dear, to help Mr. Harris in every way possible to see that my wishes are fully carried out." She reiterated to me that her children had the best upbringing and education she could provide for them, and a Trust Fund specified in her will would provide a small yearly income for each them as long as they live. "The Trust Fund begins when I die - and I'm not ready to die yet." Her words were on fire and her blue eyes flamed with an intensity I had not yet witnessed.

I held my breath while the fearsome flames subsided. I had heard all of this before, and I knew I would hear it again, but I vowed to work harder than ever to win over the children. I still refused to give credence to the blackest of possibilities that Miss Buck's adopted children cared more about what wealth they might gain from her than they cared about her. The black thought hovered, nevertheless, and I was on guard.

I met son Richard for the first time when he arrived a second time in August along with his wife Vivian and their two children. I quietly tried to win their understanding, urging a very short visit and patiently explaining that visits with anyone tired Miss Buck greatly. They must understand, I emphasized, that she will not admit to being tired and she will not show it. They ignored my pleas when finally I motioned them to please go and leave her alone. Unbelievably, after that long morning visit, Richard and family returned again in the afternoon and at my suggestion, which obviously displeased them, they reluctantly left the children downstairs so that they might visit more quietly with their mother. Their little boy, in typical little boy fashion, was noisy and active and full of good spirits. I knew the noise and the running around downstairs could be heard upstairs, so I finally took him with me outdoors and we walked up and down the road. It was altogether a frustrating visit, and I felt I had failed at my job. All my words of caution - always carefully phrased with "please understand that what we are doing is in your mother's best interests" - fell on deaf ears. They refused to believe that the patient needed any coddling when she appeared so robust and healthy looking.

Edgar, the oldest adopted son and his wife appeared one day unannounced, the first of two late summer visits. Dolphus served them lunch with Miss Buck upstairs in her sitting room. It was, again, a long visit - too long in spite of my best explanation that brief visits were best, according to the doctors. After this long visit, and after many such family visits, I saw Miss Buck collapse in exhaustion and near despair, worn out from the effort needed to keep up the charade. It would have been much easier, of course, if she had chosen to collapse in front of these family members - then they might have finally understood what Ted and I had been trying to tell them all along. But she would never give in and insisted on the big brave front. Ted and I were left with the aftermath of long visits and lack of understanding.

If extreme fatigue forced Miss Buck to lie down or try to sleep for a while, she would watch us with worried but grateful eyes as we moved about, doing the little things which we knew would ease her - little things which were no longer little luxuries. They were as necessary, perhaps more necessary than the doctors' medicines which she fought against. When she *did* ask for a prescribed valium or sleeping pill, we knew she asked in quiet desperation. We tried, as often as possible, to rely on the little things she loved and appreciated: a bowl of fresh flowers moved so she could visually enjoy their beauty, making sure that her rose-colored quilt and cushions were arranged just so - and the subtle fragrance of her favorite perfume sprayed in the air or on a nearby lace handkerchief.

On one such occasion, as both Ted and I quietly set about restoring calmness to her world after a particularly trying family session, she swept us tiredly with her eyes and said, "Thank you for understanding; my family, I fear, does not." Later in private to Ted, I both marveled and lamented at her superb acting performance. She fooled the family with her beautiful feeling-fine-and-strong exterior. She tried to fool them and she succeeded brilliantly.

She didn't fool us, nor did she try. Her act, her performance, prompted me to comment to Ted that what we witnessed, and which no one else witnessed, was the pure essence of Pearl Buck: the will to do, the will to overcome the impossible. We witnessed her kind of raw willpower, her sheer energy that had given birth to her own Foundation, once thought by so many to be an impossible undertaking. Willpower and energy are invisible forces, but here we were witnessing them in visible form.

It is now, after years of searching for satisfactory ways to explain the strong forces which moved around and within Pearl Buck that I feel comfortable with what I observed, what I witnessed.

Did Pearl Buck sense death? Was she afraid to die? Why did she do some of the things she did, like insisting on putting up a front of strength and invincibility in front of her family?

Yes, I think Pearl Buck sensed death, though we did not talk of it outright. No, she was not afraid to die. And she had already made it clear to me that no matter what she did, her family did not understand her. At this point in her life, she was not ready to die. She had set goals for herself that were not reached. There is no doubt that she was determined to finish all unfinished work, to put all her several worlds in complete order. Then, and only then, would she be ready, in what she told me was the old Chinese way, to greet death, the next world for which she had been preparing all along. Many times she related to me, in calm once-upon-a-time fashion, with no touch of fear or anxiety, how the ancient Chinese would prepare for death, by trying on the cloth shroud they would wear when death finally came, by even lying in the coffin to see whether or not it was the proper width and length. Death was merely a journey to another world, but she just was not ready for that other-world trip.

At this point she was sparring with death, showing her strength, outwitting an invisible force with forces of her own. She had to finish THE RED EARTH, THE GENIUS BOOK, and arrange all the areas of her several earthly worlds precisely and to her exact specifications before she would consent to the next trip.

Yes, after all these reflective years, I feel comfortable describing what I saw, what I witnessed in terms of Pearl Buck assuming the greatest role of her long career. The role she was playing now was death's colorful sparring partner.

Those who would not accept her on her terms never knew the pure essence of the woman who was not afraid to die, but could not die just yet because she had too much to do.

"Thank you for understanding," she said to Ted and me, her elegant blue eyes speaking words we felt rather than heard.

Chapter 33

Pearl Buck Day in Vermont

I have used the words "floating island" to describe our cloistered days at Danby House. I am not trying to be cute or coy. Miss Buck herself used the term, and it seems to come the closest to describing how and where we were in a sort of timeless state. We were detached from the usual boundaries and limitations set in the "real world." All our time tables and schedules remained flexible and subject to change without notice. All plans for the future, while optimistic, were adapted to a wait-and-see attitude.

Summer slipped away, school started, and still Danby House remained aloof. That is not to say that we were sitting around in a state of suspended animation, langorously relaxing on our island. Oh no! But my work and Ted's revolved around how Miss Buck was feeling, what she wanted to do, and what she seemed capable of doing. The doctors came and went, urging care and caution, but encouraging as much activity as the patient could handle. The aneurysm diagnosis remained unchanged, the situation seemingly stable. Our days were geared to that one thing - maintaining a stable atmosphere, while making it possible for Miss Buck to write, to walk, to ride, to carry on with her creative endeavors, whatever they might be. She even tried to resume playing the piano, which had always been such a joy to her, but it taxed her strength too much.

Beverly Drake, Sandy Baird, and Louise McCoy watching Governor
Dean C. Davis sign "Pearl S. Buck Week in Vermont"
Photo by Lazzari.

With Jean and Grace always the exceptions, the family members picked away at our carefully guarded calm. I was deeply troubled by their tactics which upset everything. But since we could not write them out of the scenario, we learned to put up with them and work around them. We had to.

Still not knowing what the future weeks and months meant in terms of Miss Buck's full recovery, needed surgery, or more of the current touchy status quo, we avoided making definite commitments of any kind, with one exception. And even that one exception held a question mark. On September 22nd Miss Buck was to be honored at a public gathering at Castleton State College (located but a few miles from Danby) with the Governor of the State declaring Pearl Buck Day in honor of the distinguished lady who had chosen to make Vermont her permanent home. The plans for this had been underway since Spring when a delegation of ladies had approached me (among them a friend from the Pen Women group) wondering whether Miss Buck would be willing to give a speech before a prominent group of women interested in her personal viewpoints on topical issues. Knowing that Miss Buck no longer wished to lecture or even appear before large groups of people, it nevertheless occurred to me that it would be a wonderful idea if the whole State of Vermont did something to honor the author on her eightieth birthday as she attempted, in her own way, to beautify and re-activate a corner of the Green Mountain State. After getting Ted's approval to pursue this approach as a surprise for Miss Buck, I set out to turn around the initial request for Miss Buck to give a speech until the turn-around blossomed into a Pearl Buck Day with speeches to be given in her honor.

When the plans were firm, we revealed them to her, and September 22nd was an occasion she anticipated with great pleasure. We worried constantly that there might be too

Pearl S. Buck acknowledging crowd at Castleton State College, September 22, 1972 - daughter Jean Lippincott and husband Joe sitting next to Ted Harris - photo by James Pauls

Pearl S. Buck and Ted Harris leaving Castleton auditorium to
attend private reception at Sandy Baird's Rutland home
photo by James Pauls

much confusion, too much excitement, but the doctors told us to go ahead and plan right up to the last minutes and hope for the best.

Ted and I worked out the details behind the scenes, telling Miss Buck that her part in the affair would be to say a gracious "thank you" and look beautiful. She laughingly insisted that she would have to have a new and very special gown for the occasion, and Sandy Stone became a frequent visitor to Danby House, quietly and adeptly fitting and refitting a handsome silver-rose brocade gown. She noted that Miss Buck had lost weight and her dimensions had changed considerably over the past few weeks. The gown, and new jewelry to go with it, of course, became a pleasant diversion. Like the Rolls Royce, the jewels were acquired for her somehow by Ted. "He always sees to it that I have the very best," she told me proudly, showing off what looked to me like a queen's ransom in what I was told were real gems. If she was aware of the financial juggling necessary to make these baubles possible (and I suspect she was), she voiced little protest but reveled in their beauty and accepted them as an exquisite gift of love and admiration.

She took some part, too, in choosing passages from her own writing which were to be used in a reading by Vermont resident Dick Noel, the well-known radio announcer who for many years was associated with news-caster and traveler Lowell Thomas. His resonant, expressive voice gave added meaning to her words, many of which came directly from MY SEVERAL WORLDS. I can still hear him dramatically intoning, "I remember when I was born - I do remember." Another passage chosen by Miss Buck was the descriptive one about Spring Haunt on Stratton Mountain, and yet another vignette about what she called the "supremely natural."

As September 22nd approached, we traveled once to Castleton for a brief dress rehearsal - more a quick look at the auditorium and the stage. On a lovely, warm golden early autumn morning, Dolphus headed the Rolls Royce towards the college, with me beside him navigating and Miss Buck and Ted in the back seat enjoying the scenery.

After a very quick look around the campus, Miss Buck announced that she did not wish to return right away to Danby, but would enjoy a longer ride. She directed a surprise question to me. Did I know how to get to a restaurant, The Portage, along the old canal in Port Ann? She said, "that restaurant serves the best baked beans I have ever eaten, and I should like some of those beans now, today." I knew how to get to the restaurant, not too far away, but I could not vouch for the baked beans Miss Buck remembered from years past. Dolphus and Ted and I stared at each other, mulling over the request. I remember Dolphus breaking the silence with his good-natured, "Don't look at me; I'm just the driver." Then, "Well, why *not* go for baked beans," Ted shrugged finally, as if it were the most commonplace request.

Miss Buck wanted to eat the beans in the car, she announced - parked alongside the canal.

"Can you believe this?" I giggled to Dolphus as the two of us went into the restaurant to order four portions of their famous baked beans to go. And "can you believe this?" I called in to Wendy back at Danby, explaining that we'd be a little late because of an *al fresco* luncheon somewhere on the New York border. Being with Pearl Buck had conditioned us to believe almost anything, so it seemed the most natural thing in the world for the four of us to be digging into hot beans served in a cardboard carton and eaten with a plastic spoon while sitting in a vintage Rolls Royce with the doors wide open. We were honked at more than once by the huge tractor-trailers that rumbled by on Route 4, and we pulled away from curious stares when another picnicker tried to share our place. "The Birthplace of the American Navy," the picnicker said, trying to strike up a conversation and pointing to the muddy canal. We smiled and drove off, leaving the scene of what we later always referred to as the "baked bean episode."

The essence of Pearl Buck: unexpected, unconventional, in her own way still tasting life; or, in this case, tasting baked beans, which she declared "good, but not as good as I had remembered."

September 22nd went smoothly and beautifully. It seems our careful planning paid off. From her appearance at the college auditorium to a private reception later at one of Rutland's lovely homes, Miss Buck was radiant. No one, absolutely no one who did not know what we knew about her ticking time bomb - would suspect that she had the slightest thing wrong with her. Her doctors were there, sharing her secret and watching while she held court - acknowledging the accolades of local and state dignitaries. Our fears of too much confusion, too much excitement seemed unfounded, for it proved to be a lovely evening and a gratifying personal tribute to Miss Buck. Aside from admitting to some weariness, she showed more sparkle than we had seen since before the birthday celebration in Pennsylvania.

Jean and Joe were the only family members who accepted invitations to attend the Castleton evening, and they stayed on the next day to visit quietly in Danby. We were all pleased, relieved, happy that the evening had been such a success in every way.

We were not prepared, therefore, for the crisis in the early morning hours of September 24th - a crisis which caused a downhill retreat from which there would be no escaping.

September 22, 1972, Pearl Buck Day in Vermont, was Miss Buck's last official public appearance.

Chapter 34

An Emergency

Getting a phone call from Danby at two in the morning could mean only one thing - an emergency. When I heard Ted's worried "This may be it," he didn't have to spell out the probabilities and statistics of what might be happening. "We're leaving now for the Medical Center in Burlington - meet us there."

Bill volunteered to go with me. There might be something he could do to help, he said. Within minutes we were speeding along the dark roads. Burlington was better than an hour's drive, and without even thinking, I threw together an overnight bag with a change of clothes in case of what I didn't know - just in case.

Burlington is Vermont's biggest city and the Medical Center its biggest and most modern facility. Whatever was wrong, Rutland Hospital had been by-passed, and Miss Buck would be in the hands of Dr. Davis and Dr. Coffin, the two specialists who had been called in for consultation back in July.

Ted and Jimmy were in the lobby waiting for us. Jean and Joe arrived next. There was no news yet except that apparently Miss Buck was in a great deal of pain. Of course we all assumed it was the aneurysm. But some hours later, after tests and x-rays had been studied, we were told that

Miss Buck had had a gall bladder attack and that she would be scheduled for a gall bladder operation in a few days. The aneurysm? There seemed to be some doubt now that there *was* an aneurysm. You mean it's gone, we asked. No, it's still there, but...but what? The doctors weren't saying, because apparently they weren't sure. They directed their attention to the gall bladder problem and told us to plan on a recovery period of some days, perhaps some weeks. It all depends.... On the aneurysm? Yes, on the aneurysm...or whatever.... Whatever? Now questions, doubts, fears stalked us.

Two empty hospital rooms were made available to us while we waited for the doctor's verdict; sleepless and worried, we paced back and forth from room to room. Jean and Joe, Ted and Jimmy, and Wendy now were with us. Finally Jean and Joe departed for Pennsylvania with their children, to return again for the operation. Bill drove home with Wendy and left me with the little Volkswagen to get home whenever. No one knew what the whenever meant, but no one now questioned the fact that Ted and I would have to stay with Miss Buck no matter for how long. Everybody else would have to be our support and back-up team.

It was a different hospital building but the same oddly familiar atmosphere in which Ted and I again faced each other in our common cause. We were allowed to see Miss Buck for brief moments in Intensive Care. Sedated, obviously in great discomfort, she kept asking, "You'll stay here? You won't leave me alone?" And we promised, as we always promised, to take care of everything.

By the end of that first day, the empty rooms we had been allowed to use were needed for incoming patients, but we talked our way into temporary quarters in the nurses' dormitory. The University of Vermont had a student nursing program housed here; there was a vacant room and bath on the second floor for me and a large visitor's suite downstairs for Ted and Jimmy or whoever else might need it. A day-to-day rental arrangement was made.

The hospital staff from day one, like the staff at Rutland, assisted us in every way possible. Our stay in Rutland had been for three weeks. Our stint in Burlington was to last three months. But on that first day there was no crystal ball, and we could only inch our way along hour by hour.

I have often thought - in fact Miss Buck and I often discussed it - that the three months spent at the Burlington Medical Center would make a fascinating story in itself. Because of our unique circumstances and the length of time involved - living there day and night - we were privileged observers as well as participants. Once again Ted and I were deputized staff members, so to speak, coming and going with a great deal of freedom, yet still set apart in our unofficial professional status. Miss Buck did not have the strength during those three months, and Ted and I did not have the time to chronicle life in the hospital, intriguing though it was. And now, as I write in retrospect, with Miss Buck gone, I can still see her waggling a finger at me, cautioning me to get on with this story about her, giving just enough behind the scenes color to put the reader into the picture.

Ever-mindful of doing this, I must mention one other thing here. Living in the nurses' quarters adjacent to the main hospital wing where Miss Buck was, put me right in the midst of student dormitory life. Giggling girls, ringing telephones, blaring radios, constant commotion over books, exams, boys and clothes. The controlled bedlam was presided over by a housemother and security staff reminiscent of my one year away from home in a school dorm. But that had been over twenty years ago and I was now the older generation living with the younger generation. Some things were the same, and I had no trouble finding common concerns to chat about as the girls and I came and went on our shifts. But some things were different. Their music, for example, and one unfamiliar haunting melody played over and over. It became a sort of theme song, and even today can conjure up all the sights and sounds of those months. There was an unfamiliar scent too. I mentioned to Miss Buck that it pervaded the atmosphere like heavy Tabu perfume or exotic incense burning. The answer came in a rush as I was awakened from a sound sleep one night by loud talking and someone shining a flashlight in my eyes. "Drug raid," growled two burly uniforms, already poking through closets and dresser drawers. I would have been instantly terrified had I not seen a reassuringly familiar housemother's face. When it was explained that they were confiscating marijuana, being smoked in the dorm against regulations, I knew immediately what I had been smelling.

"Welcome to the modern generation, ma'am," one of the burlies said to me then, with apologies for breaking in on my drug-free spartan quarters. That same haunting melody drifted across the hall. What is the name of that music I hear over and over, I wanted to know. "Nights in White Satin," came the answer. I had unknowingly translated the title as "Knights in White Satin." While we weren't knights in shining armor, or knights on white steeds, we were somehow suited to being knights in white satin. Miss Buck loved the image. I can still hear the music playing in the background.

Chapter 35

Cancer

Recovery from the gall bladder operation was slow but steady, and the press releases that were issued every few days, always with the doctors' approval, were bland but reassuring. Things like "Pearl Buck's appetite has improved, her temperature was normal today, her doctors allowed a short ride for the first time, or "her physical therapy program now includes two walks daily around the hospital corridors." And best of all, one which she especially liked, "Pearl Buck has been doing some writing and research for her next book." Her fans were relentless in wanting to hear about her progress. Many called the hospital repeatedly, and I recognized more than one name who had already written once, twice, three times or more. They were concerned when they received no answer. Some, who *had* received an answer, wanted to speak directly with Mrs. Bixby, not Mrs. Drake, or vice versa. I slipped from one role to the other and Miss Buck never failed to chuckle at the dual performance. Some very perceptive callers expressed alarm when Miss Buck's recovery from the gall bladder operation was extended and extended and extended again. "If she's all right, why is she still in the hospital and why isn't she allowed to go home?" they asked.

Complications, we said. It was an unsatisfactory answer, but the real reason behind the lengthy hospital stay had so devastated Miss Buck that she wanted us to hide it as best we could and for as long as possible. She was now fighting a cancerous lung tumor, not the aneurysm that had so long been suspected. She had to realign her forces and wage this new battle *her* way. And once again she insisted on as much privacy and as little publicity as we could insure.

She was scheduled for a second major operation to remove the tumor (hopefully all of it), but not until the doctors were satisfied that both her physical and mental state were at optimum strength. There was no negative talk of the possibility of failure, never a mention of death or dying. Indeed, her own anxiety and impatience to get on with it and get over the operation so she could get on with her unfinished business created its own complications: rapid heart beats and intense periods of frustration and anguish. I saw her weep for the first time. I wept with her in silent communion. But tears were rare and she talked only of the future, of going home to Danby. Ted and I were with her each day. Dolphus was with her each night. She amazed us with her fighting spirit, and she won over the somewhat cynical younger interns. Pearl who? they asked at first, unimpressed by this old lady author some people called a celebrity. But it was not at all unusual to look into her room and see her holding court from her throne - her hospital bed or wheel chair - flowers and cards everywhere, two or three nurses standing by expectantly, and as many as six or eight doctors of all ages in rapt attention. Did they talk about her cancerous tumor and the impending operation? Yes, but they didn't dwell on this, for she wanted to hear what they had to say about the high cost of medical insurance, and how they felt about the grueling schedule for the doctors in training, a regimen that was somehow supposed to separate the men from the boys. She wanted to know all about this. And romance in the hospital.

What did they have to say about that? They would go away from such sessions shaking their heads and using Ted's favorite expression for her: "The lady is too much..."

Both before and after the second operation was a time of much coming and going of family members. I met sister Grace and her husband for the first time. She was so gentle and caring and wondering what she could do to help. I remember being with Miss Buck alone at some point while Grace and whoever else was there talked outside for a while so as not to tire the patient with too much conversation. "My bed is moving," Miss Buck said to me, her eyes wide with alarm. "No, the whole room is moving - it must be an earthquake." A doctor quickly confirmed that Miss Buck's incredibly rapid heart beat sent the monitoring machine beyond its upper limits. No wonder her bed shook and the earth moved.

The same day Grace was there and the heart problem occurred, Bill Drake was there, offering assistance to Ted in a manner I never thought possible. From being downright hostile and distrustful of this man he had once called too smooth, too full of fancy footwork and responsible for not paying me enough salary and withholding my $350 wardrobe check for lack of funds when he could find enough money to purchase a limousine, and so on, and so on, I heard my husband tell Ted that we could probably turn some farm assets into about $25,000 cash quickly. If Ted and Miss Buck could use the cash during this prolonged crisis, they were welcome to it. It floored Ted and it astounded Miss Buck. They were more than grateful for the unexpected show of support, but refused the offer by saying that they were making arrangements to negotiate a large business loan and were doing some high echelon robbing Peter to pay Paul among their various businesses. There would be no need to dip into the

Drake coffers. "Then you have my permission to use the services of my wife for as long as you need them," came the ultimate offer. I heard this and could hardly believe what I heard. Once again I attribute this turn-about to the wiles of the goddess.

The parade of Miss Buck's family continued, with Henriette being the most frequent visitor, as she only lived about a half hour away. Henriette - tall, haughty, beautiful and black. She always caused a sensation when she glided down the hall. Looking like a high-fashion model, her concern for her mother seemed cool and detached, and her talk was of herself or oddly controversial subjects. I remember one evening visit after Miss Buck had had a particularly trying day. Henriette brought up the subject of McGovern and Nixon (political adversaries), arguing vehemently for McGovern and needling her mother to argue with her. I was uneasily present during most of the long conversation. She also talked about Edgar at that time, saying that he was impossible to do anything with and that he would never be friendly towards Mr. Harris. He was "difficult" she said of her brother.

The strained and sometimes stormy family relations concerned us only when they directly affected Miss Buck's well being. We dealt with them accordingly, always relying on Jean and Grace to be the family negotiators. Without them, our job of carrying out Miss Buck's wishes while maintaining peace within the family would have been impossible.

The over-worked employees back in Danby, meanwhile, had been carrying on the businesses as best they could without much direct assistance from Miss Buck or Mr. Harris, except by telephone. Jimmy became a shuttling message carrier and Wendy stayed in my dorm room on weekends, taking over my duties when I went home.

But wherever we were, whatever we were doing, we lived constantly with the anguish of caring for Miss Buck, person, and caring for Miss Buck, business. She herself continued to think nothing but positive thoughts of the future, and her dreams died hard. She forced promise after promise from Ted that he would keep the Danby project moving forward.

And in anticipation of her own return to Danby House and resuming her writing as her strength returned, she started yet another of her "wouldn't it be nice if..." schemes. She wanted a large extension added to Danby House - a room with a huge stone fireplace and walls of shelves to hold her books, and a walking balcony overlooking the sitting area. And she wanted all this completed by the time she left the hospital, still some weeks away but with harsh Vermont Winter weather fast approaching. Of course it was an impossible dream. No one knew that better than Ted Harris, but it was not the first time he had been asked by her to "see that it is done and done now." Lesser mortals, perhaps (notice that I did not say "wiser") would never have attempted this impossible dream. It was clear from the start that there could be nothing in it but more financial headaches and personal heartaches. If she knew what she was asking of Ted Harris, the goddess ultimately decided that seeing her pleasure would be reward enough for him. And her ulterior motive, of course, was that she wanted Danby and Danby House built up to her design specifications, not only so she could enjoy them but so that she could see for herself that all was in readiness as her gift to Ted for his lifetime.

A noble gesture, a generous and thoughtful thank you to this man who had done so much for her. But it was no gift now that she handed to Ted as he, to please her, reluctantly attempted what she asked. And employees, already squeezed and exhausted and in many cases performing double and triple duties, were rejuggled, cajoled, promised the moon in some cases to keep them going, and we all pressed forward somehow.

The large loan, negotiated to clear up past problems (like the hot Rolls Royce which had long since disappeared from the scene) would now have to be stretched to include an elaborate architectural problem which ideally could have used a whole army of slaves to complete on time. At Miss Buck's insistence and over the strong opposition of Wendy who did not take kindly to the idea of being monitored or directed by anybody but Ted Harris, an assistant business manager was hired to oversee everything in Danby, particularly the complicated (and growing more so) financial situation.

The whole complexion of Danby changed with these new and dramatic demands. Ted and I, though of course involved with the on-going hassles and complications involved, were nevertheless removed from the Danby day-to-day struggle for survival. If we hadn't been, there is no way we could have continued to provide Miss Buck with as much personal comfort and emotional assistance as we did. Once she had set the new Danby plan in motion, she considered it over and done with and devoted herself to preparing for the tumor operation.

Jean and Joe were in Burlington for that second operation, staying long enough to make sure that the patient was out of immediate danger. But it was Ted and I, as usual, who were in constant attention and who learned to cope with the touch and go emergencies which are a part of the intensive care unit - emergencies which the trained medical staff accept as a matter of course and treat with efficient calmness. The life and death situations are entrusted to the medical people. All others are forbidden entry, except for very brief look-in visits, more to comfort the visitor than the patient, who is very likely sedated and too exhausted to worry about anything, anyway.

My first recollection of Miss Buck after the operation was not of someone "out of it" and oblivious to her surroundings, but we saw her imploring blue eyes trying to say something important. She couldn't speak, for she was wired and wound about with tubes and instruments. One arm, stiffly bandaged to a rigid board holding an intravenous feeding apparatus, started banging on the metal side of her bed. The blue eyes implored even more. Ted and I looked at each other helplessly. We knew she wanted something, but what? The banging increased and the medical staff, frantic with an emergency in the bed next to hers, implored us to do something - anything - to stop the banging. We started asking her questions. Did she want something from us? Yes, she nodded. Are you in pain, are you hurting? No, she signaled. We ran through a whole series of questions until finally we hit the right one. You want us to stay here with you? Yes, she nodded, the blue eyes obviously relieved. I don't know whether we can, I said, looking worriedly at Ted. The banging resumed with a vengeance, and a nurse called out harshly, "Stop that racket - it's too distracting." In a flash I said to her, if we're not allowed to stay here with you, you're going to keep banging and creating more of a racket? She nodded yes, and incredibly we saw the hint of a wicked twinkle. We were allowed to stay, and our presence became almost common-place in this off-limits atmosphere.

The man in the next bed was desperately ill and in danger of dying, and the doctors were working over him frantically.

Miss Buck observed most of the harrowing procedures going on until finally she was wheeled to another area. As we walked beside her bed, we passed the mangled body of a young man just brought in from a car wreck. He was bloody and bent, and I caught just a glimpse of his face. I felt the floor go out from under me and I held onto the metal bedside. "My God," I whispered to Ted, "He looks just like my Tom." It couldn't be Tom, I knew. My tired eyes were playing tricks on me. Death and disaster were all around us, and that was the closest I had yet come to breaking down with the strain of emotion.

"Thanks for your help," whispered a doctor as we at last settled Miss Buck quietly. "I hate to ask you, but can you do something else for me?" It seems that the dying man was a prominent Burlington personage and his whole family was outside in the waiting room, understandably weeping and wailing. Emergency after emergency had created a chaotic scene in the Intensive Care Unit, and the tense doctor begged Ted and me to "do whatever you can to comfort those poor people; it may be some time before any of us can get to them with definite news."

So momentarily leaving a sleeping Miss Buck (the doctors told us we would be able to return any time she needed us), Ted and I next tried to ease the distraught family - strangers going through their own tragedy. We talked, we held their hands, we even asked the doctors if it would be all right to offer them a little sherry, which we always kept in the office upstairs for occasions when it calmed Miss Buck more effectively than the medicines she hated. Yes, came their instant approval. Time stands still during episodes such as the one I am describing. No, time doesn't stand still. Time has no meaning; it ceases to exist. You go on doing what you have to do whether it's morning or night, and it's only when things start to calm down a bit that you become aware of time in the conventional sense. When the distraught family was finally handed over to the doctors and we had looked in on Miss Buck and found her still sleeping, then and only then did I become aware that it was dark outside, after dinner (we had had no dinner, of course), and I had been scheduled to leave for home hours ago. I ran for the nearest phone, apologizing to my husband and explaining as calmly as I could the emergency situations we were dealing with, including the dying man. I just can't get away tonight, I said, Ted and I are going to be on call all night - right outside the Intensive Care unit. My explanations, my pleas for understanding, fell an deaf ears.

"What the Hell is going on up there anyway; just who the Hell do you think you are; I'm beginning to care less if you come home at all, etc., etc..." The understanding and sympathy which I had come to depend on from my husband and which had allowed me to keep on an even keel for Miss Buck had suddenly, cruelly, and at the worst possible time, been pulled out from under me. I was close to tears when I returned to Ted, still in the Emergency waiting room, alone and fighting for his own emotional control after the turmoil we had just experienced. In frustration, I railed at our current impossible situation. It's more then anybody should be asked to do, I exploded. And I railed at Bill Drake for returning suddenly to his old uncompromising ways. I got no sympathy from Ted, who railed back at me that I was reacting like a spoiled child. I knew he wasn't really upset with me; he just didn't need another female in distress clinging to him at that particular moment. My hysteria passed and we assessed things realistically. We couldn't leave; we had to stay. We challenged each other to a game of Scrabble, to take our minds off our problems. It helped, at least for a while. The

Emergency Room was blessedly quiet, dinner was forgotten and Bill Drake was forgotten.

One of the doctors eased wearily into a chair beside us and said, "Thanks, you two, we couldn't have done it without you in there tonight." It was high praise, followed by one of the nicest invitations ever. "The two of you come to dinner soon; you deserve to get away from this nightmare and my wife would enjoy meeting you; she's an admirer of Pearl Buck."

Into this atmosphere stormed my husband, misinterpreting our struggle for survival as some intimate tete-a-tete. He was barely civil to Ted or me. Ted waved a hand, dismissing me to the fates and saying that I should take the night off and don't worry. I looked from Ted to Bill and back to Ted. In Ted I saw nothing but understanding; in Bill I saw nothing but misunderstanding.

I think now, though I was too exhausted to think then, that the goddess was in critical danger of losing her powers and for some reason, my husband had been the first to react.

I could only hope that the loss of power was temporary. As it turned out, the goddess powers never returned completely, but remained intermittent, creating up and down havoc as time went on.

Chapter 36

Thanksgiving in the Hospital

Everything possible was done to help along the recovery period, but new complications developed in addition to the old ones. Fluid in the lungs which had to be removed often by use of what was called a "bird machine" created greater stress on the heart, which in turn created discouragement and depression. Miss Buck hated the bird machine and expressed her feelings to the insistent nurses who came and went on their onerous missions. And she gave verbal tongue lashings to those who performed what she called too much "barbarian blood-letting." It did seem that there was a constant probing and poking with needles; even her toes were jabbed when fingers and arms became over-worked.

To better cope with the medical complications and to be instantly prepared for any unforeseen emergency, special duty nurses were hired around the clock. This, of course, being all in addition to the fact that Ted and Dolphus and I were still with her and near her always. I didn't even want to think about the astronomical costs involved, and Miss Buck's only concern was that the nurses were paid promptly, no matter where the money came from. Hundreds of dollars each week went to these highly trained women. Some developed a very personal attachment to Miss Buck, and I remained in touch with one in particular for several years.

The office that Ted and I shared directly across the hall from Miss Buck's room was actually the office for the floor doctors, and almost daily they took time to share their medical expertise with us on what was going on with our patient. Talking about cancers and the kinds of operations for removal of cancers, these doctors frequently illustrated their talk sessions with diagrams on the chalk board. Some of these fascinating details Miss Buck had to miss, and she pouted good-naturedly that the doctors should move their chalk talks to her room. Secretly to me she expressed much pleasure that Ted was spending many hours with learned medical men in high-level intellectual discussions which touched on a wide range of subjects, not just her operation. Her mind remained actively interested in all that was happening, even when her body was not so prompt to respond. She often commented that she could never turn off her mind - and sometimes she tried out of sheer exhaustion - but the mind raced constantly and she could do nothing to stop it.

When I say that everything was done to help along her recovery, I mean just that - everything. It is no exaggeration to say that we left no stone unturned to try to dispel periodic discouragement and depression, the two greatest foes to her progress. We were even allowed to use the staff kitchen down the hall to prepare special treats for her - foods she especially liked but were not on the adequate but not exotic hospital menus. A certain inevitable sameness in the institutional fare was boring after a while to one as fastidious as Miss Buck. Ted occasionally bought little chops and fresh fruits and vegetables to tempt her. When her appetite and general attitude hit a particularly low point, we had someone from Danby bring up a carton loaded with her rose-colored damask tablecloth and napkins and table settings for two with the crystal and china and silver that she favored for dinner at Danby House. Ted even found her favorite sweet amber Marsala wine. The fancy dinner proved too much of an effort for her, but everything was worth a try at least once.

Sometimes our attempts at levity worked wonders; sometimes they worked not at all. But if the recovery graph was up and down on a day-to-day basis, the over-all curve seemed to be upward and satisfactory. Her own view of her progress, her frame of mind - indeed, what was on her mind, is nicely chronicled in letters she dictated to family members. Grace received one of the first messages, and it is quoted here in its entirety:

November 7, 1972

Dearest Grace:

Your letter came in yesterday morning and I was happy to have it. I am dictating this to Mrs. Drake because I am not quite up to writing myself yet. I am improving fast and should be leaving the hospital, perhaps in a week but more likely two or three.

Of course, this has been a most extraordinary experience and I have had my bad days, but have managed on the whole to keep a reasonable view of things and to realize how much my own attitude counts in my recovery.

No one can explain why I, not a smoker or drinker, should have an attack of the growth. It is just a common garden variety but would, of course, have killed me if I had not fought back.

Now the doctors have forbidden me any public activities but tell me that I can continue with my work, which is really writing, and a quiet life. All my affairs, family and financial, are in good shape, thanks to Mr. Harris' unfailing activity and concern. I am so glad Joe is in the Foundation and Jean's family lives in the big old house. The little New England village is just right for me. The air is pure, I can live as quietly as I like, and somehow I have found the right place for me.

This is a wonderful Medical Center, one of the finest in the country and I have received every attention. I am now undergoing X-ray treatments, precautionary for the future. My appetite has returned, I sleep, and am surrounded by loving people, first of all by my staff members.

My doctors tell me that within limits I shall be as active as I wish in affairs other than public. My new book - CHINA PAST AND PRESENT - comes out tomorrow and I am already getting repercussions of indignation from people who feel that the Chinese have treated me shabbily. Yet how fortunate that I did not go to China! I thought it best to tell the whole story to my readers just as it happened.

You hold a unique and special place in my life and heart, my beloved sister. Your letters are a joy and I answer when I can. I am sure you understand everything about me, as I like to think I do about you. I think of you often with the utmost tenderness."

A letter of the same date to son John and his wife Edna:

I was very happy to get your letter, Edna, and I include John in my reply because I know that usually husbands let wives do the writing and of course I always include John in my love and thoughts when I think of your little family.

It is very disappointing to me that you did not make it up to Danby on your vacation. I would have loved to have seen you and have you see the things I am busy about. Of course, I make writing my main work but it is fun restoring the old village and opening a kind of business there under a corporation. Next time you will make it, I am sure. I am anxious for you to see our very New England setting. This is the first time I have ever lived, really lived, in an American village and I am learning a great deal in the process. The children, when you come, will enjoy the waterfall in the brook behind the house where I live. When Jean and Joe brought Scott and Dale, Dale got brave and walked into the stream with his sneakers on and slipped and slid down the whole long waterfall. First he was somewhat frightened, but then he thought it was fun and they all got to do it.

I am very glad indeed that you and John are happy together. It comforts me. I do not think that John ever has realized how dear and loved a child, boy, and man he has been to me always from the first moment I saw him, and forever. His father loved him dearly, too, but they were different types and it was most difficult for the father, a pure intellectual, to understand a boy like John who has so many different sides to him. It has been a matter of pain to me that there have been times when he seemed far even from me, but I had faith in him and a good life for him and have waited, and now I am glad that he has his own people in a family life. He has done

346

so well through all his troubles and I am sure they are ended. This is for you to read, too, dear John.

I see Henriette and Bart every few days. They live quite near the hospital. Edgar and Linda came up from New York one weekend and Jean and Joe were here for the operations. Thank God they are over. They have been difficult to bear, but I expect to go home again, to Danby, in a week or two, perhaps three. This is a wonderful Medical Center and I am fortunate to have been located near it. It is one of the best in the country and everyone has been wonderful to me. My faithful and ever-loyal staff have moved into Burlington and the hospital gave them an office so that work could go on. The rest of the staff has continued in Danby doing their work, as always, with great loyalty.

This letter is dictated to my excellent secretary, Mrs. Beverly Drake. She spends five days a week here at the hospital with the other two members of the executive staff. Mr. Harris has been beyond praise in his loyalty and ability. I want you to both know him better so that you can appreciate his fine qualities. He will have worked with me ten years this year, always putting my comfort and ambitions first....

On November 13th she had this to say to son Richard and his wife Vivian:

You will have heard from Jean that I have been in the hospital.... I have taken it for granted that Jean has kept in touch. Mrs. Drake, my secretary, has telephoned her regularly and she is supposed to have let the other children know how I am getting along....

I am so glad that you and the little ones got up to Danby to see me and I appreciate your coming. The various businesses are going well and soon the ski season will be starting. We are adding a big room onto Danby House and that is being done while I am away....

I think of you all very often and I do hope that everything is going well with you. I never forget my children....

To Janice she wrote on the same date:

I think of you often, darling - indeed daily - and I am so glad for your last visit.

I am also mindful of Carol. I am writing to Doctor Jacob and asking him to see that the school provide her with Christmas presents of things she wants or needs and send the bill to us here. When I am no longer here, remember that Mr. Harris will always see to this matter and the funds will come from our business, Creativity, Inc., as does her monthly pin money check of $50 now. I do hope that you can go to see her before Christmas, however, and perhaps take her a box of candy which she enjoys. She seems to remember you and I have to confide her to you now. Of course, I hope to be able to get to see her from time to time, but of this I cannot be sure as yet. For the present, at least, it is extremely important that I stay in the pure mountain air....

To Theresa, also on November 13th:

I feel very close to you and welcome always hearing from you or seeing you. I did postpone your visit because I am not strong enough yet and I would rather wait until I am back in Danby House and living under more normal circumstances.

I do think a great deal of Chieko and have not heard from her at all. When you write if you can let me know if she is all right, it will be a comfort to me. I see Henriette and Bart every week and of course I am in touch with Jean and the others within the limits of my ability.

It certainly makes me happy to know that you are independent and comfortable in a warm house and with friends. Keep me informed, please, of anything I can do to help your citizenship status.

And finally to Edgar and Linda, a letter of November 20th quoted in its entirety:

It was such a joy to see you both looking so well and happy and I only regret that my nurse allowed you so short a visit. Perhaps next time I shall be stronger and she will be more lenient.

I saw my story in the Christmas *Good Housekeeping,* Linda, and was very shocked to see how carelessly and badly it had been cut. As it now stands, the story amounts to nothing. I am always indignant with magazine editors who allow some little snip in the office to cut a writer's work. But so it is. Space is too valuable for advertising to include the final touches of a story.

I took my first car ride since my second operation day before yesterday. I stayed out about an hour and enjoyed it very much. The snow began again and so I shall be locked in until further sunshine.

Perhaps I am too reluctant to disturb my children's lives, Edgar, so I do not tell you enough of my own life. I believe so much that children, when they are grown, should be free to live where and as they wish. I take it for granted that the bonds of love and memory always hold fast as long as life lasts and perhaps beyond, who knows! At any rate, it was a joy to see you both and you are always welcome, wherever I am.

This week the doctors will decide whether I am to have more X-rays. If so, I shall probably have to stay at least a week afterwards until the worst effects are over. If not, we will be going back to Danby when they give permission. The foul weather is holding up our building. We need about eight days of clear weather and then it does not matter what the weather is. I look forward to the increased space very much, particularly for books, and the library is to be a gallery running around the living room, a novel idea which appeals to me because this gallery opens straight from my own study. I accumulate books incredibly fast, since publishers send me copies of many of their books, hoping for a comment, which sometimes I do give to them.

I enjoy the Vermont winters with their beautiful snow scenes and of course I am eager to get back to my own domain.

Always with love,

P.S. I do not think the artist did your beautiful mother justice, Linda, but there was a certain resemblance and I feel proud to have her with my story.

Her optimism is evident in these letters, and this positive attitude is exactly what we had worked so hard to achieve. We wanted her to visualize the good side of all that was happening, including the work in progress back in Danby. Actually, things went far from smoothly behind the scenes. The new building project, for example, was plagued with not only bad weather and cost over-runs, but all the problems which beset most big hurry-up projects.

Back on the farm, my own family situation had its ups and downs and its own emergencies. On one of my weekends home, Bill developed a strange infection of unknown origins and once again, I found myself sitting nervously in the emergency room at the Rutland Hospital, waiting for a verdict of what could be wrong. As a retired Air Force officer, Bill was referred immediately to Plattsburgh Air Force Base for further examination. I was nervous, he was nervous, and the ramifications of this latest burden came close to being overwhelming. Anything I say here is but a brief and simplistic explanation of the layered emotional upheavals taking place behind the scenes.

"Get on with the story, my dear," I can hear Miss Buck admonishing here. Indeed, I discussed Bill's emergency with her - maybe I should say she forced me to discuss it with her. Actually, she would have found out anyway even if I had tried to hide it from her. I discussed the physical aspects of Bill's problems, but would not reveal to her the extent of his bitter verbal campaign against me for leaving home, neglecting my wifely duties, and so on. To counter this, I launched my own campaign to soothe and sympathize. I couldn't go home. I was not unsympathetic to my husband's problems, but I couldn't go home, not back to the same wracking circumstances I had left. I don't know and won't waste time in speculating what would have happened had I suddenly pulled away from Miss Buck during her recovery period. As it was, it was to her bedside that Bill came from Plattsburgh to announce that what he had was not cancer, which he admitted he had at first suspected. He had a persistent urological infection which required strong medication, but it was not life-threatening.

I must make it clear that my personal relationships with my husband and sons, my working association with Ted Harris, and finally my friendship with an elderly gentleman who now enters the picture and whose needs intruded on Miss Buck's needs - all these became the topics of some of the most intimate conversations Miss Buck and I had yet had. I never brought her my problems; it was always she who insisted that I share all and bare all. She would not have it otherwise.

The circumstances of the elderly friend came out one weekend when she found out that I was not going home but was flying to Delaware at the urgent request of a dear friend who was about to undergo a prostate operation (he was in his late eighties) and wanted to see me - just in case he didn't return from the operating room, he said with directness. How and why this person was such a dear friend to me fascinated her and, in typical fashion, she drew from me the background details, filing them away I knew for possible future use in some book she planned to write. The Delaware gentleman had been a gentle and kind and thoughtful friend to me and my whole family, assuming the role of revered patriarch, even though he had a large family of his own. To me, he revealed a more personal side, though always extremely correct and proper in his behavior. I enjoyed his calm influence and wise counseling and felt flattered when he read me poetry over the telephone, shared his own intimate fantasies, and sent me favorite books so we could talk about them together.

Miss Buck, who had had her own elderly friend Ernest Hocking, went on to demand whether or not I had had or could relate to the pristine love episode in THE GODDESS ABIDES. I told her that while I could relate to and appreciate the touching depths of the moonlight love scene, I had never shared any such interludes with any elderly gent. Still, when she saw that I was very fond of him, she fussed kindly, "I think I am a little jealous of him," when I flew away briefly to visit with him.

Of my husband, her admiration of him and his abilities remained undiminished, but she more and more linked him with Ted Harris in what she called their difficult and overbearing ways. Her opinion, expresssed in many different ways at many different times during our most intimate talk, was that each of them would be nearly impossible for any woman to live with in the context of husband and wife or physical lovers. "Perhaps," she mused, "that is why you seem to have more difficulty with your husband than you have with Mr. Harris." I understood exactly what she meant, but I was less sure of what she was driving at on the many occasions she offered the opinion that Mr. Harris had always been involved with the wrong kind of woman and what he really needs is someone like Mrs. Bixby....

Conversations on the good days, the bad days, and everything in between always came back to Ted Harris. I didn't question her obsession with him, not even in my private thoughts. She was what she was, who she was, and the more I was with her, the more I think I understood what she was and who she was.

"The lady is too much," I said to the receptionist at the front desk of the hospital one day as Ted wheeled a fur-swathed smiling Miss Buck out into the sunshine for a brief ride. "He lavishes attention on her," she observed, and I readily agreed. "She's very lucky to have someone like that in her old age," she added, and I agreed again, though it was impossible to think of Pearl Buck as old.

November came and went and we were still at the hospital. The vivid images that crowd my mind are as diverse as the lady we were caring for.

I see a bevy of starched young nurses coming into her room to ooh and aah over the sheer, shimmering gowns and robes Ted brought on a regular basis to supplement the hated hospital tents. One beautiful little blonde with big brown eyes whom Miss Buck liked to watch "bounce around on her gumshoes but she should do something about her body odor" - as she so colorfully said to me - modeled some of the outfits, at Miss Buck's suggestion. And there she was again, holding court with a different group of admirers and talking about their love life and babies. The little blonde with the gumshoes and the body odor asked Miss Buck's advice - and she gave it - before she jilted one beau in favor of another. Even when it tired her and she complained a little, Miss Buck loved to be involved, and it helped to keep her mind off herself and her up and down recovery.

I see her being wheeled into the radiology room, where she fumed impatiently because she had to wait while someone else was being prepared for treatments. Then her blue eyes are staring at me in embarrassment as they strap her, spread-eagled, to a tilting metal table, her indelicate position necessary to be bombarded by x-rays at just the right angle.

Then there is a picture of Dolphus working gently over the silver hair which has been falling out in clumps from the radiation treatments. He piles it high in front so when she looks in her mirror it seems normal, but she knows it's becoming thin and lack-lustre and it vexes her.

Thanksgiving in the Hospital

I watch her tracking down the hall - this time against doctor's orders - with a worried nurse pacing along beside her. She keeps going till she's exhausted, pulling along the little wheeled trolley of intravenous tubes and bottles like some recalcitrant child fearless of punishment.

I see my son Tom shyly talking to her, uncomfortably aware that too much conversation will tire her. He's in Burlington for a school track meet. She favors him with her most sparkling smile and says she wishes she could join him, his mother and Mr. Harris for dinner and more conversation, which she is not up to just yet. We link arms - Tom and Mr. Harris and I - and we skip out of her room while she laughs at our antics and wishes she could be with us. "We're off to see the Wizard, the wonderful Wizard of Oz." In a fit of high spirits which are few and far between, we continue skipping down the hall, joined by two or three others who follow us along our imaginary yellow brick road. We leave laughter in our wake and it's a welcome sound.

All three of the Drake men arrive at the hospital on Thanksgiving morning, bearing bouquets of chrysanthomums for Miss Buck's room and bright corsages for Wendy and me. At Miss Buck's suggestion the Drake family, Ted and Jimmy and Dolphus and a few of the Danby employees are eating Thanksgiving dinner together at one of Burlington's big restaurants. This is one of the few times that Tom and Jim openly fussed at my deep involvement with Miss Buck. Their own dreams died hard, and they wanted to eat their turkey dinner in their own home. Home might not have been perfect, but it was the only home they had and it was better than strangers and hospitals. They couldn't wait to get back to the farm. I well understood how they felt. It was a strange and incongruous holiday for all of us, most particularly for Miss Buck herself, eating holiday fare from a hospital bed.

ONCE UPON A CHRISTMAS, the latest collection of her short stories, arrived from the publisher. I stayed awake reading till four A.M. in my dorm room one snowy night and pondering the lady who wrote the stories. At her suggestion, we distributed many of these new books as gifts to the doctors and nurses and other staff members who had helped us so much during our long stay with them. As I write now, Miss Buck smiles at me from the bright cover of the book. She sits in her gold chair at Danby House wearing pearl jewelry and the electric blue robe Sandy Stone created for her. A glittering Christmas tree is behind her, and she's holding a copy of the book, without the cover. I think this copy must be the same one in which she encouraged Ted to keep a Treasure Book of his own. For in this he wrote, "Keep for yourself a place enshrined...A place where you can live apart...To praise or ridicule you can be blind...In this sanctuary for mind and heart...This is my place....

He starts his Treasure Book with sad words dated December 3, 1967. Is it a PSB poem? It could be, but I am uncertain.

It has been said

The heart breaks but once

From birth

Till you are dead.

Does this imply

There is no healing

Thanksgiving in the Hospital

Till you die?

And why?

Inside the heart

A single tear

Can remove the joy

From a year

Remove the joy

Erase the year

To cry a tear

To die.

But as we left the hospital ten days before Christmas, 1972, we were not thinking sad thoughts. We prepared for the holidays ahead with joy and anticipation, and we carried back to Danby boxes and boxes of joyous words from people we knew and people we did not know. Many well-wishers, wanting to thank Miss Buck for touching their own lives, quoted Ted Harris directly from the Biography, in which he said, "Thank you for giving so much of yourself to the world and to me." Someone else wrote a thank you with, "It is, I suppose, an understanding and over-flowing heart able to put into moving words what experience teaches. And so I translate it into mine - for its truths and wisdom. Warmest appreciation of the books and you, with affectionate greetings to a great spirit..."

Back to Danby we went with memories and messages and hopes for the future. The weeks of illness and isolation from the so-called real world had changed us, each of us, and as we said "Merry Christmas" the very words seemed to take on added meaning because of all the added dimensions to our thinking.

There was a great loneliness in Miss Buck that she often expressed to me in terms of being set apart from other human beings. Though love and attention surrounded her and she was never really alone, still she was lonely. She somehow felt an extraordinarily deep need to reach out and touch the world and be touched in return. The loneliness of her life's work was more poignant than ever that Christmas. I wish I had had then what I have now in the form of another artist's explanation of her creative desires. I would have shared it with her and said "Merry Christmas, you are not alone, for your work is touching everyone out there." Here is the quote, from a young blind sculptor Miss Buck never knew: "We as human beings are microcosms which reflect the great cosmos around us. We are the windows through which we look out at ourselves mirrored in the exterior world. We are not separate from each other, although we may often feel so. Linked to a network of life by our existence, our uniqueness allows us at once both beauty and isolation." (from Lynette Denney)

Chapter 37

Family Problems

I know of no better way to portray the holiday homecoming than with Miss Buck's own words, excerpts from the final entry in her Treasure Book, written Christmas Day, 1972:

Months have passed. I have spent time in the Medical Center in Burlington - two operations, both serious. Now I understand why the entries in this book have been so sad, so pessimistic. I was ill for months without knowing it! Now life has been given back to me - second life. No more pessimism. I intend to enjoy every day, every moment. First of all, I want to write down here my undying appreciation of Ted Harris and Jimmy Pauls. They moved to Burlington, endured great discomfort in food and shelter, and stood by me, steadfastly, through the long ordeal. They gave me courage to live.... My dear TFH would not let me be discouraged. Every day, all day, he was near. I knew all was being done that should and could be done - he saw to it. One after the other of the doctors and surgeons told me what a skilled, resourceful and wonderful man TFH is - as if I didn't know after all these years.

Now we are home again. I am weak but alive and happy. No more dark moods.

....I want to make this clear. This house, Danby House, is to remain forever as it is. Nothing is to be moved from it. It is to be a home for Theodore F Harris and James Pauls as long as they live and Theodore F. Harris is to decide its future at all times.

If and when, *and only if and when* the Green Hills house is declared legally and formally an historical monument is anything of furniture or pictures or any other decoration or article to be removed from Danby House to Green Hills - the Charles II screen, for example, is to stay where it is in Danby House unless and until Green Hills is declared legally and formally an historical monument, and only then if Theodore F. Harris agrees.

In short, everything in Danby House belongs to Theodore F. Harris at my death, including all that now is mine. He has the right to dispose of everything, if and as he wishes, at any time.

I state this here because I have full confidence, after many years of observations of and experience with him, in his integrity, unselfishness and efficiency.

....The big room and library are under roof. Somehow TFH has managed it. I am happy.

Today, Christmas Day, I ask only to live. My life has been given back to me. TFH has stood by me and stands by me in complete loyalty and devotion. I shall not give up. Years lie ahead, happy years of life and work.

....My rooms are beautiful with flowers this Christmas Day.

....A warm, muggy day but who cares? I am alive and I am home.

....I gained nearly two pounds this week! I now weigh nearly 132 pounds. I am wearing my silver grey Chinese robe and my jade jewelry.

....In re-reading what I have just written, I add that the Green Hills House, in perpetuity, should and must be endowed by the Board of The Pearl S. Buck Foundation..."

In sickness and health, so to speak, Miss Buck pressed forward with her single-minded purpose of putting everything in order. Her mind was constantly working along these lines, but on Christmas Day she was asking only to live.

I was home briefly with my family, Dolphus had gone South for a short visit with his family, and Ted and Jimmy prepared a roast goose dinner for a quiet Christmas celebration at Danby House.

Ted had vowed not to intrude on my own family holiday and said he would not call me or expect to see me in Danby for a few days unless there was a dire emergency. I smiled my way through the festivities, uneasy and out of touch with whatever could be considered normal. I felt guilty that I had not made the usual batch of Christmas breads and cakes; I hadn't been around to help trim the tree, and it didn't help my edginess when Bill asked me why I received no Christmas present from Danby - not even a cheap bottle of perfume from Mr. Harris, he needled. This, to me, was an unreasonable complaint in light of all we had been through. I had already presented to my family a copy of ONCE UPON A CHRISTMAS inscribed by Miss Buck "To my good friends The Drake Family," but it was useless to explain further that the exchanging of material gifts at a time like this seemed not only unnecessary but totally out of place when we had been exchanging gifts of love and support and understanding all along. I remembered what Miss Buck herself had once said that for those who understand, no explanation is necessary; for those who don't understand, no explanation is possible. So I remained on edge, especially each time the phone rang, and the dire emergency we had dreaded came on the morning of December 27th.

"Please," I heard Ted say with quiet desperation, "Meet me at the Rutland Hospital; Miss Buck's in Intensive Care again..." The sober, disappointed faces of my family surrounded me and I felt more guilty than ever when they suspected that once again they were losing me to Danby. I couldn't bear to leave; I couldn't bear not to leave, so I compromised. I promised not to be gone long. I'd just do what I had to do and return as soon as possible. And I persuaded Jim to drive with me as a sort of hostage to my quick return, knowing that he had friends to meet and places to go that afternoon.

The situation was critical when I got to the hospital. Not only was Miss Buck physically hurting; she was mentally and emotionally very depressed, and Ted was the lowest I had seen him yet in all the long months we had been involved with Miss Buck's illness. Of course I was there much longer than I had anticipated, and when I finally returned to Jim, still waiting for me in the lobby downstairs, all he said in his quiet way was "Mom, you know this is all getting to be too much."

Of course I knew it was all getting to be too much - for all of us at Danby and all of us at home, but somehow we would have to continue to find the compromise route which would allow us to carry on.

Except for the needling at Christmas and expression of concern so accurately voiced by Jim when he said that this was all getting to be too much, the situation became so serious in the weeks that followed that my family took a resigned attitude of "if you can't beat 'em, join 'em." I was consumed with the care and comfort of Miss Buck. My family accepted that and they really helped however and whenever they could.

As soon as Miss Buck returned from the hospital, she announced that she wanted to see Ted Dolmatch, her publisher from New York, and Doris Howell, a physician from Philadelphia, to discuss with them in person how she wished them to be involved for her with her Foundation, starting now, but especially in the future. "I like them; I trust them; I must have their promise of their help when I am no longer able to carry on at the Foundation." No, Miss Buck had not given up her fight with the cancer. There was no talk that the fight was lost, but it became more and more clear that she was carefully putting all the block in place - when she would no longer be around. Dr. Howell was reluctant to voice pessimistic predictions for the immediate future, but it was obvious that she saw Miss Buck's condition as very serious and starting to further deteriorate. Bill and I picked up Dr. Howell at Albany Airport when she flew in from Philadelphia, and we had the opportunity to talk with her at length as she was our overnight guest at the farm while discussions with Miss Buck and Ted Dolmatch continued. Both Dr. Howell and Ted Dolmatch pledged their future support to the Foundation, and Miss Buck expressed gratitude and relief that they would be looking after her interests there.

Let me return to my notes for that period for a more impersonal summary of the atmosphere. Miss Buck herself, as soon as she felt strong enough (and even when she did not feel strong enough), took it upon herself to try to solve a lot of the family turmoil - not mine, but hers. I wrote this about the post- Christmas emergency: After a siege of very rapid heartbeats, Miss Buck was taken back to the Intensive Care Unit at Rutland Hospital on December 27th, where she stayed for two nights and days, very agitated and upset the whole time. She was deeply discouraged that she had had this setback, thought Henriettte's Christmas visit might have something to do with it, and the constant undercurrent of Edgar calling or trying to call and visit, becoming insistent, etc. I was in communication with Edgar, Henriette, and Jean frequently at the hospital during this brief stay, trying to smooth things over for Miss Buck by suggesting to all three of these children that everything must be done to insure a calm atmosphere and anyone who could not visit and stay calm should stay away. Jean offered every assistance, including talking to Edgar and urging him to stop upsetting their mother. Edgar was in Londonderry, Vermont, during the week between Christmas and New Year's. I explained that it would be best not to try to see his mother for a few days, and all I remember him saying was "why not," even after all my explanations and Jean's too.

Before we had left the Burlington hospital, Dr. Davis had dictated to me a letter with his advice and recommendations relative to Miss Buck's family, in case we should need it sometime. He said that doctors' orders are doctors' orders, and even family members must learn to abide by them. Here is his letter, dated December 14th, addressed to Ted:

Dear Ted:

One point that we did not cover completely before you managed to escape my clutches, was the limit of Miss

Buck's activities in the near future. She should be kept from too much excitement and certainly should not be surrounded by multiple members of the family for the immediate future. I feel certain that her family will think that I am hard-hearted, but she has a long recovery period ahead, and I believe it would be in her best interest if she were not over-fatigued. Even though she may feel an obligation or a desire to see her family, I would like to keep this at a minimum.

For example, I do not believe she should go to Pennsylvania for the holidays, which would be a natural desire. I would rather she stayed in Danby and kept life relatively peaceful and tranquil, at least for the immediate future.

If you have any strong objections to this, give me a call and I might be willing to change my mind if the necessity arises.

Sincerely,

John H. Davis

Chief of Surgery, MCH

Chairman of Department of Surgery, UVM

At the bottom of this letter was added the following which further reinforces his feelings at a later date:

At the request of Dr. John Davis, the following is added January 15, 1973 - After examining Miss Buck today, it is my opinion that she continue to curtail her activities and maintain her recuperation schedule in the same manner as the past month.

I hadn't read that letter from Dr. Davis in over twelve years, but it is as clear in its intentions now as it was then. Doctors' orders are doctors' orders, but as far as Miss Buck's family was concerned, the orders were dismissed as unnecessary - except by Jean and Grace, the two whose love and understanding continued to bridge the gap which seemed to be increasing between Miss Buck and other family members.

Being with Miss Buck as much as I was, I saw her consciously rallying her strength, so shaky and unpredictable now, to work at putting the blocks in place - one by one, one by one. A good analogy here would be that she performed like a tired but determined athlete who had already completed most of the decathalon events but had to dig even deeper to finish and win the final events. One by one, one by one I watched Miss Buck's building blocks go into place. The big stumbling block which she couldn't put into its proper place remained her family, and she insisted on dealing with this herself in her velvet sledgehammer manner.

We at Danby had once again gone through the motions of putting the daily routine back to normal - she demanded it. We had tried and failed at this back in July. This time the situation was even worse than before and any semblance of routine of any kind was null and void, and we improvised through each day as it came along. For a very short period I returned to my old office on the third floor of the country store, during which time I was surrounded by the usual busy-ness of the Book Club, the antique shops, and business in general. The assistant business manager who had been hired but a few weeks before, left unexpectedly during the holidays, never to return. Even his last paychecks were sent back with no forwarding address. I didn't even speculate on this mystery, because once I returned to Danby House again, I was unable to be concerned with or involved in any business or office affairs, except when they directly involved Miss Buck at Danby House. Looking after her and seeing to her every comfort were the only things that mattered now. She knew - I know she fully knew - what a burden she had become, and it was she, over vehement protests from Ted and me, who attempted to set her family straight as to what she had to do, what the doctors advised her to do, and how we at Danby were attempting the impossible in caring for her as she desired.

It was only after Dr. Davis examined her on the fifteenth of January that we knew the cancer had been growing and spreading and, short of a miracle, there could be no hope of recovery. It would be a matter of time before the end came. Ted forced doctors to admit to him that from time of first detection of lung cancer to the end was usually six to eight months. If we used July 1st as a starting date, we were already in the end time. Behind the scenes, in a frantic search for a miracle, Ted talked to and had me talk to physicians who were experimenting with nutritional cures for cancer. I made phone calls to Canada and California and had long involved conversations with nutritionists who offered little hope that putting the patient on special diets at this late date would reverse the creeping cancer. If only we had called sooner, then maybe?....

We purposely discussed none of the January 15th diagnosis until she forced it from us during the early part of February. It is a gross understatement to say that she made the most of her good days during all of January. We knew she disregarded growing aches and pains and refused medicine when it might have eased her. But she chose the body discomforts in order to keep her mind as free and sharp as possible. Her letters to the family dictated slowly and painstakingly started early in January. Clipped to the carbon of the first letter, addressed to son Edgar, is a first draft I made so that she could make any necessary changes, including meticulous little punctuation notations, so typical of her desire to have everything just so. This first letter was dictated January second, and she insisted on having both Mr. Harris and me present. It was a laborious undertaking for her, but there was no arguing with her once she had made up her mind. She had to do what she could, and this is what she did: (with a blind copy to her attorney, Gale Raphael, in Boston)

Dearest Edgar:

It is most unfortunate that your stay here in Vermont coincided, accidentally, with a very difficult period for me. Briefly, the situation is that I do not tolerate digitalis except in minute doses and yet it is necessary for me to take digitalis for my heart. If I do not take it, my heart races at a dangerous rate, particularly if there is any stress or strain, and in a family as large and as various as ours there is nearly always stress and strain somewhere.

As it happened last week, I think on Wednesday, Mrs. Halligan, the very fine nurse who lives near us here in Danby and who comes in now and again on doctors' orders to check my heart, found that on that day my heart was beating dangerously fast. This was because the doctor had taken all digitalis away to see how I would do without it for a while. Digitalis is a poison and is cumulative in the system and the week or so previously I had been desperately ill and constantly vomiting because of the digitalis I had been taking for some time until Dr. Cross ordered a complete rest from this drug.

It is obvious, however, that I had to have some and Dr. Cross, my Internist at the Rutland Hospital, said that I must go at once to the Intensive Care Unit there and have my heart pace measured so that he could gauge what dosage of digitalis I could tolerate. I went immediately and was there for some days. If you have ever been in Intensive Care, you know that it is just hell. I was unable to think of anything except how to get through the days.

Meantime, I was forbidden any guests. Tad Danielewski had telephoned that he was already on his way up to see me and Mr. Harris told him that he might not be able to see me at all, or perhaps only for a moment. He replied that he wanted to see Mr. Harris, too, and thank him personally for all that he had done and does for me. As matters turned out, I saw Tad for a few minutes but I was so miserable I do not know what he said. He did, however, spend a very enjoyable evening here at Danby House with Mr. Harris and Jimmy Pauls. He came back to Danby House again the next day when he left but I saw him only long enough to say good-bye. I was too miserable to do more.

Meanwhile, Dr. Davis, the head of the Medical Center Hospital in Burlington and the physician in charge of my case, had told Mr. Harris to discourage all visits including and perhaps especially family visits, since family visits draw on one's strength. Mr. Harris pointed out that this would be very difficult advice for him to follow since my family naturally felt they had priorities. Dr. Davis then wrote a letter of stern direction. He wrote that he knew from experience, when he himself was ill, he preferred to be surrounded only by professionals and staff and not by family since emotional ties with family inevitably make their demands.

I must say that my staff was absolutely wonderful all the time I was in the hospital. Mr. Harris simply moved up to Burlington and with him Jimmy Pauls and my chauffeur, Dolphus Crow. Five days a week Mrs. Drake left her own family and stayed in the office across from my room and was on constant call.

I doubt very much that I could have pulled through the ordeal of two major operations so close together had it not been for the conscientiousness of my faithful friends who are also staff members of our corporation. Even while I was in Intensive Care for four miserable days, they saw to it that I had constant and special attention and were always near me. Of course, the leader and chief was and is Theodore Harris. I know of your unreasonable and unreasoning prejudice against this most remarkable man to whom I owe so much and for so many years of unselfish devotion to my welfare. He has worked with and for me for more than ten years and I have never discovered the slightest failure in him in any regard. He is courageous, honest, and resourceful. More than that, he is brilliantly efficient. His total honesty is beyond question. He will not even use the royalties on his own books for himself. The royalties for the two volumes of his biography of me he uses altogether for me, saying that he is determined not to benefit personally from his work for me.   Thanks to him, I live in complete comfort and safety. I know my children would do all they could for me but the fact is that I could not live with any of you, dearly as I love you all. Jean's life is completely absorbed in her many children and the Foundation children she also cares for and I do not want to infringe on her over-crowded life. None of the others have time to take care of a complicated person like me. Moreover, I am in full possession of my senses and I have books yet to write and I need and must have independence, which I have here at Danby House.

Of course, taking into consideration Mr. Harris' unself-ish devotion to me and to my concerns, it embarrasses me beyond words to have you behave so rudely to him. I want you to know that I feel this very deeply. I have dis-cussed it with the other children, particularly with Jean and Janice and Henriette, and while they are concerned because it concerns me, they are pessimistic about your ever being able to do away with your prejudice or to hear anything except what you want to hear.

What to do about this unfortunate and foolish situation I really do not know. I only know that the doctors warn me that I am not to allow myself to be troubled. This is more easily said than done. You are my very dear son and it wounds me that you maintain an attitude of stub-born prejudice against a man you do not even know and yet who has done more for me personally than any other person whom I have ever known in my whole life. I only consider myself fortunate, *most* fortunate, that at this time in my life when I have a most complicated business, over one hundred publishers, and innumerable con-tracts and work yet to be done, that I must also be troubled and depressed by such awkward and even ab-surd prejudice on your part. It amazes me that a man of your ability and quality could harbor such a prejudice. Henriette and I have discussed it very freely and she is very pessimistic that you will ever allow yourself even to hear any good about Mr. Harris. I can only say that I will not tolerate rudeness to him in this house. He is a gentleman and he never complains but it embarrasses me that I have to tell him when you are coming in order that he may absent himself to avoid insult.

I have written to you frankly, my dear, because I think it is best to do so. If you are determined never to find out the truth about Mr. Harris, then I shall have to consider how to handle this. I remember how wounded I was that when you came to Philadelphia after the smut article on me in *The Philadelphia Magazine* came out, that you did not immediately come to me and ask for the truth. Instead you went to the evil people who made the attack. The man who led that attack is now in jail, as you know, for a minimum of three years. He is already ruined professionally and when he comes out, if he ever does, since he is desperately ill with diabetes, he will find it difficult to live. Even his wife and three children have left him.

That is all past history. Meanwhile, all investigations against Mr. Harris have cleared him absolutely. I have perfect confidence in him and he works closely with my own attorney, Gale Raphael, who admires him enormously. I wish that the new year could begin without this cloud and I will not give up hope.

My love to you both,
(signed) Mother
cc: Henriette Teusch
Jean Lippincott
Janice Walsh
Grace Yaukey

A very worried sister Grace attempted to ease the anguish over Edgar, sending him her own letter which pleads for his understanding and help. A cover letter to Miss Buck explains her letter to Edgar. Her own anguish shows through as she gently begs forgiveness for intruding....

Dear Pearl:

I am sending you a copy of a letter I have written to Edgar.... I have kept thinking of the anxiety in your voice when we talked the other day... If I need forgiveness for writing as I have, for perhaps intruding, won't you please forgive me on the basis of my stupidity or insensitivity? Or something.

I really wanted to send a copy of the letter to Mr. Harris, too, but decided it might be better for you to show yours to him, if you think it best. I do want him to know that I deeply appreciate all that he, and Mrs. Drake, are doing through your time of illness, and that I feel only deep gratitude.

Of course nothing may help the situation, but I would certainly love to do anything that might.

My love always,

(signed) Grace

And her letter to Edgar, dated January fourth:

Dear Edgar:

I hope I can make you understand my reasons for writing you when I have never done so before.

I am writing you as the only contemporary member of Pearl's family because I feel certain that you want to do all you can to help her recover.

I believe that it is urgent that she not be worried about anything that can possibly be spared her. But she is very worried about your feeling toward Mr. Harris, even though she knows it grows out of your loyalty to her and your love for her.

Your reasons for this feeling are clear to me, but after thinking it over carefully, I find I have to write you now, sending copies of this letter to her and to Jean. Since I do not have your address, I have to ask Jean to be so good as to mail the letter on to you from Dublin.

Recently, in reading over some of the letters your mother wrote me years ago, I was struck by her particular delight in you as a small child, repeatedly commenting on your unusual intelligence and in the promise in you that she felt. Now, it is sad and ironic that she should be caused any kind of worry and anxiety during her illness by an attitude that, for *whatever* reason, one would not have expected. For I feel that this is a time when we should *all* pull together to get your mother through this low point by our love and support. This kind of cooperation is not possible if there is any kind of hostility in the air.

So, Edgar, as your ancient aunt I am writing to beg you to accept the present situation in Danby with grace and understanding, aware of the many advantages in the arrangements, and willing to overlook the things you may not appreciate. This is surely not the time to judge, but the time to help in every way we can, for her sake. Of course I do not need to argue this point with you. Won't you help?

As ever....

* * *

One would think that *all* family members would cease and desist any attitude, (for *whatever* reason, as Grace so beautifully put it) which could possibly upset or worry Miss Buck. One would think that now at least Edgar would accept the present situation and give his mother the needed strength of a son's love and compassion. I could hardly believe it when, after the letters from his mother and his aunt, he sent another long involved message dated January eighth, again bringing up old wounds and continuing his harangue. This letter marked "Personal and Confidential"on the envelope, still trying to by-pass anyone who would open his mother's mail, unnecessarily upset and annoyed his mother. Miss Buck did not want to read this next letter from Edgar and instructed me to send the following to her attorney Gale Raphael:

Dear Mr. Raphael:

Miss Buck has requested that I send you the enclosed copy of a letter from her son, Edgar Walsh, and she has asked me to retain the original in our files here.

Miss Buck has also asked me to tell you that she has not seen the contents of this letter, nor does she wish to, and that the letter was purposely not given to her by me, as I was following the instructions of her daughter, Mrs. Jean Lippincott. She wants it clearly understood that I was following Mrs. Lippincott's specific instructions, and was not acting on my own or taking instructions from anyone else.

Sincerely,

(Mrs.) Beverly Drake

Secretary to Pearl S. Buck

The family - Edgar in particular - continued to be the cause of much worry and anguish but one by one, one by one, the building blocks continued to go into place. While she directed a great deal of energy towards trying to resolve the family misunderstandings, she simultaneously demanded personal consultations with Mr. Raphael, who came from Boston more than once during the month of January. He came armed with not only the statistical facts and figures she demanded, but also all the legal and personal assurances he could muster to convince her that her affairs were in order and that legally no one, either now or in the future, could upset or overturn what she had set in motion.

She had one last demand before she was satisfied that her legal documents were in order and as strong as she could make them to insure that her personal wishes were carried out. After this legal business was out of the way, she told me she could get back to the business of trying to regain her wobbly strength so that she could finish her unfinished books. She discussed with the attorney the possibility of having me, Colonel Drake, or both of us named as executors of her will in place of Mr. Raphael, who was already acting as both her attorney and accountant. I alone, without Ted, was present during most of these discussions and when my opinion was asked, I replied that I was ready to do whatever would strengthen Miss Buck's position in order that her wishes were carried out to the legal letter.

"Next to Mr. Harris," she said, "no one knows me better than Mrs. Drake. She knows what I want and I trust her implicitly to see that my every wish is carried out fully."

Those words seared my brain then and they sear it now as I repeat them. The complete trust and confidence that had built up between Miss Buck and me she was now going to rely on further to see that her will was obeyed. Did she expect trouble after she was gone? I can only assume she did, for no one could have worked more diligently to stave off trouble in whatever form it might appear. That uncommon invisible fellow called Destiny was sitting uncomfortably on my shoulder as Miss Buck probed me with her worried blue eyes. The legal expert Mr. Raphael reassured me once more. "Everything legally possible has been done to insure that Miss Buck's wishes will be carried out." He further said that the executor's job should be pretty cut and dried because all the documents were legally sound and it would be difficult to challenge them. The will states her wishes clearly and succinctly and she has provided a small inheritance for each of the adopted children, just as she wished. Bill and I were not connected in any way with her business in Danby or Philadelphia so there was no conflict of interest and we were not mentioned as beneficiaries. Ultimately it was decided by Miss Buck that having both my name and Bill's written in as co-executors would strengthen her cause. And that is how the papers were drawn up in a Codicil dated January 23, 1973 - the Codicil to her very carefully drawn up and unchanged Will dated April 9, 1971 (before I was employed by her). Everything in that last will remained exactly as she wanted it, with the Codicil naming the Drakes as executors.

Bill was wary of the involvement this might possibly necessitate, but we were both assured by Miss Buck and Mr. Raphael that everything was in legal order and there should be no problems whatsoever. With a bit of her old humor, she told us that there would be a bit of pin money in the job. Mr. Raphael estimated this to be maybe $1500, based on the current estimated worth of her estate at about $150,000. I certainly wasn't interested in any pin money, of remuneration of any kind, and I laugh bitterly now when I remember how I was later accused of conniving with Miss Buck to get my name on her will because I would gain millions. Years later a rumor reached me that Pearl Buck owned the Drake farm and we had only lived there as caretakers. An even uglier rumor reached me that Bill Drake and I had known Pearl Buck for as long as Ted Harris had known her, and we were all involved in a very sophisticated conspiracy to inherit her wealth. I won't dignify this ugliness with further comment.

How my name, and Bill Drake's name were put on Miss Buck's Will at her insistence I have decribed exactly as it happened. The Will is explicit, with the first four items leaving no doubt as to what she wanted:

"FIRST: I leave my engagement ring containing seven small diamonds to my daughter JEAN WALSH LIPPIN-COTT, and I leave all the rest of my jewelry to my associate THEODORE F. HARRIS, since all of the rest of my jewelry was given to me by him.

SECOND: I leave all the rest, residue and remainder of my property, whether real, personal or mixed, wherever located, to the Trustees of the Pearl S Buck 1971 Trust, created under indenture of April 9, 1971, for the uses and trusts declared in said trust.

THIRD: I do not leave anything to my children, JANICE, RICHARD, JOHN, EDGAR, HENRIETTE, CHIEKO OR CAROL, nor do I leave anything to THE PEARL S. BUCK FOUNDATION, INC., as my children and the Foundation have been provided for by other means.

FOURTH: In the event that any legatee under this will contests the validity of any transfer made by me during my life to any person, corporation, trustee or foundation, then such legatee shall not be entitled to any distribution from my estate."

The 1971 Trust, entered into between Miss Buck and Gale Raphael, involved income from domestic copyrights and royalties, which belonged to her during her lifetime. Upon her death, she stipulated that one-seventh of the net income of the trust, but not more than four thousand dollars annually shall be paid to each of the seven adopted children, Janice, Richard, John, Edgar, Jean, Henriette, and Chieko during their respective lives. Her only birth chid, Carol, in the institution in New Jersey, was provided for separately.

The Will, The Codicil, The Trust, all her legal papers prepared for the time when she would not be around to oversee her affairs, were clear, forthright, foolproof - or so she thought.

At the risk of interrupting the chronological events which were taking place, I must pause long enough to remind the reader that these legal affairs were being conducted because Miss Buck insisted. While her physical strength was failing in spite of her best efforts to get it back, her mind was as sharp and keen as ever. We still had great difficulty in hiding the undercurrents of business or family problems behind the scenes; she usually uncovered the most minute annoyance we tried to keep from her. So I must emphasize that all through January, as paper after paper was meticulously composed and signed by her, she was doing this because she demanded it so and not because, as it was later unjustly and falsely suggested by jealous and vindictive individuals, that she did these things under duress. Indeed, if there was any duress involved, we were the victims - mainly Ted Harris and me, the two people who were the closest to her then during that very active time of *her* letter writing and *her* legal maneuvering.

No one at any time could possibly ever coerce Pearl Sydenstricker Buck into doing anything she did not want to do for whatever reason. I can feel sorry now, though I felt fury then, for the insecure family members of Miss Buck's clan who ghoulishly circulated the preposterous abomination that 1) Pearl Buck was incompetent at the time she wrote all those poignant family letters and the Codicil to her Will and 2) that certain individuals, namely a fiendish Theodore F. Harris with a willing but naive secretary helping him, forced a rich old doddering soul on her last legs to sign documents against her will. I sense that my sorrow is in danger of turning to fury again, so I will return to the chronological thread of the story - the way it was. Tell it like it is. There will always be those who have sense enough to believe it and understand it, said Miss Buck, so I must continue....

The legal matters were put to rest and Miss Buck was satisfied that all was in order.

But the fretting and fussing about Edgar continued. The following long and agonizing letter, addressed to the whole family, was preceded, at her insistence, by a long conversation with Ted and me. She said she was tired of hearing and thinking about Edgar; it was agitating and bothering her unnecessarily, and interfering with her own creative work, hard enough to cope with because of her physical lack of stamina. She said she didn't know whether it would help or hurt to write her feelings to the family. Then she asked me directly what I thought. I replied that if, as she had so often stated, her displeasure with Edgar went back years to when he was a small boy and long before she met TFH, then perhaps the family should be told in her words. Others could describe how she felt but her own words would be strongest and most effective. We talked, perhaps two or three hours (more accurately I should say that she kept Ted and me in her presence bombarding us with ideas and opinions as to what she should do). When she asked Ted directly how to proceed, he said why didn't she dictate a letter to Mrs. Drake saying the things she had just said to us. She did, making at least two subsequent drafts, deleting a passage or two and adding several strengthening points. Even after the final draft she asked both Ted and me if the letter was forceful enough. There is no doubt that she valued our opinions and trusted our judgment. We offered both only when she asked for them. After her long letter was dispatched, again the ghoulish suggestions started to circulate by certain family members that Ted and I had coerced her into writing it or worse, we had written it ourselves and forced her to sign it. I have in front of me now the carbon copy of the final draft which she signed "Mother," as she did on all the other copies. This effort, this last arduously written letter to her family at large crackles with her spirit and determination. It is pure Pearl Buck:

January 24, 1973

To My Dear Family:

Somehow or other, I don't quite know how, an absurd situation has arisen with certain members of the family. This absurdity manifests itself at the moment in a feeling among some of you, and I don't quite know how many, that Theodore F. Harris, my Business Manager, has alienated me from my family. Nothing could be further from the truth and I should like to state the facts as I know them and as they present themselves to me.

This morning Mr. Harris has reported to me a conversation between him and Edgar, which Mr. Harris initiated. He called Edgar last night after I had retired and determined to do what he could to dispel the entirely false situation which is causing me distress at a time when I should not be asked to endure any stress whatsoever, by doctor's orders. This morning he had a conference call wtih Edgar and Jean in which he stated what I know to be truth, that he has no personal animosity whatsoever toward any of my family. Indeed, he has always respected and followed my permanent principle of total separation between business and family.

The present situation as regards Edgar, however, goes back many years, long before I met either Tad Danielewski or Mr. Theodore F. Harris, both of whom had and have a business relationship with me. It is quite true, as you all know, that I have always separated firmly and permanently my professional life and my family life. Let me say that no one has valued family life and does value it more than I have and do. I came to this country a stranger and to that extent I have not been fitted to be a good mother to my children. I grew up in another culture, not American. I never went to school until I came to the United States to go to college in a very secluded girls' college atmosphere. I returned to China immediately after graduation and began my adult life there, which ended abruptly in 1933, when the rise of Communism forced me to leave China. At that time my great professional success had already been proved. I had become famous overnight with the astonishing success of THE GOOD EARTH.

Certain changes, already inevitable, were now timely. I could provide for my retarded child, and I was the only one who could or would do so. My unsatisfactory first marriage could and did end amicably. I married again a man intellectually and emotionally congenial. We both loved children. Indeed, my children have been the love of my life. I could have no more by birth and I have always had the warmest, even the most tender, feelings toward those unknown women who gave me my children, not knowing what a gift they bestowed.

We made a very happy home at Green Hills. I had always the two lives running parallel to each other and my husband perfectly understood this and cooperated with me as I did with him. I have been most fortunate as a professional woman in being able to do my work at home. I could see my children off to school in the morning, taking pleasure in packing their lunches myself - even though I knew that probably they would trade their good homemade bread sandwiches with some other child who had baker's bread.

My children always went to private school. In our neighborhood the best private schools were Quaker schools.

The public schools were not yet established to be what they are today. The children had excellent teachers, to which each child responded. According to his or her abilities, each achieved or under-achieved. Since this letter deals chiefly with Edgar, I must say that my deepest concern and in some ways disappointments have been roused by his almost consistent under-achieving. Of him who has much, one expects much - perhaps too much. This talented and brilliant boy from the very first resisted, for reasons not known to me, and still not known to me, all opportunities available to him for excellence in performance.

I never stressed the importance of marks or grades but I did stress the importance of doing one's best. My husband perhaps did not help because he did not believe in homework or its importance. To this degree we were not helpful to our children. We spent the evenings in games, in reading aloud, in music, rather than in homework. For consequent lack of achievement I take the blame. I remember one day when Edgar was in the grades he came home with a ridiculously low mark in some subject. When I expressed surprise, not to say shock, knowing his intelligence, he said, " I thought you didn't care about grades!" Years later, when he was in prep school, he complained that he had no "motivation." This astonished me again for I myself have always been self-motivated. I have always had a great pride in myself. If there were a high mark to be had, I wanted it because I had faith in myself. I was always sure I could do it. That alone was my motivation. It was difficult for me, therefore, having realized to the full Edgar's enormous potential, to know what caused the years of consistent under-achievement. This has been the source of my disappointment and my not knowing what to do about it.

I have never forgotten the beautiful June morning at George school when we, the parents, went to Commencement, where our four younger children were to graduate from high school. Three graduated. The fourth one, Edgar, did not receive his diploma. When I asked Mr. McFeely, the excellent headmaster, why Edgar failed he said, "Great potential but consistent underachieving." When I asked why, he said, "Lack of self-discipline."

Thousands of dollars went into tutorial fees. I paid these faithfully. On his potential, Edgar was accepted at Harvard. I remember the day he called me up to tell me he had been accepted. He seemed happy and I thought "perhaps now he can find self-motivation." Harvard did not provide this, however. It was the same story. At the end of his junior year he was asked to withdraw for a year on the grounds that he had "slept his way through college." I felt that somehow I had been at fault or perhaps the failure was in the home. By this time the father was sinking into the long years of decline which none of us had foreseen. Indeed, we had planned, when the children had finished their education, to do the traveling we had denied ourselves through all the years. I should not say *denied,* for we loved every minute of the children's life with us.

I made mistakes, of course. Jean's hands, for example, were too small for piano lessons and I should not have insisted that she keep trying. Music has been such a joy in my life, however that I wanted the children at least to have a chance to know enough about it to enjoy it. The two older boys, it was soon obvious, had no wish for music. Edgar, always talented, had a real talent for music, I was told, but again it was under-achievement. He did not want to practice and he gave up lessons.

A year behind his class, he graduated from Harvard. Later, of his own accord, he wished to go to Harvard Business School but his record was not such as to gain him admittance. He did well in his military service, although he never went abroad. His work in the place where he was put was good and I had my first moment of real satisfaction in my son's great natural intelligence. Later I rejoiced in his marriage. His wife is a charming woman and a lady born and bred. Her family has been excellent for Edgar and I am eternally grateful for the way they have welcomed him. It warms my heart that they truly like him. He found his own first job in banking, and so far as I know he had a successful career there for a few years. It ended because he said he felt he had learned what he needed to know about the handling of money and financial affairs. His real interest - at that time, at least - was in motion pictures and quite by chance I was able to be of use in finding him an opportunity to work abroad in that field for some years. He was promoted and finally left of his own accord and, he said, for his own reasons.

I do not need to continue this record. It will be seen that it centers chiefly about Edgar. This does not mean I have not been equally concerned with the other children's lives. I have indeed. John has been through great troubles. I have known about them, I have helped as I could, I have sympathized even when I could not approve, knowing what he was suffering. Richard ended his military service abroad, returned, and made a second effort to go to college, which was unsuccessful. He is now married, he is an excellent citizen, a good husband, and a wonderful father to his two children. John is married again and I consider both of these sons successful within their area.

I could not now be concerned about Edgar except in some ridiculous fashion he has become entangled rather than involved in my professional life. There seems to have arisen an animosity on his part, at least according to other members of my family, against my business associate and manager, Theodore F. Harris. Mr. Harris has no animosity toward any of my children, nor indeed, any relationship to my family life. I repeat, I have steadfastly maintained the distance between my business life and family life. I am a professional woman and a successful one. I am the head of an enormous business. I have one hundred publishers in ninety countries. I employ a staff of some twenty to twenty-five persons, among them three secretaries, a bookkeeper, an attorney and others who carry on my business, under my final direction and supervision, with Mr. Harris as my very efficient executive.

It became evident to me some ten years ago that I could not continue my writing, which I have every intention of doing, and at the same time manage this huge business organization. When I returned from India, where I had been working on a film with Tad Danielewski, I realized I must find someone, a young man trained and successful in business, to help. Quite by accident, I found this man in a most unlikely place, the Arthur Murray Studio in Jenkintown, Pennsylvania. I had taken the four girls then living with me, two of them adopted daughters and the other two my wards, for dancing lessons. I went with them, since I love dancing, and I had not indulged in this pastime for a number of years. The young man who was in charge of our dance programs was Theodore F. Harris. I will not go into his personal history here, as that is no concern of my family, except to say that his real talents lie in the field of business management. At the time I met him he had had, for a number of years, his own group who went to studios which were failing, made a thorough examination of their management and brought them back to a sound and profitable business. They worked with many well-known studios - Xavier Cugat, Fred Astaire, Patricia Stevens, Arthur Murray, etc. When I discovered what he was really doing in the Jenkintown studio, which had indeed nearly gone into bankruptcy and from which position he had brought it back to prosperity, I told myself that this was the man for whom I was looking.

He began with the Foundation which I wished to establish. This story has already been told and I need not repeat it here. After a period of consideration, he decided he had long wished to devote himself to a worthwhile cause. He made it clear to me that he would not take the job for any personal reasons since people, as he put it, "are always temporary." Upon this basis, he set up the Foundation. I need not go into all that this entailed but it entailed Business with a capital B. There were the matters of property, legal problems, banking matters, fundraising, building a staff - which staff is still there, I might say - and the setting up of foreign offices. All of this Mr. Harris did in an incredibly short time. The Foundation stands and will always stand as a monument to his efficiency and integrity.

When the Foundation suffered under unjust, untrue and false attack, centering upon me but using him as an excuse, he resigned. The Board accepted his resignation under the circumstances, but I had no intention of losing this man's great talent for business organization. I asked him, therefore, to remain with me and to take charge of my professional and business corporations. This he has done with the utmost integrity and efficiency.

It is not necessary for me to go into more detail concerning my business life. I love and enjoy my children and my grandchildren but they are independent of me and I am independent of them. This is as I wish it and this will continue. Suitable provisions have been made in all ways for my wishes to be followed after my death.

I want to say here quite firmly and clearly that it has never been and it is not now my intention to live with any of my children. I will visit my family home. It delights me to have Jean and her family enjoying the life there and I shall always maintain my room and offices there but I shall never live there permanently. I like the mountain air of Vermont, I feel well here, I am near one of the finest medical centers in the world, I have medical attention within fifteen minutes of Danby House and a trained nurse always available only minutes away. I have a devoted staff who give me all the independence and privacy I wish but are at my beck and call when I need them. Mr. Harris has maintained the position I wish him to have, that of my chief business executive in charge of the staff and my business affairs.

In my personal life, needless to say, I am completely independent. I have my own rooms. Whatever I want I have available. At the same time I have complete freedom to be alone and to continue my work. This is as I wish it, since, as I have said, I have always maintained a clear division between family and business. Should anyone accuse Mr. Harris of being responsible for feelings of alienation between me and any members of my family, I can only say I am not aware of any such alienation. If the children feel alienation, I do not understand it and it springs from their own imaginations and misinformation. My concern about Edgar, as with my other children, goes back a long way and has nothing whatever to do with Mr. Harris. I do not remember Mr. Harris ever discussing any of the children with me. The two areas have nothing to do with each other. Children are family. He is business. Although the two are completely separate and have always been, today it is natural that I am more professional woman than I am the mother or even grandmother. It would be impossible for me to live with any of my family, children or sister, dearly as I love them all, because I would be too much for any of them. When I was in the hospital, for example, over 10,000 fan letters were received. These had to be acknowledged somehow. The Book Club, Mr. Harris's creation, has thousands of members now, the number constantly increasing. It is set up as a separate corporation, among others. It has a separate staff under the general management of Mr. Harris, as do all of the corporations. Hundreds of telephone calls, contracts to be studied and signed or rejected, constant reports demanded by the press - all these and many other activities would make it impossible for me to live with anyone at all. As Mr. Harris has put it, I am not merely a person but an institution and his function is its efficient manager. My books are much more widely read now than they were ten years ago when it was said by my stepson that I had a "slowly dying audience." Today I am the most widely

translated author in the history of American literature.
That my work thrives is thanks to Mr. Harris's good efforts. The idea that any of my children could do what he
is doing is absurd. None of them is experienced enough
or fitted by disposition to undertake this management.
I would not welcome it nor indeed allow it, for I maintain more firmly than ever the total separation between
family and business. I do not think any of us could function under any other circumstances. Mr. Harris has
never taken any interest in the family, to tell the truth,
and has neither helped nor hindered the relationships I
may have with the family. During my illness he felt he
had to let the family know what was happening and he
did not wish to assume entire responsibility for major
decisions. Being what I am, I made all major decisions
and the family was informed through Jean and Janice.

I might add here that it is a great relief to me that Janice
and Jean have taken over the responsibility of my
retarded child, Carol. Janice is in charge, in the main,
and has taken my place on the Board of the institution.
This pleases me very much.

As to the nonsense that any of my staff has made efforts
to separate my family from me, I can only say that this
is sheer absurdity. Their concern is with the business
and this more than occupies their time. While I was in
Burlington Mr. Harris and Mrs. Drake simply moved the
main office to the hospital which kindly granted them a
room and Mr. Harris was able to be present when his
presence was necessary. Fortunately he had provided
amply for medical insurance, one of his wise business
decisions made immediately when he found how little insurance I had, and I have been so amply covered that I
can only be grateful. But this has been part of his duty,

of course. He has been entirely correct in his behavior toward the family. He has never in any way sought to divide me from the family, nor from anyone else I wished to see. Indeed, I am sure he would consider it presumptuous and absurd. If, as my sister has reminded me, there are always natural jealousies within a family, then perhaps these have operated in ways of which I am unaware. Mr. Harris has certainly had nothing to do with them and I doubt he knows anything about them.

One more point: my staff cannot assume responsibility for relaying to me, or not relaying to me, family problems sent by letter or telephone or visits, this in view of doctors' instructions to spare me when possible. Example: it was not the staff's responsibility to decide whether Edgar's recent letter should be shown to me. The secretary, therefore, called Jean for advice and Jean took full responsibility for deciding against showing it to me. The letter therefore was simply put on file. I happen to have heard of it only through Henriette.

In summary, let me say that I am quite happy with my two worlds. I love my family. I delight in my grandchildren, I am interested in every one, of course, I am proud to be your mother. I am happy that the family home is being continued under Jean and Joe and houses not only their children but also two Foundation children. From that house and from Jean and Joe's care, there has begun the happy marriage of Karl, our half-Japanese, half-American boy, and a lovely American girl. They have their own apartment now and are beginning their own life. Two other Foundation children are still in the house and, in the office once used by Mrs. Shaddinger, the Adoption Department of the Foundation now functions. This unusual combination of family and

Foundation brings me satisfaction.

I am equally pleased with the strong consolidation of my business affairs. Personally I have never been in as good shape, business-wise, as I am now under Mr. Harris's most efficient management. He has been in constant consultation with my attorneys, accountants and tax experts throughout the years of our association and he works very closely with Mr. Raphael today and always.

Mr. Harris has never in any way said anything to me about the family side of my life, and certainly he has never sought to keep me from seeing any member of my family. It would not interest him to do so, and he would consider it beneath him. I consider it an insult, not only to him, but to me that any child of mine could suspect any of my staff of such an act. In this case, it not only insults Mr. Harris's integrity but it insults my intelligence, and I do not take such insults lightly. I want to hear no more of it from *any* of you.

Now I have said my say. Come to see me if you like and stay away if you like. You are each and all as free and independent as I am!

Love as ever, and forever,

(signed) Mother

P.S. A chatty (female) member of our family informs me that on the day of distress at the Foundation, you, Edgar, did try many times to get me by telephone and were unable to reach me. I am sure this is true. People all over the United States were trying to reach me and so were our foreign office staffs in other countries. The switchboard, therefore, had been told to put no calls through. The simplest thing would have been for you to do in the morning what you did at night, which was to ring the doorbell. I was there alone all day with the junior staff, faithful souls who are with us still and carry on their daily work at the Foundation. But we may now all relegate this to the past. P.S.B.

What this letter cost her in terms of physical discomfort and mental anguish can only be known by Ted Harris and me. The will to win - the will to convince her family that she was doing what she wanted to do and how she wanted to do it and they must understand - this will was very much with her at this point. I believe that she thought her carefully composed letter would once and for all halt any and all family misconceptions and misunderstandings about her life. Convincing the family about herself was the final stumbling block she had to eliminate so she could feel at ease that her life now and whatever lay beyond was in order. It is nothing short of tragic that her eldest adopted son could not or would not accept what she had to say - what she so desperately now wanted her family to comprehend. Edgar persisted with more written messages marked "Personal" which she was never shown.

I doubt that any reader at this juncture in the story could be unaware that Miss Buck was not getting better in terms of her illness - she was getting worse. Edgar, along with all of the adopted children, had been kept informed of her condition.

After that last long letter which was an all-out effort on her part, she fought no more, she tried no more to turn around anybody or anything. She was now fighting for her life. It was now that she handed over her velvet sledgehammer to me as surely as if it had been an inheritance written into her will.

Chapter 38

The Red Earth

Once the lengthy legal discussions were over and the rash of family letters relegated to finished business, Ted and I braced for what we knew was coming. Dr. Davis' grim report of the examination on January 15th had not been broached while important business was being conducted. But early in February Miss Buck lowered the boom with a vengeance. Her physical condition showed a steady decline. She went through an uncharacteristic period of silence and solitude, dismissing both Ted and me with "leave me alone for a while." During this time we were worried but did not intrude. Finally came the hour when she very formally asked me to get Mr. Harris immediately. "I want to speak to him alone," she announced, "and then I shall speak to both of you together." She didn't just speak to us - she poured out her heart to us and there was nothing we could do but stand by and listen helplessly. "I'm dying," she said, "I'm dying and you lied to me. You knew, you knew all along; you knew I was dying. I'm dying, and there's nothing I can do about it."

There is no way at all to soften the blow, to mitigate the anguish of such a declaration. Pearl Buck had been sparring with Death for quite a while now. She knew it; we knew it. We hadn't lied to her; we never lied to her; we just hadn't told her the extent of that last examination. And she wasn't angry at us or disappointed in us. She was angry at Death, angry because she now wouldn't have time to complete THE RED EARTH and THE GENIUS BOOK, angry because she wouldn't see the completion of Danby House. She was angry because time was running out and she still wasn't ready for that final journey.

"I'm still not ready to get into my waiting coffin or try on my waiting shroud," she said, refuting what was happening to her. She talked to Death as some big mean person dragging away a small protesting child. Indeed, as Ted and I watched her and listened to her with aching hearts, she became a helpless child pitting her last strength against a giant. She had no hope of winning. Her last visit to Burlington had revealed another tumor, probably more than one starting to grow in other locations. This meant the cancer was spreading, had already spread and there would be no containing it.

"I would like to live to see my next birthday in June, when the flowers are so beautiful," she announced. And in the days that followed Ted asked me not once but dozens of times whether I thought Miss Buck would be able to celebrate another birthday. It became the ultimate goal to reach and sustained us more than once when things seemed at a grotesque standstill - not moving forward, not going backward.

Work on the addition to Danby House had stopped, mainly because first one thing and then another began to bother her. First it was the smell of the kerosene heater the workmen used to ward off the cold; then it was the unbearable sound of their tools. Even a small hammer or drill annoyed her. Music was still a pleasure, but there were times when any noise was too much. The few starting pages of THE RED EARTH remained always nearby. She talked about the story often enough and, talking about the actual manuscript of this book and others in progress, demanded that I "watch over them, keep them safe from harm," was the curious way she put it. "All of my possessions, of course, belong to Mr. Harris, but you must help him all you can. If things should become too much for him, help him - help me. Take the manuscripts and those personal papers I would not wish to fall into the wrong hands..." What wrong hands? When? And why was she talking this way? I promised, of course. The handwritten manuscript of THE RED EARTH lays before me now, and it seems more than appropriate to drop it into the context of those last difficult weeks. It begins so simply, as many of her stories do, but do not be misled by the simplicity of the surface story. The peasant hero in THE RED EARTH is waging a one-man battle, and his story is designed to illustrate what one determined human being can accomplish if he set his mind to it. How the Communists took over the giant China would have been a later part of the book, with one man still combatting great odds - what a difference one human being can make in the world. Be not deceived by the simple man Liu Sheng. Be not deceived by the simple woman Pearl Buck. They are one and the same and they are not simple.

THE RED EARTH

by Pearl S. Buck

Liu Sheng leaned on his hoe and stared up at the sky. The hoe had a long handle. He had made it himself from a wooden carrying pole. Until he had thought of making a long handle for his hoe, he had bent his back over a short handle as his ancestors had done for many centuries. Then one day, straightening his aching back, he had muttered to the earth and the sky, "Why should I bend my back year after year because of my short-handled hoe? From now on I will use a long handle."

His neighbors, all peasants like himself, had been amazed when they saw the long-handled hoe. They had laughed and taunted him.

"You!" they had cried. "You are too good for your ancestors! Who ever saw a man stand straight to hoe his land? The soil will be too shallow for the seed to sprout."

"Harvest will tell!" he had shouted back.

The harvest that year, however, told nothing. There had been no harvest. In this endless high plain of north China the soil was dry as dust. As dust it was swept by the winds of Mongolia all winter, on air so dry that in spite of bitter cold there was little snow, though as every peasant knows, a snow is better than any fertilizer, especially if it falls on spring wheat. And rain, when it came as it did in summer, it came in torrents, drenching the fields into gullies and flattening the growing wheatfields. Wild rain it was, and the Yellow River rose high as it plunged eastward to the sea. When it receded again, it left piles, even hills, of silt, raising the riverbed many feet above the fields. Thus Liu Sheng lived in a continual state of anger against Heaven and Earth.

"How can man live, between these two?" he shouted often to his wife.

"As we have always lived," she always said.

She was a strong young woman, as strong as Liu Sheng himself, and she worked in the fields at his side. When, therefore, the strangers came to the village of Ta Chen, and calling the villagers together, they preached to them of a new time which they called "liberation," Leu San-Tse Liu Sheng's strong wife, was the first to listen and believe what they said. It is true, she did not believe at once, for she had heard foreign preaching before. In their distant village, far from Peking, and in the bitter lands of Shansi Province, there had often been other preachers. They, however, were from foreign lands, especially America, and they preached of strange gods. One foreigner even brought strange medicines. The people of the village were not interested in the new gods but the medicines were often good, after they took courage to try them. Indeed, when the foreign doctor came with his medicines they learned at last to welcome him, though he spoke their language as a child does, with few words and little understanding and many signs.

"What is your country?" Liu Sheng's father had asked long ago when the foreigner first came to their village of Ta Chen and Liu Sheng himself was only a small boy.

"I come from America," the foreigner said. "I am a doctor."

"Why did you leave your country?" Liu Sheng's father had asked next.

The foreign doctor had smiled, a strange, somewhat sad smile. He was at that moment examining a blind child's crusted eyes.

"Perhaps," the doctor said. "I may say that I had a mandate from Heaven.... Ah, it is too late for this poor little one! Yes, I had a mandate from Heaven."

He had sighed and put a soothing ointment on the child's eyelids. "I should have come earlier," he murmured. "Well, there are always others - many others."

He came so often then through the years that the people of the village grew accustomed to his coming and going. He rode a donkey and stayed at the village inn, eating the food it served, noodles of wheat or buckwheat flour, and garlic stir-fried with vegetables. The soil was poor and vegetables scanty except for turnips, sweet potatoes and cabbage. He carried his medicines in an old black leather bag strapped to the high back of the Chinese saddle and only he knew what they were. There was magic in them, nevertheless, and as the years passed, the villagers learned to trust him.

Thus year passed into year in the village of Ta Chen. The times were not good in the outer world. The villagers heard of the death of the old Empress in Peking but they were indifferent. Peking was far away and the less they heard of rulers the better, since rulers always meant taxes. Landlords were worst of all, for they were nearer and at least once a year the Kung family which for generations had owned the lands about Ta Chen sent their men to watch the weighing of the grain when it was harvested, this grain being chiefly barley, wheat millet, corn and a kind of sorghum. The province was too far north for the growing of rice. Many villagers never tasted rice, unless at a wedding feast, when it was imported from one or another province from the south, or perhaps only from the grain markets in the city of Taiyuan, the capital of the province. Neither Liu Sheng nor any of his family had ever been in that great city, nor indeed had anyone in the village except the aging school teacher, Mr. Chang, who had in his youth gone up for the Imperial Examinations and, having failed, became the village school teacher. He was a distant relative of the Kung family who were the landowners, but so distant that they gave him no sustenance except a few bushels of grain at harvest time. Except for this, Teacher Chang was entirely dependent upon the small amounts of cash which the families in the village gave him if such a family had a son who seemed too clever for the land.

There were a few such lads in Ta Chen and the brightest of them was Liu Sheng's son, the eldest of his four sons. His two daughters need not be mentioned. They were born after the four sons and they took care of the house, washed the grain and vegetables for the two meals a day, and fed the pig and the four hens. Like most village girls nowadays their feet were not bound, even though it was before Liberation. Liu San-Tse's feet had been partly bound, but her mother died when she was still a child and after that no one bothered to bind the child's feet.

The villagers lived in peace, although the people there heard of many wars and troubles in the world beyond. Such wars and troubles they took for granted, however, since the province itself was in a perilous place, and the elders often told the younger ones, on summer evenings when folk gathered on Liu Sheng's threshing floor because it was the largest in the village.

Thus all villagers heard their own history. Even the children were quiet when the elders told of the past.

"Our province," they said, "is the head of this great empire of The Middle Kingdom. We protect our mighty people against the enemies of the North. When they attack, as they did during the time of the warring kingdoms, we remain firm. Again and again we remain firm. We have our own gods, the Buddhas in our temple yonder. We have our own mines - we have iron and we have coal. Our lands yield us food, the Yellow River brings us water. True, its floods are evil. It wanders where it will. This river is at once our blessing and our curse."

Thus the elders taught the people, generation after generation, for hundreds of years. Of what happened beyond they heard little and knew nothing. At the turn of the century when Liu Sheng was a small child, some great evil occurred. This the villagers knew, for no more white men came to preach of their gods. Only one white man came. It was the foreign doctor and he came to find refuge.

"Hide me," he had gasped. "The old Empress has ordered all of us killed. Only I am left. I escaped, only I. Let me live here in secret. If it is known that I am here? Ah - I will not put your lives in danger, too! Let me die!"

The villagers were aghast at the sight of him. His donkey was staggering under him. He had not eaten or slept. Liu Sheng at this time, though young, knew the doctor was a good man, foreign though he was, and his father took the foreigner and hid him. Yet he could not save him. The man could not eat or sleep. He was speechless or if he spoke, it was to tell of the horrors he had seen - the white men, the white women and their children, cut into pieces and their bodies thrown to the wild dogs by the Chinese Boxers.

"They, my friends, who came here to save, to teach, to heal, cut into pieces. I tell you! Oh the children! Had we the right to let children be born here? They should have been born safely in our own land! How dared we have children?"

The villagers had listened awed and silent, not knowing what had happened, not daring to ask. No one told beyond his own door that the foreigner was in their village, hiding day and night in Liu Sheng's father's fuel room, among the bundles of grass cut for the kitchen stove.

It was not for long, however. One morning in early autumn, the air already chill with the north wind, Liu Sheng went in with food and found the foreign doctor dead. Child though he was, he was sad and he ran back to tell his father.

"The white man, the foreigner, will not wake! He is dead, he is dead!"

Every member of the family went to see, and it was true. The foreigner lay peacefully and forever still upon the bed. It was scarcely even a bed. It was only an old quilt laid upon bundles of grass. But there he lay, his pale mouth ajar, his faded eyes half closed, and his scanty reddish-white hair awry.

What to do with him then had been a question not to be answered by one man or even one family. Liu Sheng's father had been one of the village elders and must call together the other elders.

"Do not touch him and tell no one," Liu commanded his own household who had gathered about to stare at the dead white man. Leave him to me."

The family had obeyed him and after pondering a day and a night, Liu Sheng's father, then a strong man in his prime and a silent man, decided after pondering for a day and half the night, that he would tell no one, neither family nor neighbor. Instead, in the darkness of midnight he had dug a hole under a date tree on the south side of the northen wall that surrounded his house and there he buried the white man. Liu Sheng had been asleep on his pallet bed in the room where his younger brother slept, and he was waked by the howling of the dog. It was not a loud howling but a whine, even a moaning, and rising half asleep he had crept to the small window in the earthen wall and in the dim light of a waning moon, he saw his father in the dusty earth, digging, digging - and when he had dug, he saw his father lift the dead body wrapped in the old quilt and lay it into the hole and cover it with earth and flatten the earth with his spade and cover the earth with weedy sod he had peeled off and laid to one side, the dog watching and whining until his father struck him silent with the spade.

When this was done, Liu Sheng made haste to crawl into his bed again and cover himself head and all until at last he slept.

When at dawn his father woke him to take the yellow sow out to graze on the high bank of the river, he asked no question of his father, nor did anyone in the family ever ask such a question. Simply, the white man was gone. If any knew, no one spoke of it, and Liu Sheng went on about his days, working, eating, sleeping, to rise and repeat such days until his father and his mother decided what young woman he should marry. It must be a young woman from another village, since a man cannot marry a woman of his own surname. Thus he was married when he was seventeen years old, a small wedding for it was a year of evil from the river. The winter snows had been heavy in the far away mountains, the river had spread itself and left fields covered with muddy silt.

As if this were not evil enough, a sickness had come with the flood and both his father and mother had died. Liu Sheng gave them decent burial on high land and then, with only his younger brother left, he and his young wife whom he called not even by name, but only "You!" when he was hungry or thirsty, he took his father's place in the village. And not one in the village knew that a white man's bones lay buried at the foot of the crooked date tree - not one except Liu Sheng himself.

In the years that passed, years of war and disturbances but always far off, the country without a ruler, and invaded, so Liu Sheng heard, by Eastern Sea always, and then by white men, Liu Sheng would think to himself of the white doctor lying among the roots of the date tree. He would wonder whether in some far country a family mourned this man and puzzled to know why he never came home again or if he were dead, was he buried somewhere or had he been eaten by dogs as many white people were when they were left where they were killed and no one buried them.

Such questions; if they were asked, could never be answered and Liu Sheng kept to himself what he had seen that night of the waning moon. He told no one, not even his wife after he was married to her.

....In what way is Liu Sheng's life different from that of millions of other men? When he looked back over the years, it seemed that his life was like that of all others until the day when he thought of making the long handle to his hoe. At that moment it occurred to him that something new could happen to a man out of himself, with no help from a god or even from another man. For this was what happened to Liu Sheng. When he hoed his field now it was not with his back bent. Instead he stood and his hoe rose and fell....

Chapter 39

The Music Episode

The bad days were beginning to outnumber the good days, and it was becoming increasingly difficult to schedule anything more than a few hours in advance. All activities - even phone calls and reading through the mail - hinged on how Miss Buck was feeling, how strong she seemed to be. Ted and I had long ago become super-sensitive to her slightest sign of distress or fatigue. We consulted constantly on how much or how little activity, both mental and physical, she seemed capable of. In keeping with her own insistent wishes, we tried to organize each day's routine to be as "normal" as possible. This became an impossible task. And all the while we were trying desperately to mask our own mounting worries and fears about her declining condition.

It didn't make matters any easier that we were still smarting from her recent sharp rebukes the day she lashed out at us for hiding the whole truth, what the doctors had been telling us, about her illness. What we had been doing for as long as possible was to protect her from the final irreversible truth. We were futilely trying to buy time for her at a terrible emotional price - our emotions as well as hers. The final truth was, of course, her impending death - the final unwritten page which none of us wanted to consider or discuss until we had no choice. She had been struggling all along to accept the awful reality of what was happening to her. She would not, could not, give in until her tremendous spirit finally crumbled and failed her. She knew that we knew and we knew that she knew. It was all a desperate game and we three were playing out our moves as best we could. When the old rules didn't work, we discarded them and made up new rules on the spot, bravely keeping the game going until it was time for the next inevitable change.

We shuffled and reshuffled each day's activities, rearranging and discarding as a dealer manipulates a deck of cards. Only we knew we had been gambling now for a long time and luck was running against us.

I have described several times before the blue intensity of Pearl Buck's eyes and how we relied on them as a remarkably accurate window to her inner emotions and physical condition. What I am going to state now sounds crazy and impossible, I know, but the bright blue eyes suddenly and without warning turned gray. The pigment actually changed color. Ted and I, thinking our own tired eyes were playing tricks on us, independently consulted with the doctors, who listened sympathetically and accepted our blue-to-gray description. While they did not think we were crazy, they could offer no positive reasons for the color change which was so obvious to those of us who were with her and observed her constantly.

Once we noticed the startling gray, the bright blue eyes we had known never again returned. For brief and infrequent periods, Miss Buck's eyes went from gray to a pale blue, a blue that seemed merely a faint and pathetic imitation of the brilliance that once was. I relate this strange phenomenon with no further explanation, for I cannot explain it further. I only know that the bright blue eyes disappeared and we were left with the new problem now of trying to decipher what was going on behind the alarming gray and the pale blue.

The pale blue seemed to appear, or so we thought, on her good days. And so it was on one of those pale blue good days that we decided to go ahead with an appointment that had been scheduled and canceled twice before. The appointment was for a young pianist to come to Danby House to play for Miss Buck. Marlee was the young girl I had mentioned to Miss Buck last summer, when I had heard her perform brilliantly in Rutland. Shortly after that Marlee's teacher, whom I knew through association in a national artists' organization, had contacted me to inquire whether or not I thought Miss Buck might enjoy having Marlee give a personal program for her in the privacy of her home. Marlee was leaving the area soon to pursue her own career as an aspiring concert pianist, and it was thought that performing for such a musically knowledgeable and famous person as Miss Buck would be an enjoyable, worthwhile experience for the young musician. I was enthusiastic and so was Miss Buck right from the beginning. But after two cancellations, I was doubtful that the anticipated musical program could ever take place.

However, the pale blue eyes prevailed on a February day in 1973 and Marlee arrived as scheduled in mid-morning. Ted and Miss Buck sat in their accustomed places in the gold velvet chairs chatting amiably with the young visitor. Observing this pleasant and familiar scene, I almost forgot for a moment the bittersweet seriousness of the whole situation. I doubt that a stranger, observing Miss Buck's lovely and calm appearance would have been aware that she was so very ill. Her bright exterior hid the truth, I believe, from all but the most practiced eyes.

As Marlee moved to the grand piano on the far side of the room in back of the gold chairs, Ted's eyes caught mine and I saw his ever-present concern and worry. But so far so good, I thought. Miss Buck was smiling, sitting comfortably it appeared, and apparently looking forward to hearing some Beethoven and Chopin - her choice of composers.

I sat down at the very end of the long sofa facing Miss Buck and Ted and took a quiet deep breath. I returned Ted's steady glance - there was that look of worry again, and I smiled my best "everything's going to be all right" smile.

Marlee opened her program with something light and lively by Beethoven. I relaxed a little and concentrated on the music - familiar to me from a far-away time and place, for it took me back to my own girlhood when I had spent many hours practicing one or another Beethoven sonata.

Sneaking a look at Miss Buck, I wondered what thoughts she was thinking. I saw that her hands were folded quietly in her lap, but one finger was beating time to the music. Her head was to one side and her eyes were down. Or maybe they were closed - I could not tell. At any rate, she seemed comfortably settled and at ease. A silent signal of relief passed between Ted and me. Always prepared for the worst, I breathed a little easier as I realized that Miss Buck was relaxed and enjoying hereslf. It seemed that the music was turning out to be a good idea.

The Beethoven ended and after some appreciative comments by Miss Buck, Marlee swept into the undulating and sensuous strains of a Chopin Nocturne, one that I knew well and loved to play myself.

I was unprepared for what happened next. Listening to the flowing, achingly beautiful melody, I was horrified to discover that tears from nowhere had filled my eyes, in fact were blinding me and actually spilling down my cheeks. I took a very deep breath and fought for control. Pretty adept at hiding my emotions under any circumstances, I hoped desperately now that she of all people would not see how the music was dissolving me inside. My being upset would risk getting her upset and through a blur of tears I tried to blink away, I was relieved to see that Miss Buck was still calm and quiet - apparently unaware of my little turmoil. But Ted? He was observing me intently with a worry that was almost an anger; when I met his direct gaze, I saw my own emotion mirrored in his dark and troubled eyes. Would I let him down? his eyes seemed to be saying. Would I let Miss Buck down? What was happening to me? I must remain calm. I must. I must.

It certainly didn't help to realize that the same intense emotions sweeping over me seemed to have affected Ted much the same way. Chopin was just too much to cope with under these strained touch-and-go circumstances. Although I didn't see actual tears in Ted's eyes, I saw my own scattered fragments of fear and fatigue and frustration of the past agonizing weeks and months.

Ted continued to watch me worriedly, wondering of course whether I would succeed in controlling and turning around the forces which had caught me unaware. I drew on the strong and silent rapport that had existed so long between us - the rapport which meant "we must carry on for her no matter what." Slowly the tears subsided and I knew that the bad moment had passed. The music ended, and once again I turned my whole attention back to Miss Buck. She appeared unaware of my momentary loss of control. She had enjoyed the music very much, she announced, but admitted she was now a little tired.

411

Taking this cue quickly, I rose to see if Dolphus had coffee ready to bring in along with the pound cake I had made at home the night before. I thought of what Dr. Cross had said on his last visit to Danby House. One of the reasons why so many terminally ill patients die in a hospital is because the family cannot stand the constant strain - the unexpected ups and downs and the emergencies that occur in endless cycles. Miss Buck wanted to stay at Danby House. It was up to Ted and me to stay strong enough to see her through the bad times as well as the good.

Marlee was one of the very few visitors Miss Buck was well enough to have in February. When she left, I do not think she knew how fatigued Miss Buck had become toward the end of her visit. Supreme actress that she was, Miss Buck had sustained another of her memorable performances. We knew that the show would go on for as long as she could endure the terrible effort. We dreaded the up-coming visits by members of her family, for our efforts to protect her from exhausting conversation and physical activity would, we knew, be brushed aside as unnecessary. They would not know - they would not see - they would not understand - but worst of all, they would not trust us. We would be left, as always, to carry out her wishes no matter what others said or thought.

Marlee left and as Ted and I helped Miss Buck upstairs - practically carrying her, she all but collapsed in our arms. She smiled wanly at us as we eased her into bed. No words were spoken. No words were needed. Her eyes were no longer pale blue now. They were gray.

Chapter 40

"Dearest Edgar"

The day-to-day agonies of a dying cancer patient are not pretty - not pretty at all - and setting down a journal of such agonies is neither fitting nor proper, if I am to follow what Miss Buck would have wanted; which is what I have been trying to to do from the beginning of this story. I know Miss Buck would consider it undignified for me to tell readers of her final suffering, except as it is necessary to further reveal what she considered her strengths, not her weaknesses. I know she would want me to gloss over most of the weaknesses now, as she did then. "Tell them," I can hear her pleading, "that I wanted to appear strong, invincible, unwilling to give in, even to Death." All right, I answer her now, as I did then, though it may be impossible to convince anyone, especially your family, that this is what you wanted for yourself and this is what provided the most consolation as you lay dying. All right, I repeat, she wants me to tell you of her strengths, not her weaknesses, so I shall continue. At least I can take comfort that in truth, there is dignity.

In my personal files I find a synopsis of the last month with Miss Buck. I offer it here as a brief and factual framework for the emotional details which follow:

The last four weeks of Miss Buck's life were difficult ones; she went downhill swiftly and the nature of her illness evidenced itself in different things at different times. Often she was physically weak to the point of not being able to stand unsupported. Edgar, Linda and Janice came up on a Sunday morning a week before she died and Miss Buck met with them in the sitting room - a tremendous effort during which time Ann Halligan (Nurse) and I were both present. Because they stayed on and on, Ann and I both had to quietly but firmly insist that they please leave. They were unaware that their mother was fatigued beyond all reason but would not give up while they were in her presence. The next few days were an agony of trying simply to keep the patient clean and as comfortable as we could. Jean remained the go-between with Danby House and the rest of the family. She said she would handle any problems in the family, for I had my hands full. Sister Grace, her husband and children visited and were quiet, sympathetic and understanding, and made their visits brief and said they would do whatever we thought best and whatever the doctors wanted. They were completely cooperative at all times. Grace offered assistance constantly, finally coming up to Danby and staying toward the end so she could be available if she could be of help. She stayed two nights at our farm, as did Jean, on different occasions. She was not in Danby when Miss Buck died, but Jean and Janice were. How the rest of the family was kept informed during the last few days was left up to Jean.

Facts, truth, but little emotion. I wish l could leave the story here and say it's done, over, farewell. I cannot do that, for the final beautiful essence of Pearl Buck remained behind the scenes. During those last few weeks, indeed, those last few days, she wrote her own synopsis, and it was packed with emotion and strength.

It is perhaps fitting, though sad, that her last dictated letter was to Edgar, the adopted son who had caused her so much vexation in past months. It is to me an incredible measure of her strengths and the depths of her love that this last letter mentions none of their past tensions and focuses only on the future - a future that was not to be. Read this letter and you will think that it was written by someone in mild discomfort, getting over an illness and anticipating recovery in the near future. Is it any wonder that she confused those whom she kept at arm's length and those whom she had not allowed to know her?

February 21, 1973

Dearest Edgar:

When I woke up on Valentine's Day the first sight I saw was a beautiful pink cyclamen. The cyclamen is one of my very favorite flowers and pink is my color here in my rooms. The flowers have not faded at all and I have enjoyed every minute of them. They stand on the center table in my little sitting room facing me where I sit and eat my meals and are thoroughly enjoyed. Thank you very much, my dear.

I have still not reached the point of writing my own letters and so you must excuse the typing, which is very exasperating to me.

I have had a little set-back, the cause of which seems to be unknown, but I am getting over it. My main problem seems to be that I do not wish to eat but this, of course, will not go on forever and the doctor tells me it is mainly because of the medicine I have to take for my heart. I am allergic to digitalis altogether and this is very difficult. I dare say I shall get over it as I do all my problems.

Jean and Joe came to see me and brought me lovely flowers from the camellia house, and Janice came, also. She and Joan have started a shop which seems to sell almost everything including a lot of junk which cluttered up their house. It seems to be working out very well.

I am glad to say the doctors are unanimously in favor of my progress and that is satisfactory. I am very lazy, sleeping a lot, but I thought out a short story for next Christmas for "Good Housekeeping" magazine.

We are having a very odd winter but then everything seems odd this year. Only my love for you remains the same.

As ever, (signed) Mother

To which I must reply: How can I, who was with your mother so constantly, tell you now, Edgar - for I couldn't tell you then so you would understand - how can I tell you now that this chatty, loving little letter was written during a brief time of great clarity and lucidity. You did not believe me when I told you that this letter was preceded and followed by long periods of deep, troubled, drugged sleep for your mother. Drugged sleep because strong medicine was needed to fend off the creeping pains which engulfed her more and more; troubled sleep because the cancer was metastasizing throughout her body and finally reaching her brain no matter how hard she fought to keep the brain immune. Deep troubled sleep is actually a way of saying that starting a few days before February 21st and all the remaining days, she slipped in and out of a coma. You never saw this - she did not want you or any of her family to see her in a coma. She wanted you to think she was taking a little nap.

Let me tell about that day, February 21st, when she wrote that last letter. She was no longer able to dress herself, bathe herself, walk or even stand unaided. I could not coax her to swallow even a bit of broth. In frustration she threw a glass of water at me after I told her I could no longer bathe her in the bathtub; it was too dangerous and I was afraid I couldn't lift her out after she got in and therefore I had to bathe her in bed. She didn't like bed baths - not home, not in the hospital. She once threw another glass of water, or maybe it was hot tea at somebody else those last few days - probably it was Wendy, who was sleeping on the floor next to her every night, in case Miss Buck called out or needed anything at all.

I should mention here that there were times, the bad times, when Miss Buck did not recognize any of us around her, and one morning it was so bad that I sat with her quietly for over four hours pretending with her that we were at some big hotel in New York City and she was waiting for her driver to arrive with her limousine so she could go for a ride in Central Park. She didn't know who I was, but accepted my presence, did not recognize Ted Harris and wondered who the red-haired stranger was and what he was doing in her sitting room. Anyway, the terrible lapses of memory were caused by the metastasizing cancer. They were intermittent and went off and on unexpectedly like someone flipping a light switch. As a room can go from light to dark if the electric current is interrupted, so a mind can flip from on to off. Maybe it too is an electric current. From one of those deep troubled sleeps lasting so many hours that I had called the doctor to report the length of time involved, Miss Buck emerged on February 21st to write a letter to Edgar - and only to Edgar. I had left her briefly to go downstairs to phone the doctor and when I returned she was miraculously sitting up in bed, a satin bed jacket around her shoulders, reading glasses on and a book held in front of her. The book was upside down. I gasped as I tip-toed into the rooms, expecting to see her comatose as before.

"Mrs. Drake," she said loudly and clearly and imperiously, her glasses slipping down her nose. She peered at me intently and demanded that Dolphus bring her breakfast immediately, that Mr. Harris come upstairs instantly with the day's agenda, and that I should get pad and pencil because she wanted to dictate a letter - perhaps several letters. The scene was beautiful, wild, incongruous, so sad, so impossible to believe. I wouldn't have believed it if I hadn't seen it myself. In minutes she returned to a helpless state, the brilliant flash of old reality gone. I wish the whole family, the whole world, had seen this incredible lady sitting imperiously on her throne wrapped in white satin and commanding that her will be done.

A day or two before the cyclamen arrived and the visit from Edgar occurred, Edgar called Danby House and wanted, as always, to speak with his mother in person. I explained patiently that she was unable to speak with anybody, she had been slipping in and out of a troubled sleep and was in a great deal of discomfort. I had tried so hard to make Edgar believe and all he said to me was, "Tell my mother I would like to see her before she is dead." Horrified, I suggested that such a message would break her heart (indeed, I would see to it that such a message never reached her). Controlling my emotions, I suggested that she would instead appreciate a loving message and perhaps a plant or some flowers. When Edgar did arrive with the plant and marched upstairs to see for himself that his mother was indeed sleeping and unable to speak with him, he asked me for paper to pen this message "Dearest Mother, I know that you are fond of this color and I hope this small floral display will cheer you. Love, Edgar."

The plant and the message pleased Miss Buck and she made a great effort to express her pleasure in her last letter. But nothing Edgar could ever do would ever erase in my mind, his unfilled directive "Tell my mother I would like to see her before she is dead."

It is infinitely painful for me to write of such things, but the pain goes away briefly when I recall the smiling lady looking at me over her glasses and holding her upside down book and wondering why I was tip-toeing into her room when she was quite all right. She was indeed quite all right. It was just the cancer and a few insensitive people who were all wrong. The picture of her, Lady Peasbee, as a knight in white satin is quite all right as a picture of strength, not weakness.

Chapter 41

"Thank You - I Love You"

The ministrations of doctor and nurse, the presence of Wendy each night, and the efforts of Ted and me each day were comforting but futile attempts to ease the end of one long journey as another was about to begin. We did what we could and always wished we could do more. Her speech, usually so precise and proper, became slurred and guttural and foreign-sounding, when she was able to speak at all. She insisted (over my most vehement protests that she should rest and not try to speak) on telling me of a very vivid incident in which she was both participant and observer. She had roused, she said, from one of those nightmare painful periods, and with great clarity and awareness had been suspended up above her bed, looking down upon her other self, the suffering self. She was, she continued, in a light and lovely place where she had never been before but was yet familiar and friendly.

"How could I be suspended up above, safe and secure, looking down on another me, all tired and worn?" Haltingly, she posed this question and of course I had no answer. When her mind slipped away again, I hoped it was to that light and lovely place she had seen so clearly.

I later found out that what she described to me is a rather typical experience related by many patients on the thresh-

420

hold of that next long journey. Had she succeeded in fighting off the cancer which was ravaging her, this incident would very definitely have found its way into a future book, just like the reincarnation episode in MANDALA. Perhaps that is why I find it important to insert it here, and perhaps that is why she went to great pains to tell it to me just the way it happened. I believe she was telling me that I was to repeat it for her.

Pearl Buck's last big speaking effort was directed to Ted Harris, the man in whom she had put such great faith and trust, and to whom she had given such love. Because it was such an agony for her to try to make herself understood (apparently her mind knew exactly what she wanted to say but the motor part of speaking was garbled, with the message from brain to tongue being short-circuited somewhere along the way), she requested my presence as translator-interpreter. In a heart-wrenching scene, we three became a surrealistic trio - passionate and passionless. I had great difficulty understanding her, but was able to translate what she had to say if I let it sink in for a few seconds in delayed comprehension. Following her slow but careful instructions, I propped her against me on the edge of her bed and Ted sat in front of us at her feet. She was too weak to sit alone, and I held both my arms around her to keep her from toppling. She tried to speak directly to Ted, but he kept shaking his head in frustration and looking to me in agony because he could not understand. Quietly, slowly, with periods of hesitation in between, she spoke and I translated, speaking the most beautiful words of love from this woman to this man. Her voice faltered and faded frequently, and my own voice followed in unconscious imitation. I looked into the very depths of Ted's dark eyes as I translated Pearl Buck's farewell. "Thank you - I love you," she whispered again and again. "Thank you - I love you," I repeated for her again and again.

Lest anyone doubt what I did or that maybe I was improvising and ad libbing, let me assure you that what I said was what Miss Buck said and wanted me to repeat exactly. I paused between sentences and she nodded agreement or disagreement of my accuracy. She would not have tolerated my making up her words of love.

"Thank you - I love you," she whispered over and over. That is enough for the world to hear. I choose to give the rest of what I heard and translated the dignity of privacy. I was an interpreter, not an interloper.

Pearl Buck died in the early morning hours of March 6, 1973. There were no more farewell speeches; everything she wanted to say had been said. But I think she would very much like it if I chose a few words by Ted Harris, and then in my book, as in his, *she* shall have the very last word.

"Future generations," writes Ted Harris in Volume 1 of THE BIOGRAPHY, "will know and love her, not only for her books but for the heart out of which they flowed, leaving still more love for her fellowman. Is this not the true meaning of all life? Is this not pure worship of whatever creation is?.... She has lived, she has written her own life into her many books, and we can all read and know that someone, somewhere, has been through our own joys and sorrows. We can take comfort because she survived in triumph, and so, perhaps may we. I can think of no better way to end this record of her life than with her salute to the world in her poem, "Essence"–

"Thank You—I Love You"

I give you the books I've made,

Body and soul, bled and flayed.

Yet the essence they contain

In one poem is made plain,

In one poem is made clear:

On this earth, though far or near,

Without love there's only fear.

Chapter 42

Requiem

An eloquent song without music was composed and spoken by Theodore B. Dolmatch in final formal tribute. I listened through the hushed sunlit atmosphere of that long ago Spring morning in Green Hills, Pennsylvania. Standing side by side with members of Pearl Buck's large family, only Bill Drake and I, Wendy and Dolphus represented her Vermont world. Following to the end her specific instructions, Ted Harris was not present. In his place was a single red rose of exquisite beauty. In stark contrast to the simple beauty of a rose and perhaps meant to complete a subtle symbolic reference to her own spirit, there was a large stone brought from Vermont. This stone, which she had insisted should be of the simple garden-variety type from the earth she loved, traveled with us from Vermont to Pennsylvania - a living entity to mark her final resting place.

Pearl Buck's several worlds came together in formal farewell. Time and Destiny would prove whether those several worlds could exist in harmony and accept the legacy she bequeathed.

PEARL S. BUCK

by *Theodore B. Dolmatch*

"For each of us here and for millions of others across time and place, Pearl S. Buck was many things. She did everything. Knew everyone. Received every honor. She had the confidence of the mighty and kept the confidences of the lowly. She was mother and friend, artist and craftsman, public figure and private person. In short, she was a most complex and important lady. I knew her for most of my life the way most people knew her - through her work. I don't know when I first read *The Good Earth*. The book and the film are irrevocably merged in my mind. Two illuminations out of my past are one. As she intended, I *lived* with those men and women of China. They were compelling more for their humanity than for their exotic land or their culture. They became part my own life and (in testimony to her art) part of the world's heritage as well. She was tireless, as Jason Lindsey said in Stockholm, in her efforts to 'bridge the awful gulf which separates mankind from itself.' Those efforts insure her immortality, as indeed they should.

"Slighty more than a year ago, I came to know her in a new way: Through a variety of accidents I became her publisher; she, my author. What a proprietary-sounding phrase! All it really means is that her words reached her readers through my colleagues' efforts and my own. She was so alive to our task, so aware of all those little things that add up to that one very big thing - a book. As ill as she was a few weeks ago, she took the trouble to say how much she liked the jacket design of her newest novel.

"She was the quintessential professional. Not one book, but more than eighty. A generation of writing. Her books rang true to her readers, who went to them to get just that which books can give: vicarious joy as well as sorrow, both refuge from the world and a mirror for it, understanding of the self and others - and faith in both. She was *such* a problem for the critics: Artless in her art. Transparent in her humanity. What *does* one do with her? In what pantheon is she placed?

"In several. For example, with all the current cant about women's liberation, here was a *truly* liberated woman. She wrote and mothered, spoke and dreamed, achieved and lived. I know of no fuller life, and she did all this naturally, with a finely-tuned awareness of the fact that both men and women have much to learn from one another, to give to one another, to add to one another. Her humanity was never exclusive.

"And for another example, the children. How she tried to help *them!* The ones that needed help the most - the weak, the lost ones - but *not* with charity. She said she hated charity, meaning, I think, *dependency.* Her goal, and the goal of the Foundation she created, was to build independent, strong children - for they needed strength to survive. A proud woman, Pearl Buck was proud for others, too.

"Finally, China, the country that formed her, fed her, shaped her. She could not see it again. But she helped her fellow Americans to see it. She played a part in bringing the two great peoples of China and America together. She did so by recreating their universal humanity - through her own. Her *universal* humanity. She was not Chinese - although it pleased her to say so. She was a part of all of us — 'under Heaven, all are one.' And she felt it:

" 'I do not pray' she wrote, 'if prayers be words or pleading or searching. If the process must be explained, it was simply that I gave myself wholly to a universe which I do not understand, but which I know is vast and beautiful beyond my comprehension, my place in it no more than a hollow in a rock. But there is the hollow and it is mine and there is the rock.' This was in *A Bridge for Passing*. At *this* 'bridge for passing,' we know that her place is *more* than a hollow in the rock of time. It is a hollow in our very being, deep within each of us who knew her personally or through her work. That hollow is hers too, and in some ironic way we are all the fuller for it."

Chapter 43

Coda

Since I began this story with Once Upon a Time, the ending should read "And They Lived Happily Ever After." The lady I came to know so well worked so hard to achieve this kind of ending, but I cannot write that because it is not the truth of what happened. In spite of all her carefully laid plans, backed up by what she considered to be the finest legal advice available to her, the adopted family - the infants she had raised to adults with their inter-racial, international origins - her adopted family, in the end and in sad truth, did not know her well enough to understand her. Whose fault this was, or whether it was anybody's fault, or whether it can simply be dismissed as genetic inheritance or fate, matters not. The fact is that Pearl Buck touched the world with her great love and concern, and I think it fair to say that the world responded in kind. She touched her own adopted family with that same love and concern. That they did not respond with the depth of love and understanding one might expect may be, simply, that they were children, she was mother. They saw her in one context, intimate and complex; the world saw her in another context - intimate and complex, yet at a distance.

The person Pearl Buck was, by her own admission, difficult and complicated and capable of disrupting comfort and calm in other persons. Especially her family, whom she loved and treasured but chose to keep at arm's length - for her own comfort and calmness as well as theirs. Pearl Buck was an institution and a legend. How does one live with an institution and legend? And she was a goddess. How can anyone live with a goddess, much less understand one? The analysis of Pearl Buck and her relationships could go on and on and on. The infinite variety of her long life could be viewed from many vantage points and could be the subject of scholarly explorations touching on the psychological, physiological, educational, literary, even the occult. The list of possibilities is quite endless.

But enough of what if's and could be's. Miss Buck herself steered away from such analytic speculations and musings. "Continue to tell the story the way it happened, my dear," I can hear her admonishing me now, "tell the story the way it happened, even though the ending is hard to relate."

The ending is painful, but reaps its own reward of beauty and dignity.

It was July of 1975 before Bill and I knew that the lawyers had reached the end of the legal road in their fight to keep us as executors of the will. During the more than two years since Miss Buck's death, Edgar had relentlessly pursued and pressed to first have us removed as executors and second, to have his mother's will overturned. He questioned everything his mother had done and suggested foul play by those associated with her at the end. The doctors tending her testified to her soundness of mind. It should have been enough, but the voices of reason were not loud enough. Threatening letters and phone calls, smear tactics in the press. There is no nice way to say what Edgar wanted - what he insisted was rightfully his. He wanted the money, jewels, furniture, real estate - the so-called riches his mother had unfairly, under duress, he said, handed off to the nefarious con- man Ted Harris. An adopted son wanted the spoils of his mother's fruitful life. It was his birthright, as his lawyer so charmingly put it. Everything that Pearl Buck willingly gave to Ted Harris as her thank you to this man who had performed so magnanimously and selflessly for her, Edgar coveted. He wanted the material possessions of his adoptive mother, for himself and his brothers and sisters. They deserved the spoils and he fought to get them away from Ted Harris.

And now comes the most personal part of this story. Where was I when all this fighting and legal wrangling was going on? Why didn't I jump in and tell the whole world what Pearl Buck wanted? If I had come forward in 1973 with the story I am telling now, wouldn't it have made a difference and couldn't I have written the ending, "And They All Lived Happily Ever After?"

Bill Drake and I stayed together for as long as Miss Buck needed us. When we were legally removed as executors in the summer of 1975, it was shortly thereafter that we were legally separated. And it was my human frailty, my inability to stand up under the emotional buffeting of a crumbling marriage coupled with the ugly battles surrounding Miss Buck's estate that caused my own demise from the world for a time. Quite a time, and it has taken me these long years to summon the strength and fortitude to tell all of this. It's not pretty, it's not nice, I keep emphasizing; it shouldn't have been the way it was.

And now, although I am not proud of those years after Miss Buck's death and what happened to me personally, I am proud now that what happened to me gave me the added perspective and maturity and humility to share the truth.

When I went to work for Miss Buck, I had run away from home. That is, I had run away from an impossible situation and I was trying to make the best of it. I believed in marriage, I sincerely wanted to help my husband, and I had two growing boys I adored. I did what a lot of women were doing in those days - keeping one foot in one world and one foot in another, uneasily seeking solutions and trying to keep everything precariously balanced. Those of us who tried that made a lot of mistakes, but we learned a lot about ourselves and we taught a lot to others who followed in our footsteps.

Pearl Buck's estate was left in the hands of the lawyers. They were fighting the battle. I would have been one individual with no money and faltering strength to stand up to the battery of legal people Edgar Walsh mustered to overturn the will, smear Ted Harris and drag his mother's name and reputation through the courts month after month. Here the reader may ask why I couldn't see that even as one individual I could have battled the giants and won. Isn't that what Pearl Buck's last book, THE RED EARTH, was all about? Isn't that what her own life was all about? The tremendous strength she had as one woman allowed her to form the Foundation, start the Danby project, write her books in spite of criticisms and stumbling blocks all along the line. Where was I, who claimed to know her so well, with my fighting spirit as one woman who had the truth to slay the giants?

Well, the truth is I fell down after plowing doggedly ahead too long. I couldn't re-commit myself to my marriage, though I tried, nor could I commit myself then to fighting Edgar and his pursuit of money. My world crashed in on me, and for a long time I merely went through the motions of living, staggering this way and that in search of what I should do, where I should go. I wasn't searching for the truth. I had that. I just didn't know what to do with it.

When Ted was hospitalized in the summer of 1973 with depression and exhaustion, I visited him in the Rutland Hospital. I vowed then that no matter how bad everything seemed, how badly Miss Buck's dreams were being shattered and trampled by people who just did not know who she was and what she wanted, I vowed that someday the world would know and understand the truth.

That summer and fall, I stood in a little book store in Danby which we had started to feature her books and talk about her work - I stood in that little store and had people pour out their hearts to me about what a great lady she was and what a terrible thing had happened that her secretary, her business manager, and all those evil people with her when she died had forced her to sign over all her possessions to them. I listened and talked back to them, sometimes revealing that I was that evil secretary they had read about in the newspapers. Of course, I reminded them sarcastically, everything you read in the newspapers is always true. Sometimes I did not reveal who I was, taking the stings and the nasty barbs, for I was too weary to fight back.

At home, I moved out of the bedroom I had shared for so many years with my husband. I moved as a last resort to salvage what dignity and peace I had left. My exit created repercussions that ended in my husband brandishing a shotgun first at me, then at himself. It was our son, Tom, who rushed in to protect me and his brother, and his father too, from bodily harm. It was Tom who turned around that terrible incident so that we were not hurt, any of us, except in dreadful emotional scars which took a very long time to heal. And it was that occasion that saw the re-entry into my life of an old friend who had long stayed away because he and my husband always argued when they were together. The old and dear friend later became my wise and understanding husband, without whose constant encouragement I would not now be writing these words.

Such a horror as the gun-brandishing can sometimes become the straw that breaks the camel's back. I think it was then that my back was broken and things became too much, too complicated, too entangled, and I was too exhausted to even try to straighten them out any more. I sought escape from the personal agony. I started drinking with a vicious disregard to moderation and the little glasses of sweet sherry I had always enjoyed, sipped delicately from a Waterford crystal glass, became bottles and bottles of the insidious poison, guzzled at first secretly in desperation, then consumed blatantly anytime anywhere. Little did I know at that time that I had no tolerance whatsoever for alcohol; the extent I drank even though it was for a relatively short period of time, swiftly sent me over the edge into the alcoholic oblivion known as black-outs, and I stumbled through the next three years in a semi-conscious state. The terrors of creeping alcohol addiction cannot be adequately described. Alcohol in any amount never solved any problems and creates more and more on its own. But at terrible expense it does succeed in blotting out the real world for a while, turning off the brain and the heart in a brief respite. It is not respite, not a rest, but a living Hell, and I shall spare the reader the Hell I went through in order to climb back up again into the real world. It is probably coincidence that once I had made up my mind to tell this story about how I met Pearl Buck, how I went to work for her and all the tangled things that happened after that - once I had made up my mind to tell the whole story, the need for alcohol - my need for escape - vanished completely. Coincidence? Miss

Buck would say it is something else.

I almost killed myself on three separate occasions in three separate autombile accidents, and by a miracle I never injured anyone else. Once I was left for dead by the side of the road and covered with a blanket. I was tired, I was exhausted, I wanted to be left alone. I wanted the problems to vanish. I wanted me to vanish.

But the problems didn't vanish and neither did I. A night in jail, weeks in hospitals and alcohol rehabilitaion centers with caring people who had lived through a worse Hell than mine, gave me the will to be me once again. My sons believed in me and only backed away temporarily when they saw they could not help anymore; and my dear and wise friend who is now my husband believed in me even when he sent me away from him in desperation when his own great love was not enough to help me. I survived, and I am very proud to be at the end of this story now, for the world has a right to hear it and I almost vanished before I told it.

Ted Harris is the only other person who could have told this, but when Miss Buck died, he too was exhausted and wanted only to retreat from public life, from the cruel and probing eyes that so long had sought to damn him and degrade him, questioning him on everything from his name to his sexual preferences, totally ignoring his humanity. Why didn't he fight Edgar personally? It was beneath him and Miss Buck would not have wanted him to do so. They had both walked away from getting personally involved with the Philadelphia story years before.

Ted Harris ultimately walked away from Danby, leaving the spoils to the son who fought for his "birthright" for himself and the adopted siblings. Stranger than fiction, the truth of it all. Ted Harris didn't want Danby, didn't like the harsh

Vermont climate, but Miss Buck wanted it for him, and he would have acquiesed for her sake. It's nice to have a home to come back to, even though you wander the earth.

The legacy Pearl Buck left Ted Harris is beyond measure, beyond money and gold.

The legacy Pearl Buck left me is also beyond measure. She left me a dignity and understanding, which was almost beyond my understanding, but I have lived to tell about it and so maybe she knew me better than I knew myself. She was very wise, was Pearl Buck, and she knew a lot of people better than they knew themselves. She died virtually penniless, as she wanted it. What she was actually worth, in terms of book royalties, real estate, and material possesions, turned out to be far more that the $150,000 estate she laughed about at the time of her death. Had she known her estate was worth many times that amount, her distribution of it would have been exactly the same. Her will stated her wishes to the letter.

One man named in her will walked away from her money and retained her love, which can never be taken from him. Another man named in her will walked away from her love and retained her money, which can always be taken away from him.

Stranger than fiction, bigger than life, Lady Peasbee was a command presence a knight in white satin, and a goddess to the end. Pearl Buck defied classification in life; she transcends it in death. I was with her on her last intimate journey. I'm proud I knew her and I treasure the legacy she left me - the dignity of truth.

Photo By Bruce Curtis

THE

Pearl S. Buck
BOOK CLUB
DANBY, VERMONT 05739

```
" IF MEN COULD ONLY

              KNOW EACH OTHER,

     THEY WOULD NEITHER

              IDOLIZE NOR HATE. "


                              Elbert Hubbard
```

For
Mrs. Naomi Bixby
the very first copy
of this book

Theodore F Harris
and Roberts Edwardsen
and Carter McNiel
and Steven P. Michaels

DISCOVERING THE WORLD
with
Pearl S. Buck

Six Americans have won literature's most coveted award ... The Nobel Prize.
They were one woman and five men. Of the six only one remains alive and
is writing today ... the lady recently referred to by The Saturday Evening Post
as "The Empress of American Literature" ... Pearl S. Buck. In 1938 her
citation for the Nobel Prize read "For rich and genuine epic portrayals of
Chinese Peasant Life and for Masterpieces of Biography". She has become the
most widely translated author in the history of American literature. Only Mark
Twain comes near her in translations and she has doubled him. About three-
fourths of her reading audience is abroad reading her work in languages other
than her own. There has to be a reason for this overwhelming acceptance of
her work and, of course, there is a simple explanation. Her books are of
major importance universally ... and more so today than when they were written,
as one can see with a little understanding of how and why she has written
what she has written. First let us take a look at the woman ... and then her books.
It is important to see her as she sees herself, as nearly as possible, with regard
to her work. She has over two hundred humanitarian awards; she is a teacher; she
is a philosopher ... she is a great artist ... but what does she consider herself?
She considers herself first and foremost and completely a novelist ... and nothing
more. Her life work has been to write novels and all else has been incidental
to that chosen pursuit. She herself has expressed her belief that the first and
only duty of a novelist is to entertain and she has obviously succeeded in this
area for more than forty years ... as one can clearly see when one remembers
that in 1931 THE GOOD EARTH sold 1,811,000 copies and in 1971 she had
three major Book Club selections with two novels: THE THREE DAUGHTERS OF
MADAME LIANG was the Reader's Digest Condensed Book and Book of the Month
Club selection, and MANDALA, a novel of India, was The Literary Guild selection.

Her novels, however, attain a greater than literary importance when one considers how she writes. She does not, as some novelists do, sit down and make up stories through imaginary events that take place with make-believe people. Instead she writes out of her own life about events that have taken place during her lifetime to people she has known. Now consider what that statement has proclaimed. First, the events that have taken place during her lifetime. Perhaps the most important single occurrence in relation to world history is the decline and eventual fall of the Imperial Government of China, creating the void into which Communism firmly entrenched itself. She has gone from travel in a sedan chair to men walking on the moon. She has seen American involvement in Asia from its beginnings with businessmen and missionaries to our present tragic involvement with troops.

She lived forty years in China where she was definitely a part of life in a Chinese community and where Chinese became her native tongue, for she spoke Chinese before she spoke English. And what an important forty years they were. From 1892, when she was taken to China as a three-month-old infant, until 1911 she lived under the last Empress of China, the true facts of whose life she wrote into her novel, IMPERIAL WOMAN.

She lived through the ten-year void, when there was no central government, until when, in 1921, the Communist party was officially recognized. In 1927 she almost lost her life at the hands of the Communists in the Nanking Incident, after which she fled to Japan for a year, returning to China in 1928. She lived there under the Nationalist Government of Chiang Kai-shek until 1933 when she saw that there definitely would be a Communist rule, under which she could not live, and then she returned to the United States.

When she arrived she accepted speaking engagements and wrote at length about what she had seen and learned, in order that Americans would be aware of potential danger. All of her books on Chinese subjects, though most are classed as fiction, and indeed are novels, are an historically accurate account of events that took place during those strategically important years. A good example of non-fiction on the subject of China is the book CHINA AS I SEE IT which is a collection of speeches and essays from 1933 through 1970, and allows the reader to see in how many ways she has been prophetic and in how many more ways she is likely to be. There is no better teacher than experience, and she has looked into her own unique past to predict the future.

While all of her books are autobiographical to the extent that they contain at least one character with whom she can identify, they fall rather loosely into two large categories. Other than fiction and non-fiction, these two groups are, of course, the long historical novel, some spanning generations, and those written on a less vast scale, or what could be referred to as more personal books. These two large categories can be divided into five groups.

One group is her long historical novels and include THE GOOD EARTH, SONS, A HOUSE DIVIDED, THE PATRIOT, THE PROMISE, DRAGON SEED, IMPERIAL WOMAN, THE LIVING REED (about Korea), and one with an American background, THE TOWNSMAN. Into this group of important historical novels, I would place three of her non-fiction works: MY SEVERAL WORLDS and the two "masterpieces of biography" from the Nobel Prize citation, THE EXILE and FIGHTING ANGEL. These books in group one are large in scope and are set in a panoramic historical background and provide either information about an entire period that leads up to an important event, or they deal with the important event itself. Considered together as a group, except for THE TOWNSMAN, they give the reader a clear and concise understanding of Asians, of American involvement in Asia and the effect it has had on Asians and on Americans, and why Americans must be involved as we are today.

The rest of her books fall into other groups that are no less enjoyable and knowledgeable but which are smaller in scope, expressing human emotions perhaps to a greater extent than historical fact, though they are no less historically accurate and important. Into this group we place PAVILION OF WOMEN, COME MY BELOVED, PEONY, THE MOTHER, THE THREE DAUGHTERS OF MADAME LIANG, THE NEW YEAR, COMMAND THE MORNING, THE HIDDEN FLOWER, GOD'S MEN, PORTRAIT OF A MARRIAGE, THE LONG LOVE, THE ANGRY WIFE, and EAST WIND-WEST WIND.

The third group contains books almost entirely autobiographical as THE TIME IS NOON, LETTER FROM PEKING, THIS PROUD HEART, and OTHER GODS. Into this group I would place her autobiographical account of her first year of widowhood, A BRIDGE FOR PASSING, and the completely philosophical non-fiction TO MY DAUGHTERS, WITH LOVE and THE KENNEDY WOMEN.

The fourth group contains books she refers to as her summer novels, dealing with a specific person or incident such as KINFOLK, VOICES IN THE HOUSE, BRIGHT PROCESSION, and DEATH IN THE CASTLE. The rest of her books, all non-fiction, were written to inform either herself or others. To inform others: FOR SPACIOUS SKIES, THE GIFTS THEY BRING, THE JOY OF CHILDREN, THE CHILD WHO NEVER GREW, WHAT AMERICA MEANS TO ME, OF MEN AND WOMEN, AMERICAN UNITY AND ASIA. Those written for her own information are her talk books: AMERICAN ARGUMENT, TALK ABOUT RUSSIA, HOW IT HAPPENS, and TELL THE PEOPLE.

Theodore F. Harris
Biographer of Pearl S. Buck

1. THE GOOD EARTH:
From the first page the reader is swept into the lives of Wang Lung and Olan, strong courageous peasants, typical of the population living under the Imperial Government of China in any period before 1911. Very important background for understanding subsequent events. The Pulitzer Prize 1931, Best Novel of the Year; The William Dean Howells Medal 1935, Best Novel in Five Years.

2. SONS:
The opening lines of this book begin action where THE GOOD EARTH ends, with the death of Wang Lung. It carries the reader through the lives of his children during the War Lord era when the government went into fragmentation at the end of a dynasty, as it has traditionally at the end of every dynasty.

3. A HOUSE DIVIDED:
The action here centers around the grandsons of Wang Lung and the generation gap in China during which the youth rebeled against their parents and tradition. It was this division that broke down the strongest element in traditional China, the family-centered social structure. A book that makes one think of campus riots and burnings in the United States today. The final book in the trilogy, THE HOUSE OF EARTH.

4. THE EXILE:
A personal portrait of the author's mother, written after the death of the subject in order that her own children could know and understand their grandmother. This was the author's first book, written in 1921 but not published until 1936.

5. FIGHTING ANGEL:
Sub-titled PORTRAIT OF A SOUL, this is the biography of the author's father. FIGHTING ANGEL and THE EXILE together give the reader valuable insight into the earlier years of the life of Pearl S. Buck, and he gains a true understanding of American missionary involvement in China.

6. THE PATRIOT:
This book deals with the coming of Communism and the imprisonment and even the beheading of many youths rebeling, fired with the new patriotism. An important step in understanding American involvement in Asia today.

7. THE PROMISE:
"In their despair men must hope, when a promise is given, though it be only a promise". This is the opening line of the story of a promise made by leaders of the West and the devastating effect it had on China when the promise was broken.

8. DRAGON SEED:
The action, based on history, begins shortly before the Japanese attack on Nanking and describes in detail the rape, humiliation, and unbelievable brutality suffered by the Chinese. After reading this book, one will understand the traditional hatred these two peoples have for each other.

9. IMPERIAL WOMAN:
Though listed as a novel, this book is also a biography of the last Empress of China. In youth she was a concubine, in middle age a strategist, in old age a Goddess, and always an astute, mischievous, gay combination of beauty and intelligence. She ranks in history with the greatest rulers.

10. THE LIVING REED:
One of the most important books ever written for Americans who wish to understand why we have troops in Southeast Asia today. Entirely factual, only the leading characters are fictitious, and they are composites of actual persons the author has known. Finally one can understand the why of the Korean conflict and much more.

11. MY SEVERAL WORLDS:
While not an autobiography, this book is a factual autobiographical

personal recording of the author's span of time. This book will enable the reader to understand how a woman can write with the powerful historical impact with which Pearl S. Buck writes. A thoroughly enjoyable, informative, non-fiction work.

12. ALL MEN ARE BROTHERS (SHUI HU CHUAN translation):

While this is not an original writing, it certainly ranks among the most important works of Pearl S. Buck. The author spent four years, 1928-1932, after the Nanking Incident in 1927, translating this classic novel because she foresaw the Communist rule and knew American men would eventually be fighting on Asian soil. The book details the guerilla warfare being used to kill American men in Asia today. Indeed it is said SHUI HU CHUAN is the handbook of the Communist leaders.

13. THE TOWNSMAN:

Written under the pseudonym of John Sedges, this book is to Kansas what THE GOOD EARTH is to China. In the author's opinion it is not the cowboys who are the heroes of the old west, but the men who stayed behind and established villages and towns and set up schools and businesses. THE TOWNSMAN is the story of such a man. In a review the "Kansas City Star" wrote, "This book could only have been written by someone who had spent a lifetime in Kansas".

14. THE THREE DAUGHTERS OF MADAME LIANG:

This book is borderline between groups one and two, and deals with the immediate effects Communism has had on China and her people. For this reason it is a very important book. Communism has had only 50 years in China, so rather than dealing with a large historical element, the book involves actual incidents that happened to persons. There was a woman such as Madame Liang, and she did have daughters, and the incidents that take place in the story did occur.

15. COME, MY BELOVED:

This book is another which is borderline between historical and personal. It is historical in that it shows one of the reasons why the Christian missionaries have had little permanent impact on Asia. Asians are apt to judge one by what one does rather than by what one says. The book deals with a romance between an American girl, the daughter of a missionary, and his East Indian assistant. It is personal in that it expresses much of the author's own philosophy.

16. THE MOTHER:

This describes in detail and universally what it is like to be a woman and to need and want a man. It was the third novel the author wrote in China, and when she finished she threw it into the wastebasket as being too difficult a subject. The houseman was away that day and the next morning it was still in the wastebasket, so she took it out and put it away, not for publication. It became her fifth published work and a great success.

17. PAVILION OF WOMEN:

The author has told the reader a great deal about herself in the character of Madame Wu. This book is a study of a woman of pure intellect, and Madame Wu is one of the strongest of Pearl Buck's autobiographical women.

18. PEONY:

Peony is a bondsmaid, and this is her story of being in between family and servant. More important, however, is that it is the story of the Jews in China. The account is factual and required many years of research. A beautiful and enlightening story.

19. THE NEW YEAR:

The true story of a child born between the races in Korea, this book deals with the difficulty of mixed race children in Asian countries, as well as in the United States where this boy joins his father.

20. COMMAND THE MORNING:
This is the powerful story of the drama
behind the making of the atomic bomb.
The author was friends with Arthur Compton
and she sent him the manuscript. After
reading it he sent this note:
"This is a good job. I am naturally pleased
that you find in me a suitable "hero" around
whom to build your story. But I had better
not comment about what you say about the
hero. After all, this is your story! Except
for a few minor factual corrections, the only
significant change I have suggested is on
the last page, where I alter the words quoted
from me to make them more in character."
An absorbing account.

21. THE HIDDEN FLOWER:
An American officer marries a Japanese
girl - a story of racial prejudice in Japan
and in the United States, this is a heartbreakingly true book.

22. PORTRAIT OF A MARRIAGE:
A story of a marriage when one marries
beneath himself intellectually. A beautiful
book, largely autobiographical.

23. THE LONG LOVE:
The inspiring story of one woman's liberation from herself. A beautiful, important
and timely book.

24. THE ANGRY WIFE:
A factual probe into a white man who marries a black woman and their struggles and
joys, this book allows the reader to understand both the white and the black viewpoint.

25. EAST WIND-WEST WIND:
This is the author's first published book
and deals with eastern traditions and
western traditions, their differences and
their effect on each other. An important
book today when we need to understand
Asia more than ever before.

26. THE TIME IS NOON:
The somewhat autobiographical story
of the author's first marriage. Written
in 1936 her publisher, also her second

husband, at the last moment declared
the book too personal for that stage of
her career and this novel was not published until 1967, seven years after
his death. An invaluable aid in understanding Pearl Buck.

27. LETTER FROM PEKING:
Elizabeth is one of the most autobiographical characters the author has
created. All of the characters and incidents are based on fact. An important book
for philosophical appreciation of Pearl Buck.

28. THIS PROUD HEART:
Susan Gaylord is a talented and brilliant
woman. This book deals with the dichotomy
in the author's own life, the struggle between
the talent and the woman, the career and the
wife and mother. A probing thought-provoking
account.

29. OTHER GODS:
This book tells the author's own amazement
and disbelief at the form of hero worship
practiced in the United States where the
public creates a God and then tries to
destroy him.

30. A BRIDGE FOR PASSING:
The heartbreakingly autobiographical
study of the author's first year of widowhood ending with a note of hope based
on her own faith.

31. TO MY DAUGHTERS, WITH LOVE:
A mother speaks to her children with
wisdom and respect and with never
swerving firmness tempered with love
and understanding. A book to be valued
by every parent.

32. THE KENNEDY WOMEN:
A probing study of American society
today using the Kennedy family as an
example. One quote from the book gives
insight into some of the wisdom expressed:
"Greatness demands a heavy price in self-
sacrifice and self-discipline. Moreover,
ours is not an age of great men. Once
upon a time history was made by unique

men, and when it was written down it was the story of exceptional men and what they did. Now history is made up of events shaped not by strong and powerful personalities but by haphazard effects, one upon another. The full danger of the human situation can only be comprehended when one realizes that ours is a time of giant events and grave issues, but not of great men."

(33, 34, 35, 36) Group four contains KINFOLK, VOICES IN THE HOUSE, BRIGHT PROCESSION, and DEATH IN THE CASTLE, and they are thoroughly entertaining novels. A lively evening's entertainment can be found in any one of these.

37 FOR SPACIOUS SKIES:
A step-by-step account of the founding of The Pearl S. Buck Foundation written while on tour to fifty American cities on behalf of the Foundation. This book has revealing autobiographical passages.

38. THE GIFTS THEY BRING:
A study of the valuable accomplishments for mankind that have been made as a direct result of the tragedy of mental retardation.

39. THE JOY OF CHILDREN:
A deeply personal account of the author's own feelings for children and their rights. A beautiful picture book.

40. WELCOME CHILD:
The picture story of an adopted Korean-American child and her adjustment to an American family.

41. THE CHILD WHO NEVER GREW:
The author's personal account of the years of the discovery of her daughter's mental retardation. A deeply moving, revealing book.

42. AMERICAN UNITY IN ASIA:
A book of East-West relationship.

43. AMERICAN ARGUMENT:
Written with Eslanda Goode Robeson, a mature, successful American Negro

woman, this book expresses the problems of racial differences in the United States.

44. HOW IT HAPPENS:
Written with Erna Von Pustau. A Talk About the German People, 1914-1933, this book reveals a picture that might be one of America in the years just ahead. The after-math of war, families split by conflicting ideas, and group set against group.

45. TELL THE PEOPLE:
Talks with James Yen about the Mass Education Movement.

46. TALK ABOUT RUSSIA:
Written with Masha Scott. A book to help Americans understand what sort of people the Russians are.

Pearl S. Buck has published fifteen books for children, most of which have won major awards. It was her practice while her children were growing up to tell them stories each evening, and once a year the children would choose the story they would like to have put into book form. Parents and teachers have written to her declaring her children's books are useful in inducing young people to read. The most newly published of these books if THE CHINESE STORY TELLER. Other children's books are:
THE BEECH TREE
THE BIG FIGHT
THE BIG WAVE
THE CHINESE CHILDREN NEXT DOOR
THE CHRISTMAS GHOST
CHRISTMAS MINIATURE
THE DRAGON FISH
JOHNNY JACK AND HIS BEGINNINGS
MATTHEW, MARK, LUKE AND JOHN
ONE BRIGHT DAY
STORIES FOR LITTLE CHILDREN
THE WATER-BUFFALO CHILDREN
WELCOME CHILD
YULAN: FLYING BOY OF CHINA

This is not intended as a complete bibliography of the works of Pearl S. Buck (which can be found in Volume 1 of PEARL S. BUCK: A BIOGRAPHY), but is offered as a guide to greater enlightenment to her works.

PEARL S. BUCK: A BIOGRAPHY
Volume 1, by Theodore F. Harris

Pearl S. Buck says of Theodore F. Harris, in a preface to this book:

" ... As to his qualifications for the task of writing this biography, I can only say that he knows me better than anyone else does. Ours is an unusual relationship, based upon mutual confidence and understanding. The result is that I have been able to talk with him freely and at length and to answer his questions with complete frankness ... He has researched my books thoroughly and with intuitive insight that is satisfying, at least to a writer."

PEARL S. BUCK: A BIOGRAPHY
Volume 2, by Theodore F. Harris
Her Philosophy as Expressed in Her Letters

"In this book the most significant and interesting of her letters have been culled from her entire file, with connectives and background notes. Included also are a few other papers, such as confidential memoranda and unpublished articles that enlarge on some of the same topics as the letters.
"The result is a collection that is as absorbing as the straight biography of the previous volume. It fills out and deepens the portrait of its subject."

From reviews of PEARL S. BUCK: A BIOGRAPHY

"A full and inspiring life has been lovingly, yet objectively portrayed, and truly reads as dramatically as her own creations. Recommended."
                                                                    Library Journal

"Pearl S. Buck, the only American woman ever to have won the Nobel Prize in literature, ... is a woman of varied talents ... To gather some impression of the range of her preoccupations you have only to read her realistic, thoughtful and eloquent biography, PEARL S. BUCK by Theodore F. Harris ... This is a book that will bear re-reading, for it holds vision as well as love, dedication and hope and the very fundamentals of life."
                                                          Boston Herald Traveler

"Pearl Buck's reputation would thrive even without the nourishment of a published biography, but Harris has done a first-rate job in making the person of a public figure come alive."
                                                            Louisville (Ky.) Times

"The volume has excerpts from her personal journal never before published, numerous letters, delightful poems and erudite lectures including a fascinating history of the Chinese novel. The highlight of the book is the discerning parallels between the author's fictional characters and their actual counterparts."
                                                            Atlanta (Georgia) Journal

"An absorbing account of her life and of those who played a part in it."
                                                                    Seattle Times

"A warm, admiring biography ... Fresh perspectives and details."
                                                  Booklist (American Library Association)

THE

Pearl S. Buck

BOOK CLUB

offers personally autographed
Pearl S. Buck books by mail
to members.

VILLAGE SQUARE BOOK SHOP, INC.
Main Street
Danby, Vermont 05739

Short piece for the Literary
Guild Bulletin. Winter 1.
July 20, 1970. PSB.

MANDALA

The story of MANDALA took ~~seven~~ ~~eight~~ years
to mature in my mind. Once a story is clear
in my mind, its characters defined, its conclusion
plain, then the physical task of writing is performed
swiftly enough. The real work ~~had~~ already been done.

The story of ~~MANDALA~~ MANDALA began, then, seven
years ago. I was in India. I was with a company
of Indians making a film version of R.K. Narayan's
~~the~~ his prize-winning novel, ~~THE~~ GUIDE. The director,
Tad Danielewski, and I were the only Americans. The
setting of the first scenes were in Rajasthan, a
beautiful province in the north west of India. In a
blue lake about ~~set in~~ ~~among~~ rounded desert hills,
a marble palace was being re-created into a
modern hotel. I was its first guest. The setting,
therefore, is authentic.

During the months I spent there, surrounded
by the people of India, in village and palace,
the story of MANDALA began to grow in my mind.
It was on the periphery, for another novel, one of
modern China, had preference in point of time.

That, I knew, had first to be written and published and, so to speak, out of the way. That done, however, the people of MANDALA, waiting in the shadows, came quickly to life and in strength. I had research to do, for I take pride in historical accuracy, but the period was right, for I had been in India at the time of the Chinese attack and had seen the anxiety and the self-sacrifice of the people, their unpreparedness and their patriotism. I had met princes, too, who had ~~given as~~ yielded their ancient rights and wealth and were compelled therefore to find new ways to supplement their shrunken income.

All this was as familiar to me as were the peasants ~~villagers~~ in the ~~studio~~ desert ~~forms~~ villages and the modern young men and women in ~~teen~~ Delhi and Bombay. I wanted to express more than such contrasts however. I wanted to catch the atmosphere of India now; its beliefs and half-beliefs, its brusque modernity ~~its~~ entangled by ~~with~~ the myths of the crystalline ancient. The last three words of the novel ~~express,~~ I believe, this atmosphere.

As for the individual characters, they